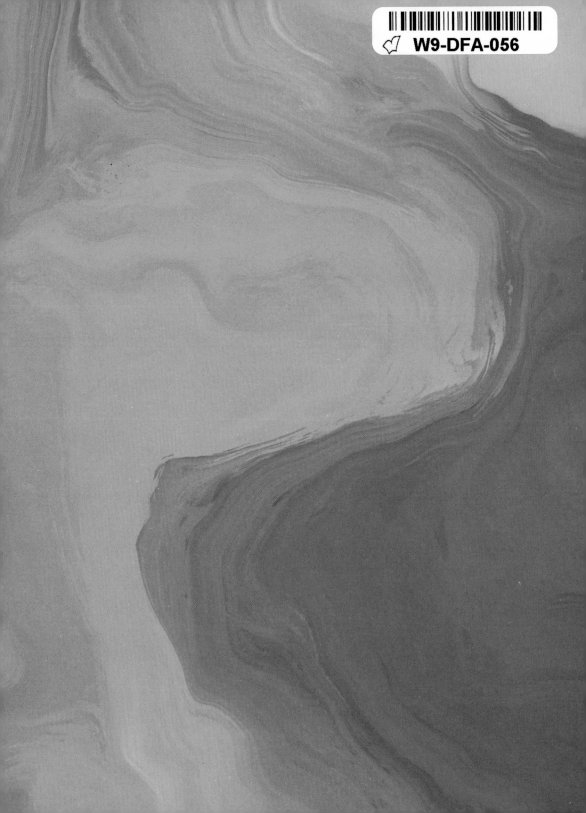

ADVANCE PRAISE FOR
FEELINGS: A STORY IN SEASONS

"A VISUAL AND EMOTIONAL TREAT, FULL OF GORGEOUS ARTWORK AND SOOTHING INSIGHT. MAKE SOME TEA, CURL UP WITH THIS BEAUTIFUL BOOK, AND LET MANJIT'S WARMTH, SINCERITY, AND INTIMACY WASH OVER YOU. YOU'LL UNDERSTAND YOURSELF A BIT BETTER, AND YOU'LL FEEL LIKE YOU'VE MADE AN INSTANT FRIEND."

MARI ANDREW, NEW YORK TIMES BESTSELLING AUTHOR OF
AM I THERE YET?

"A BEAUTIFULLY ILLUSTRATED, EVOCATIVE LOOK INSIDE THE EMOTIONS THAT LIVE AND TAKE ROOT INSIDE US. FEELINGS IS SIMPLY GORGEOUS—LUSH WITH THAPP'S SIGNATURE COLOR PALETTES AND EVOCATIVELY PROFOUND, IT FILLS THE READER WITH A LONGING TO CLIMB INSIDE EACH PAGE AND STAY AWHILE. THIS BOOK IS A NECESSARY REMINDER THAT THE ENTIRE SPECTRUM OF EMOTION SERVES PURPOSE, THAT EACH FEELING IS VALUABLE, AND, MOST IMPORTANT, THAT WE ARE NOT ALONE."

MEERA LEE PATEL, BESTSELLING AUTHOR OF START WHERE YOU ARE,
MY FRIEND FEAR, AND CREATE YOUR OWN CALM

"FEELINGS MAKES ME FEEL UNORIGINAL IN THE BEST WAY. IT REMINDS ME THAT DESPITE THE SPECIFIC EXPERIENCE OF MY INDIVIDUAL HUMANITY, THERE'S A SHARED ONE TOO, WITH THE PEOPLE AROUND ME, BUT ALSO WITH THE EARTH. IT'S A COLORFUL ROAD MAP OF HOW WE ALL CYCLE THROUGH THE SEASONS AROUND US AND INSIDE US, A CONSTANT OSCILLATION BETWEEN RAIN AND SUN AND RAGE AND RELIEF. I'D GIVE THIS BOOK TO ANYONE AND WOULD BE CONFIDENT THEY WOULD FIND THEMSELVES SOMEWHERE INSIDE IT."

OLIVIA GATWOOD, AUTHOR OF LIFE OF THE PARTY

"FEELINGS FILLED ME WITH A DEEP SENSE OF NOSTALGIA, WARMTH, AND COMFORT. MANJIT THAPP'S ILLUSTRATIONS ARE BREATHTAKINGLY BEAUTIFUL. EVERY SINGLE PANEL IS A MASTERPIECE IN ITS OWN RIGHT."

POLLY NOR, ARTIST

"A VERY THOUGHTFUL AND WILDLY BEAUTIFUL BOOK. MANJIT THAPP'S DISTINCTIVE USE OF SPACE AND COLOR EXQUISITELY EXPLORES WHAT IT MEANS TO BE A SELF, AND THE POWER OF OUR FEELINGS."

LIANA FINCK, AUTHOR OF PASSING FOR HUMAN

ILLUSTRATED BY MANJIT THAPP

THE LITTLE BOOK OF FEMINIST SAINTS

FEELINGS

FEELINGS

RANDOM HOUSE
NEW YORK

FeeLiNgs

A STORY iN SEASONS

Manjit Thapp

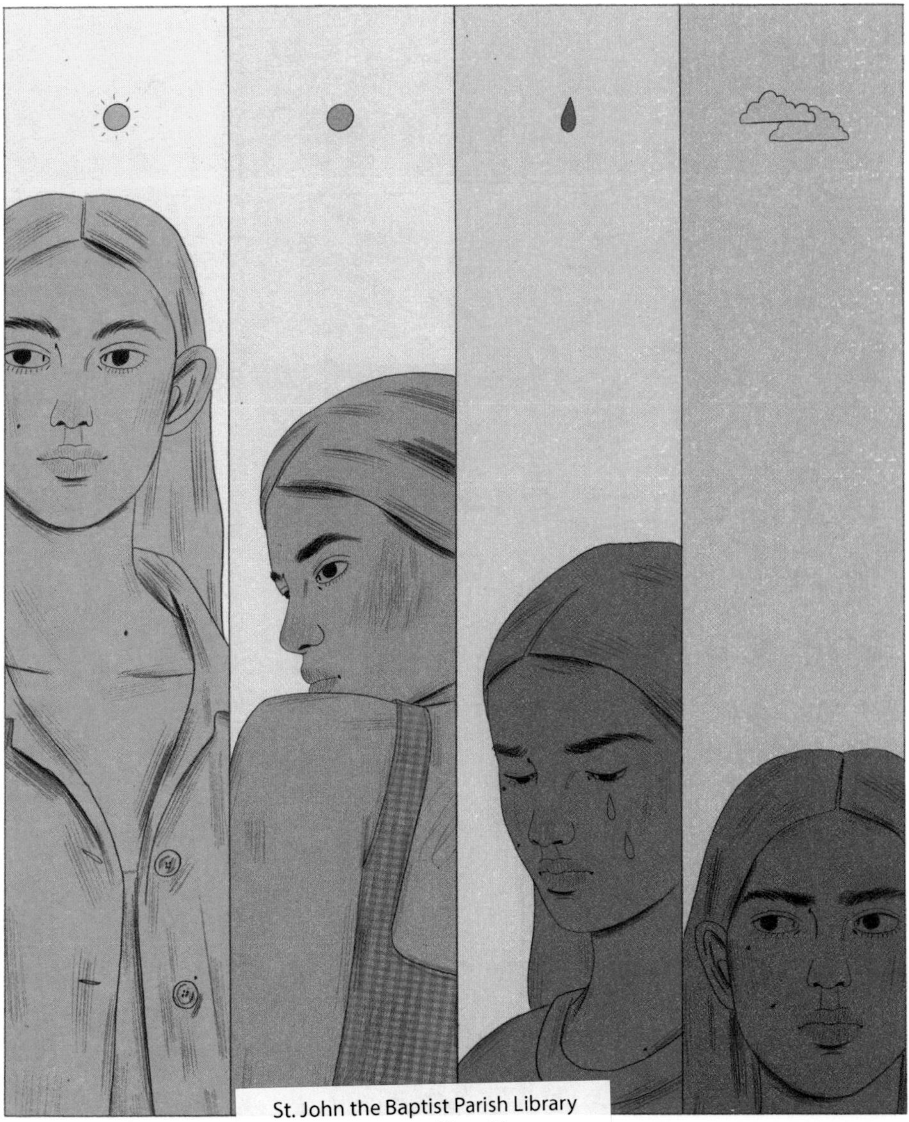

Published in the United States by Random House,
an imprint and division of Penguin Random House LLC, New York.

RANDOM HOUSE and the HOUSE colophon are registered
trademarks of Penguin Random House LLC.

Library of Congress Cataloging-in-Publication Data
Names: Thapp, Manjit, author, illustrator.
Title: Feelings: a story in seasons / by Manjit Thapp.
Description: First edition. | New York: Random House, 2021.
Identifiers: LCCN 2020020687 (print) | LCCN 2020020688 (ebook) |
ISBN 9780593129753 (hardcover) | ISBN 9780593129760 (ebook)
Subjects: LCSH: Thapp, Manjit—Themes, motives. |
Emotions in art. | Seasons in art.
Classification: LCC NC978.5.T53 A64 2021 (print) | LCC NC978.5.T53
(ebook) | DDC 741.941—dc23
LC record available at https://lccn.loc.gov/2020020687
LC ebook record available at https://lccn.loc.gov/2020020688

Printed in China on acid-free paper

randomhousebooks.com

2 4 6 8 9 7 5 3 1

First Edition

Book design by Elizabeth A. D. Eno

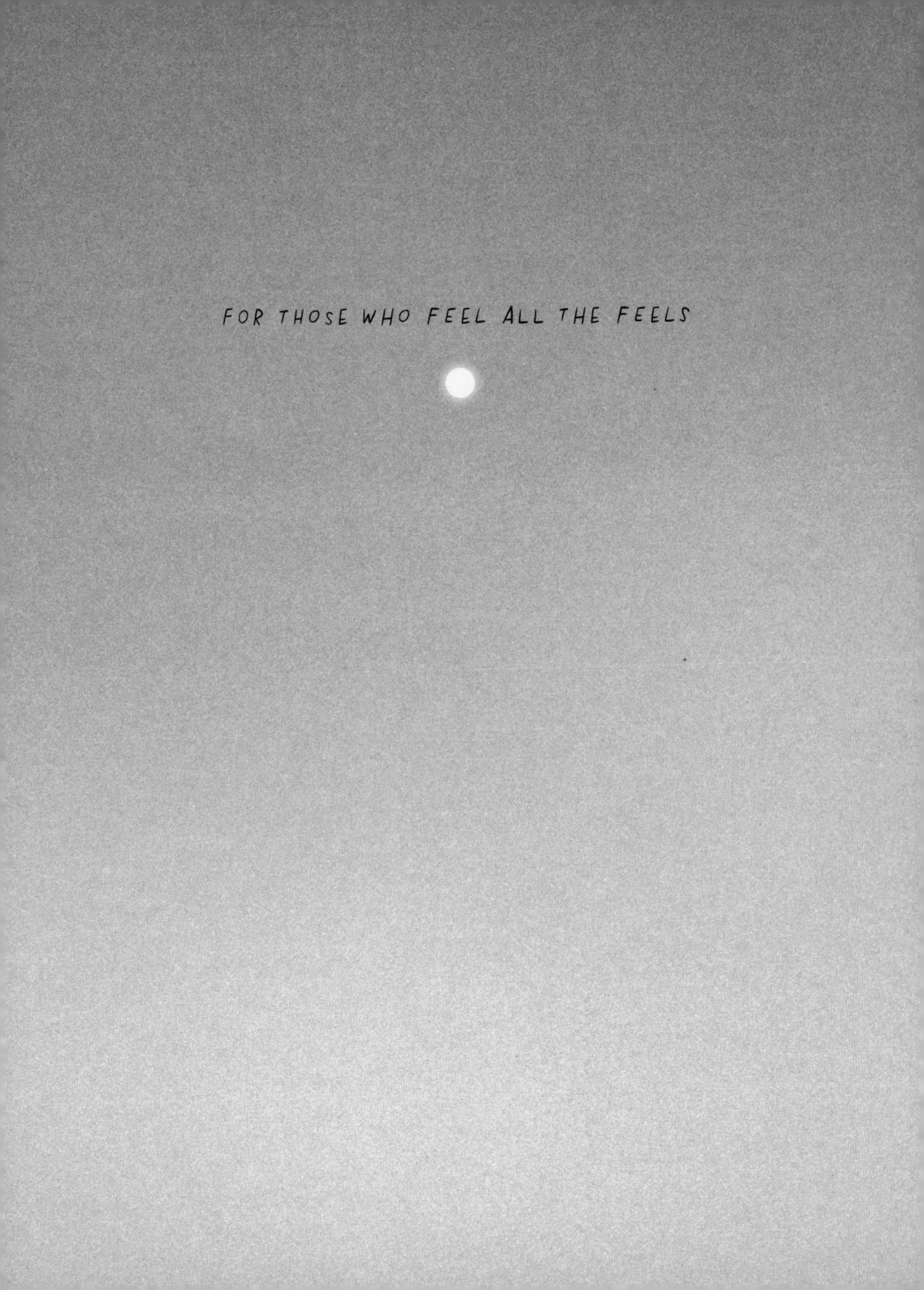

FOR THOSE WHO FEEL ALL THE FEELS

A NOTE FROM THE AUTHOR

THE WOMAN YOU'LL MEET IN THESE PAGES IS NOT AN EXACT MIRROR OF MYSELF, BUT SHE REPRESENTS MANY IMPORTANT PARTS OF ME. ABOVE ALL, I STROVE TO CAPTURE THE EMOTIONAL AUTHENTICITY OF MY SEASONAL EXPERIENCES WITH ANXIETY. PERHAPS YOU'LL SEE YOURSELF IN HER TOO.

THE BOOK'S STRUCTURE IS INSPIRED BY THE SIX-SEASON CALENDAR USED BY SOME COUNTRIES IN SOUTH ASIA, WHICH INCLUDES A MONSOON SEASON AND, DEPENDING ON THE REGION, SPLITS EITHER AUTUMN OR WINTER INTO TWO.

FEELiNgS

CHAPTER ONE

HiGH SUMMER

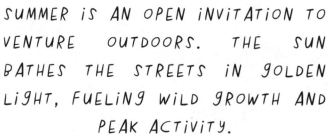

SUMMER IS AN OPEN INVITATION TO VENTURE OUTDOORS. THE SUN BATHES THE STREETS IN GOLDEN LIGHT, FUELING WILD GROWTH AND PEAK ACTIVITY.

THERE'S A CAREFREE FEELING IN THE AIR. THE SEASON SEEMS TO OFFER ENDLESS POSSIBILITY WITHIN EASY REACH.

THE KNOWLEDGE THAT THIS WEATHER WON'T BE HERE FOREVER MEANS CHANCES ARE TAKEN TO SOAK UP EVERY BIT OF THE SUMMER SUNSHINE.

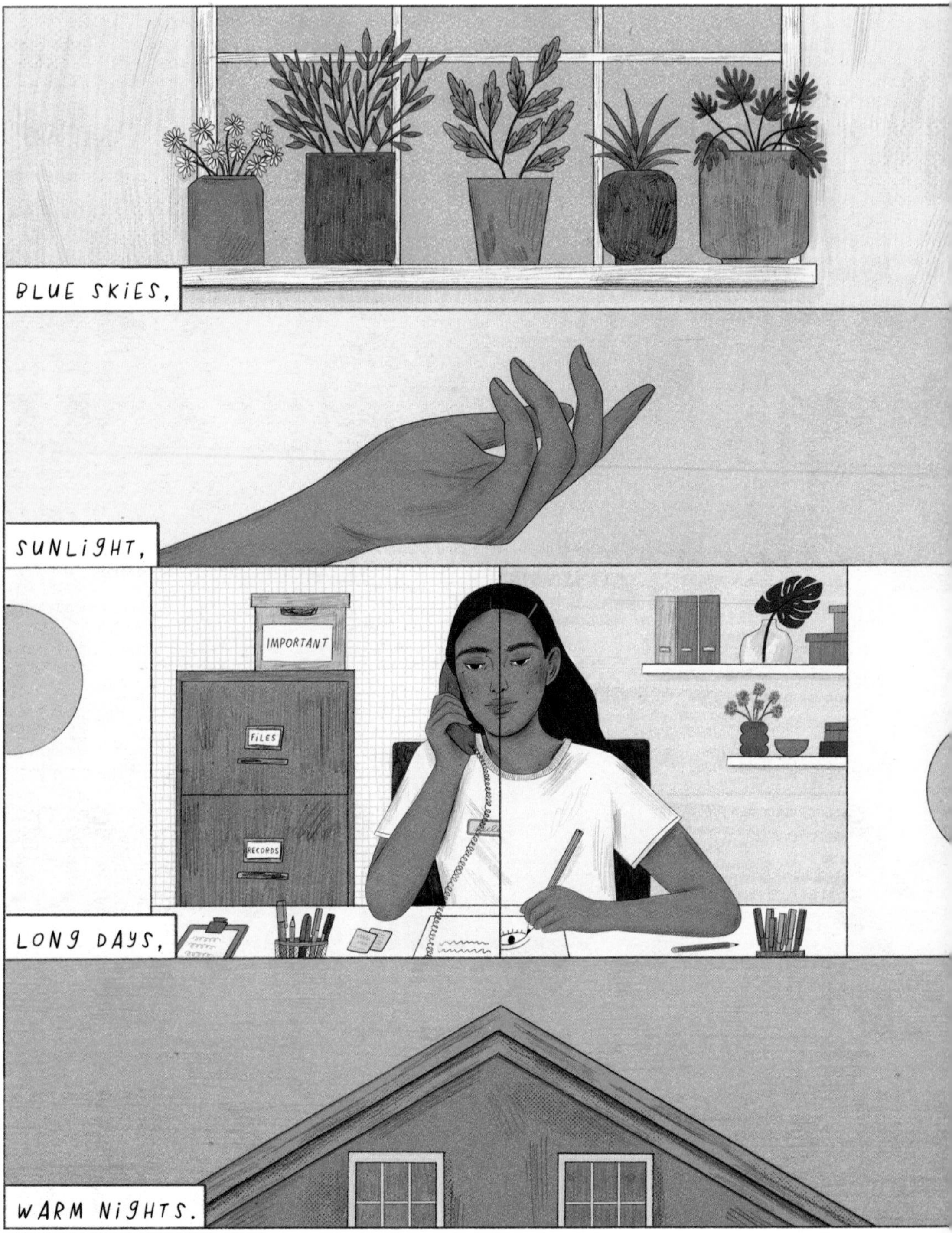
BLUE SKIES,
SUNLIGHT,
IMPORTANT
FILES
RECORDS
LONG DAYS,
WARM NIGHTS.

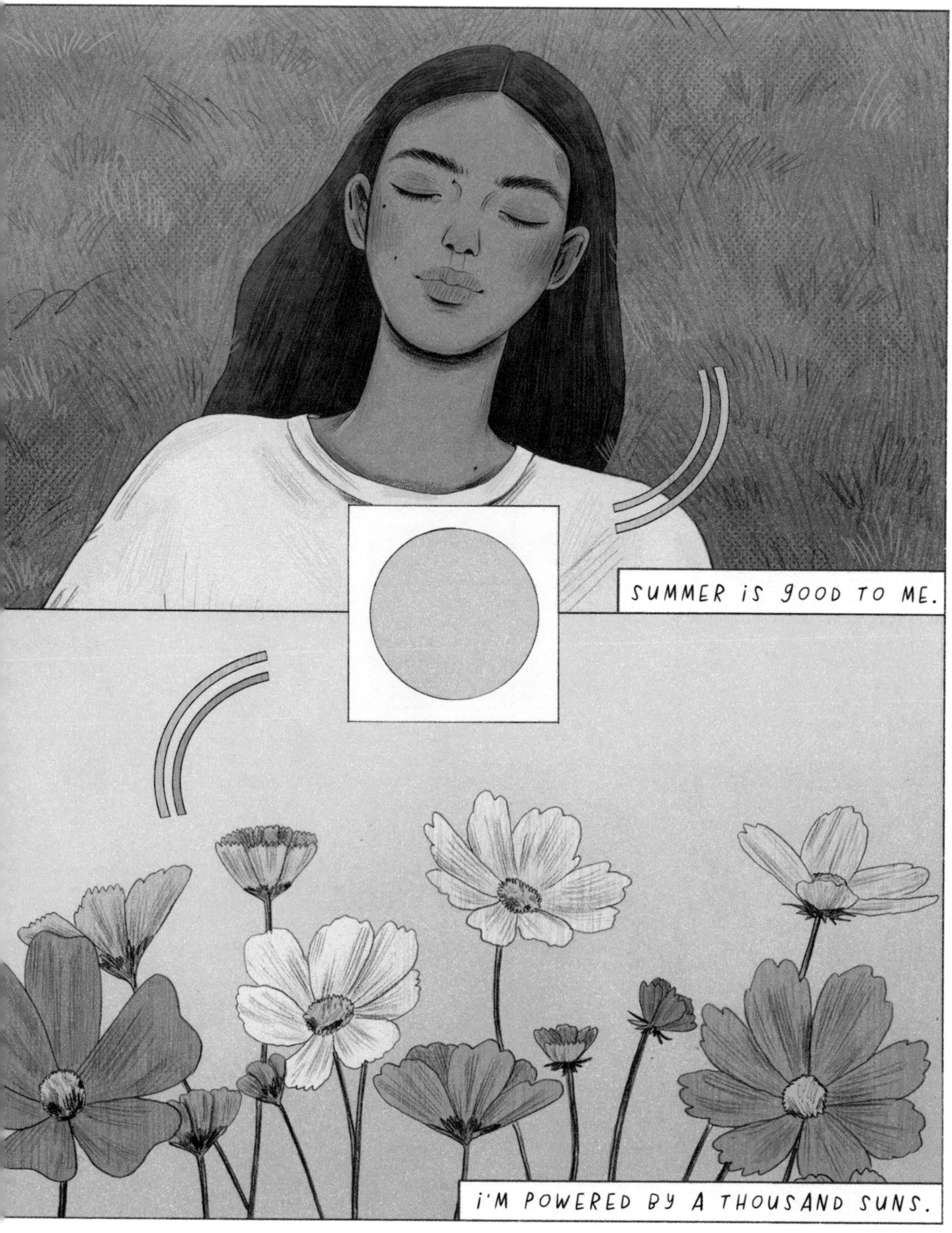
SUMMER IS GOOD TO ME.
I'M POWERED BY A THOUSAND SUNS.

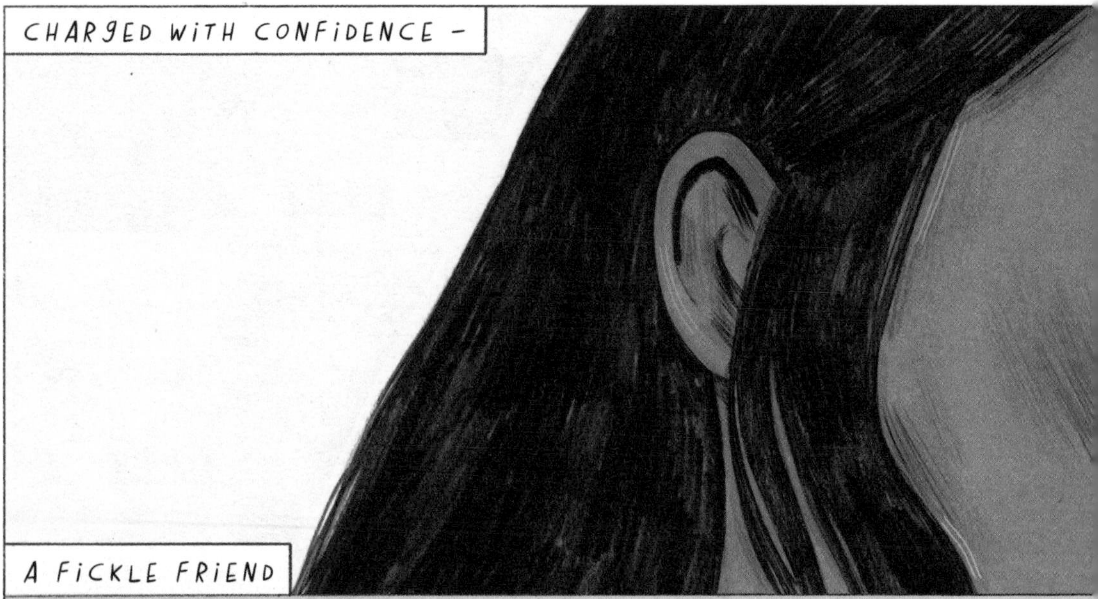
CHARGED WITH CONFIDENCE –
A FICKLE FRIEND
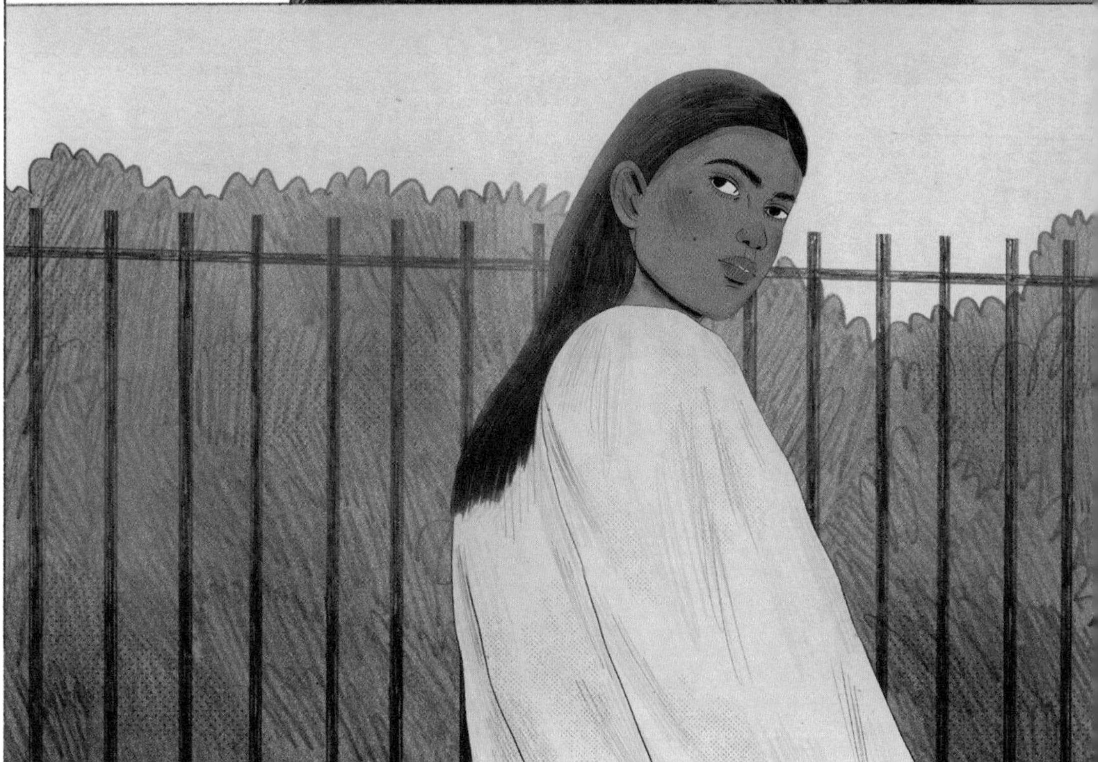
THAT ONLY COMES OUT

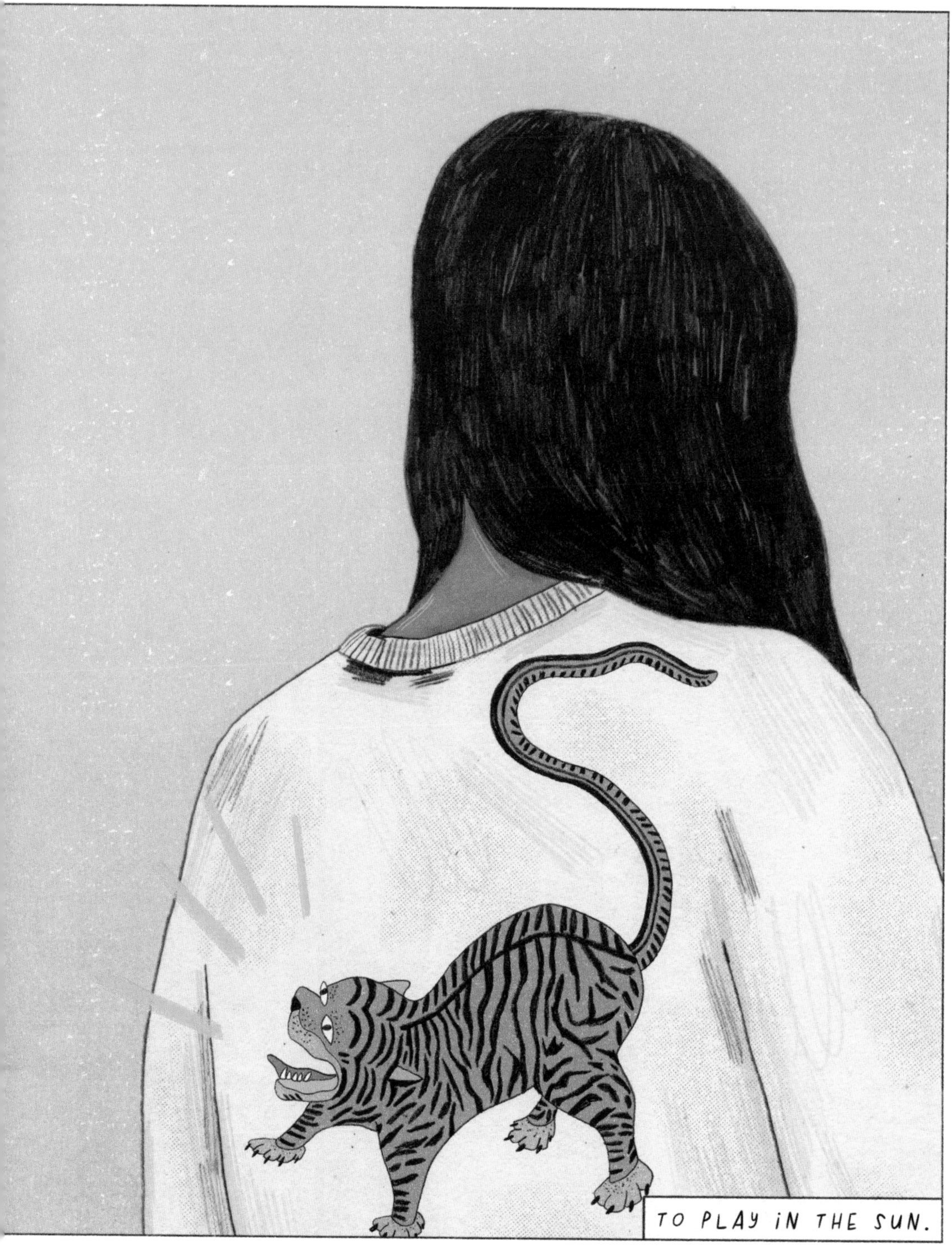
TO PLAY IN THE SUN.

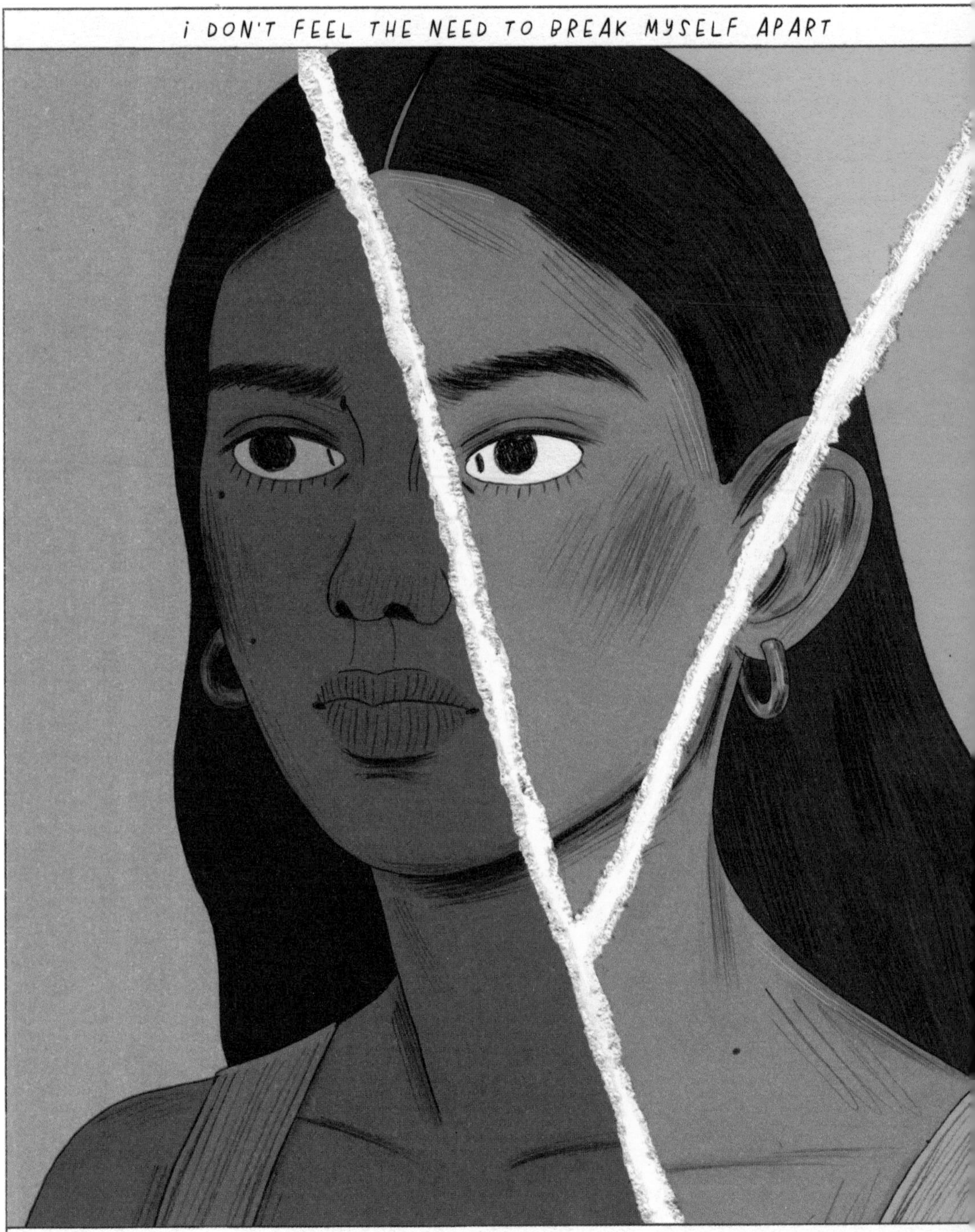
i DON'T FEEL THE NEED TO BREAK MYSELF APART
TO FiT iNTO ANYONE'S SHADOW.

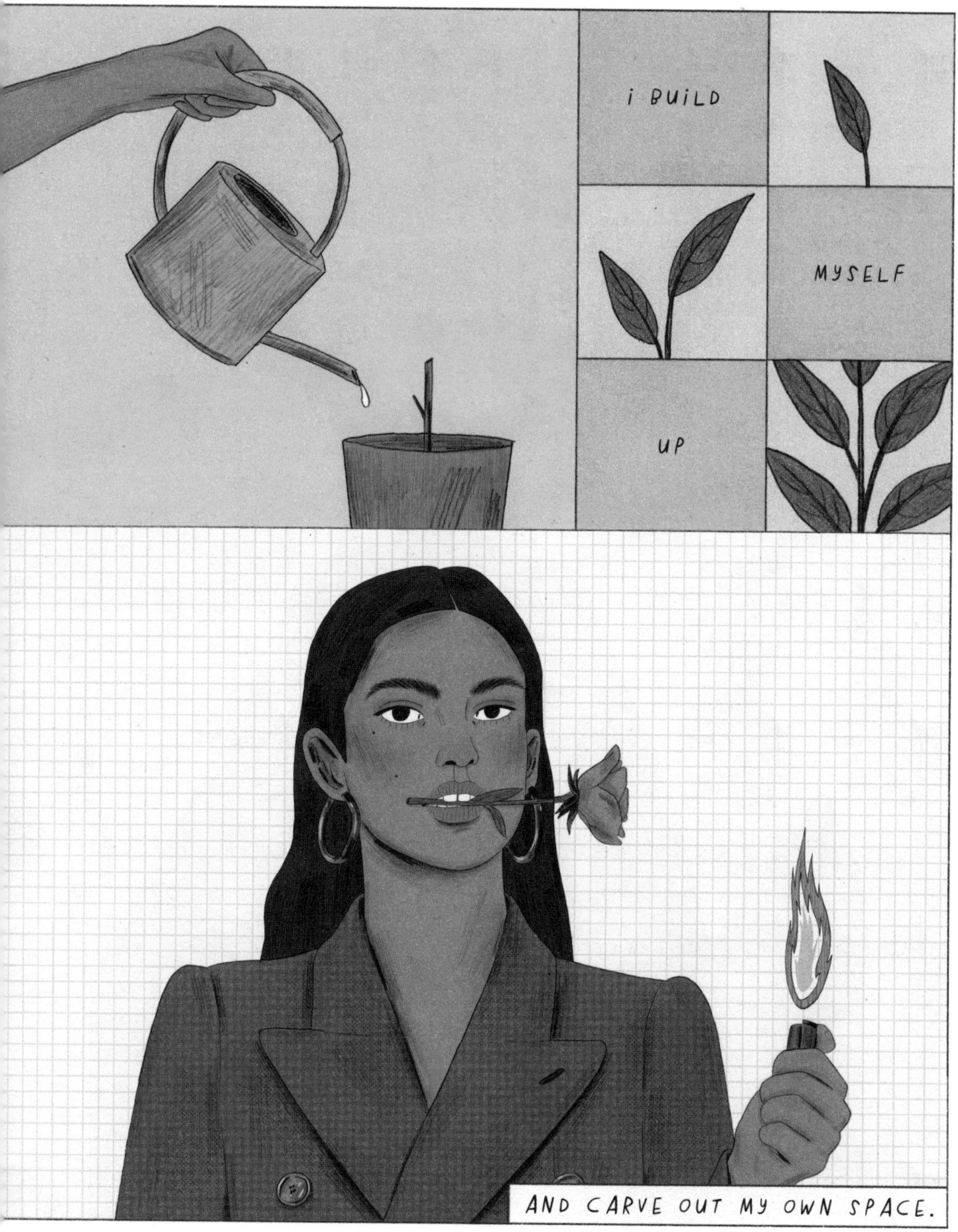
i BUILD
MYSELF
UP
AND CARVE OUT MY OWN SPACE.

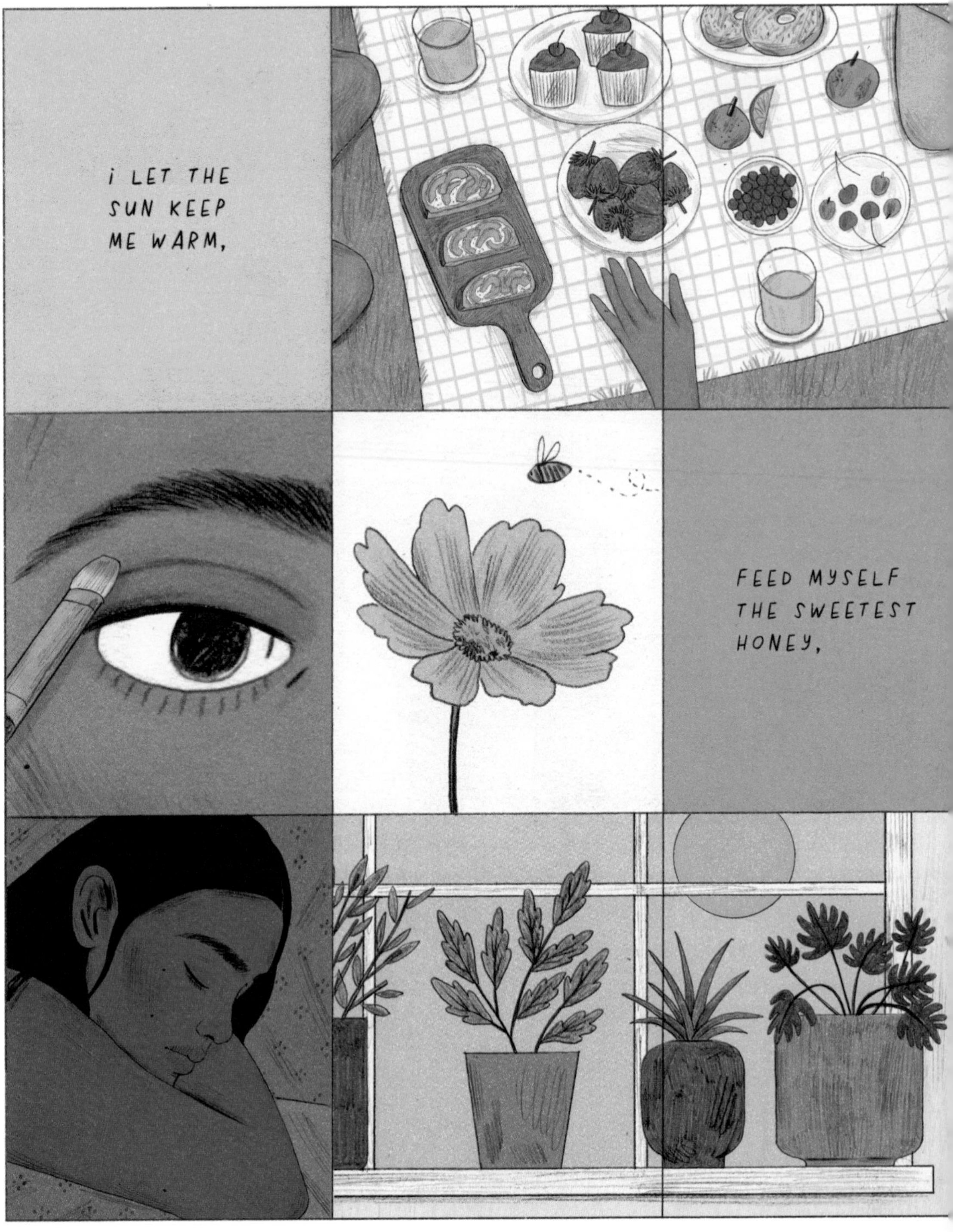
i LET THE SUN KEEP ME WARM,
FEED MYSELF THE SWEETEST HONEY,

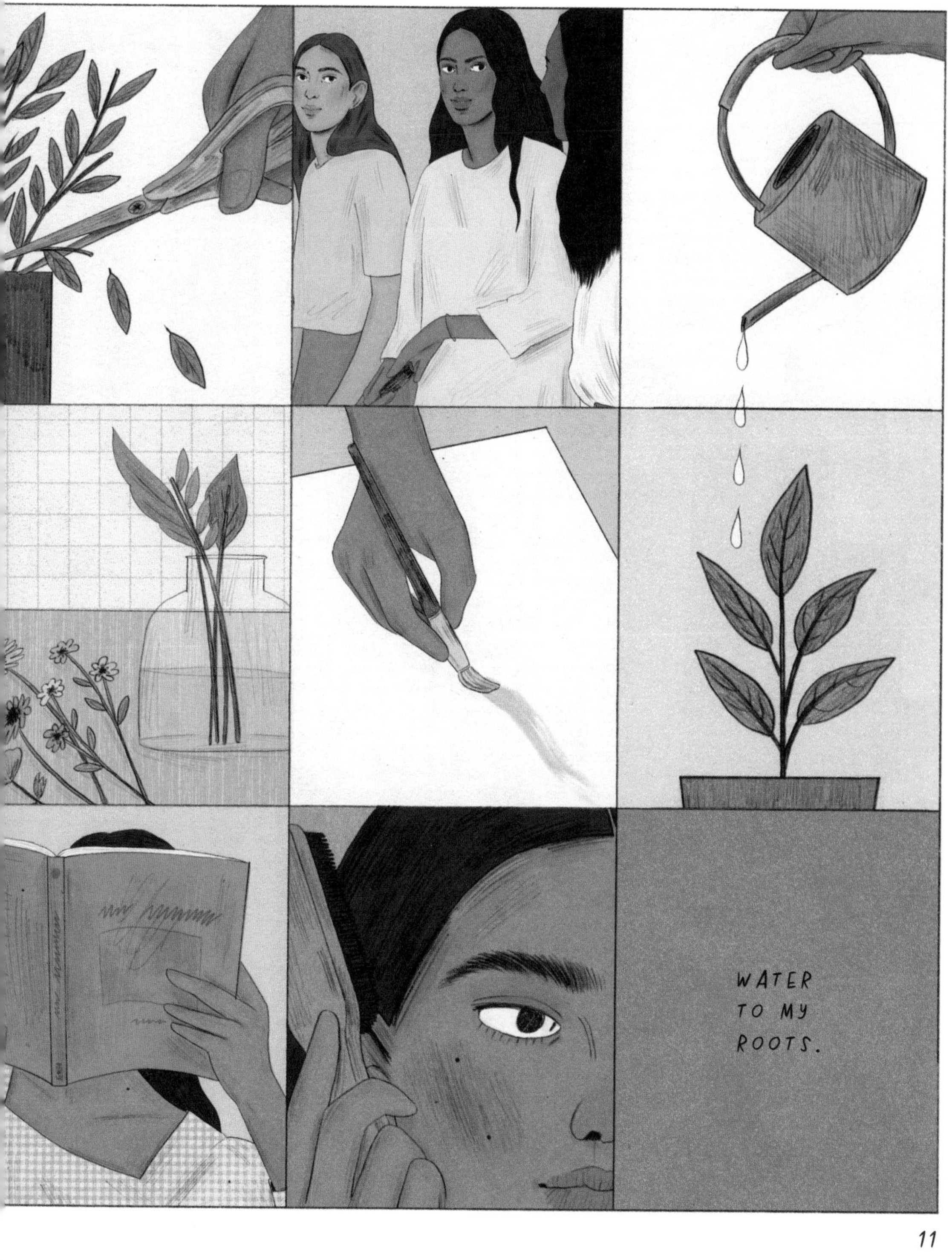
WATER
TO MY
ROOTS.

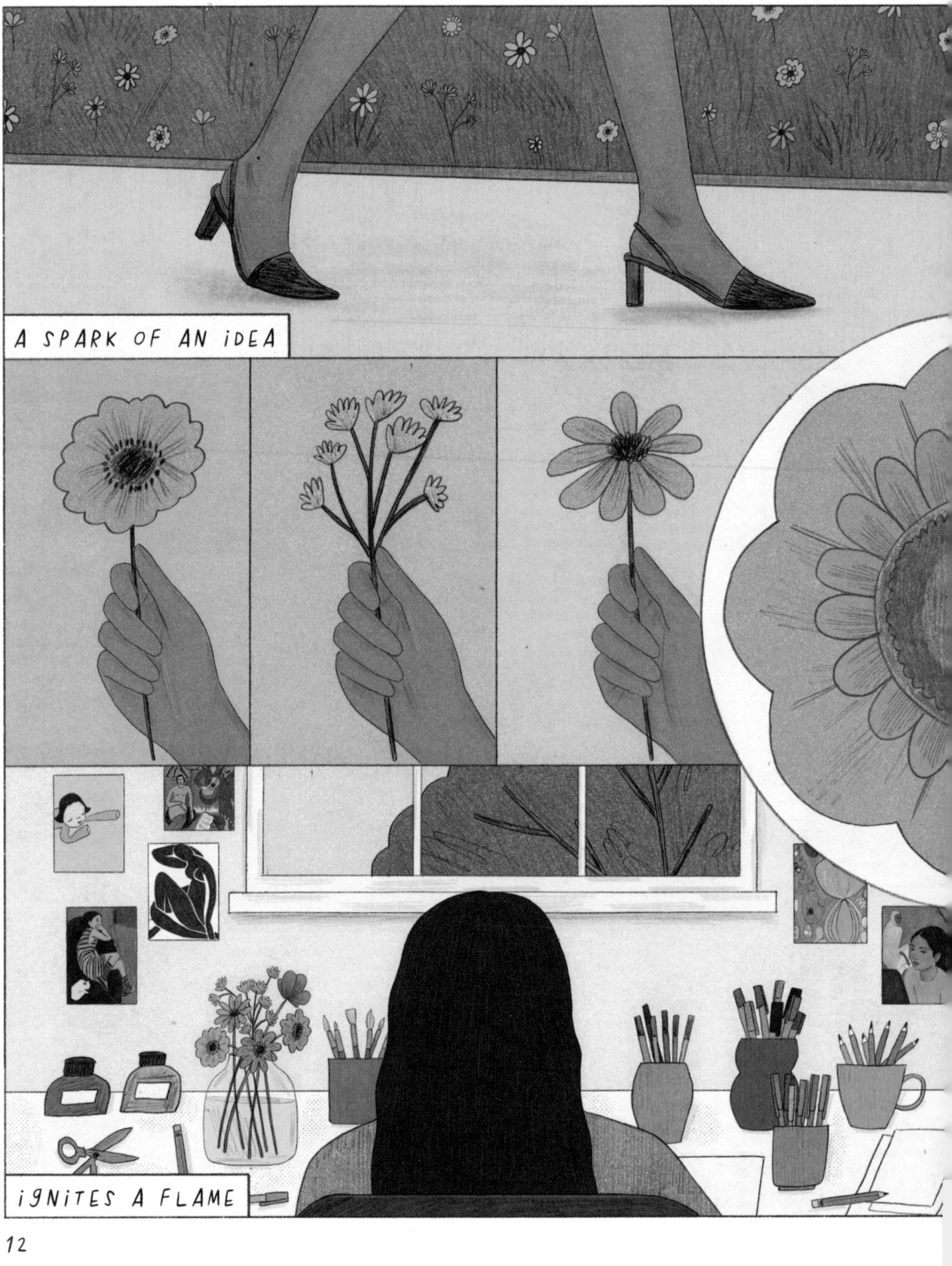
A SPARK OF AN iDEA
igNiTES A FLAME

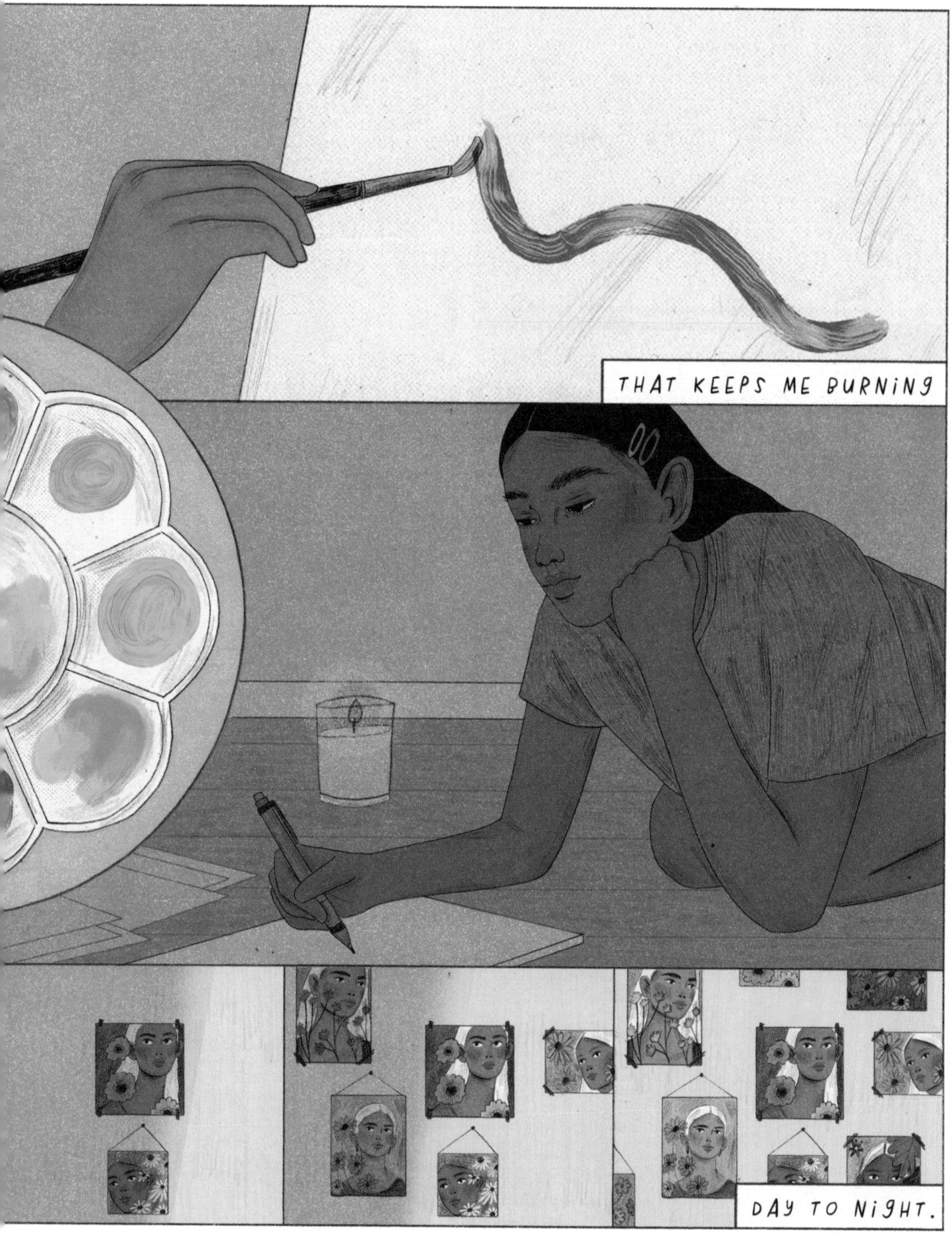
THAT KEEPS ME BURNING
DAY TO NIGHT.

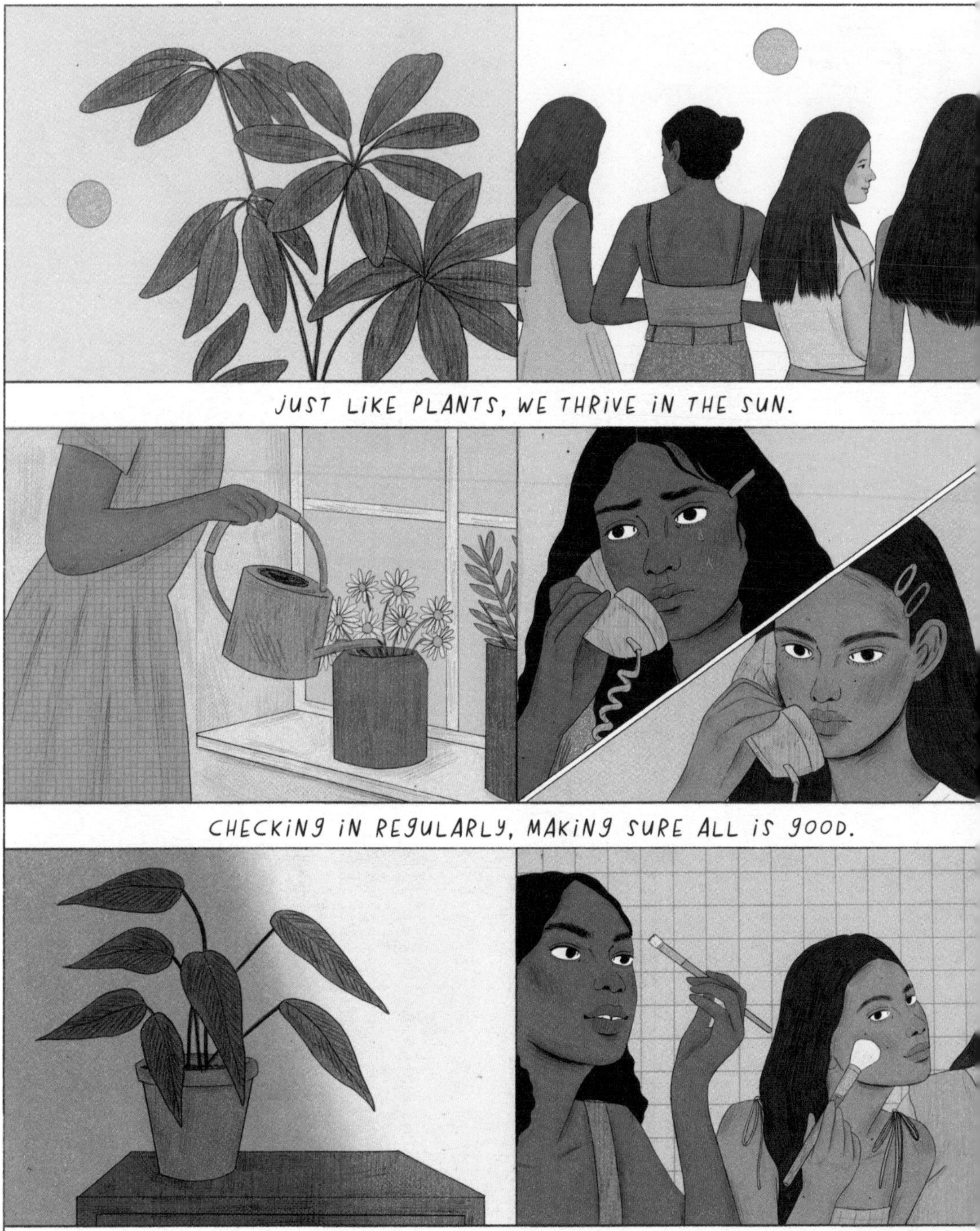
JUST LIKE PLANTS, WE THRIVE IN THE SUN.
CHECKING IN REGULARLY, MAKING SURE ALL IS GOOD.
AND IF ONE OF US IS STUCK IN THE SHADE, WE PUT IN THE TIME TO GET THEM OUT

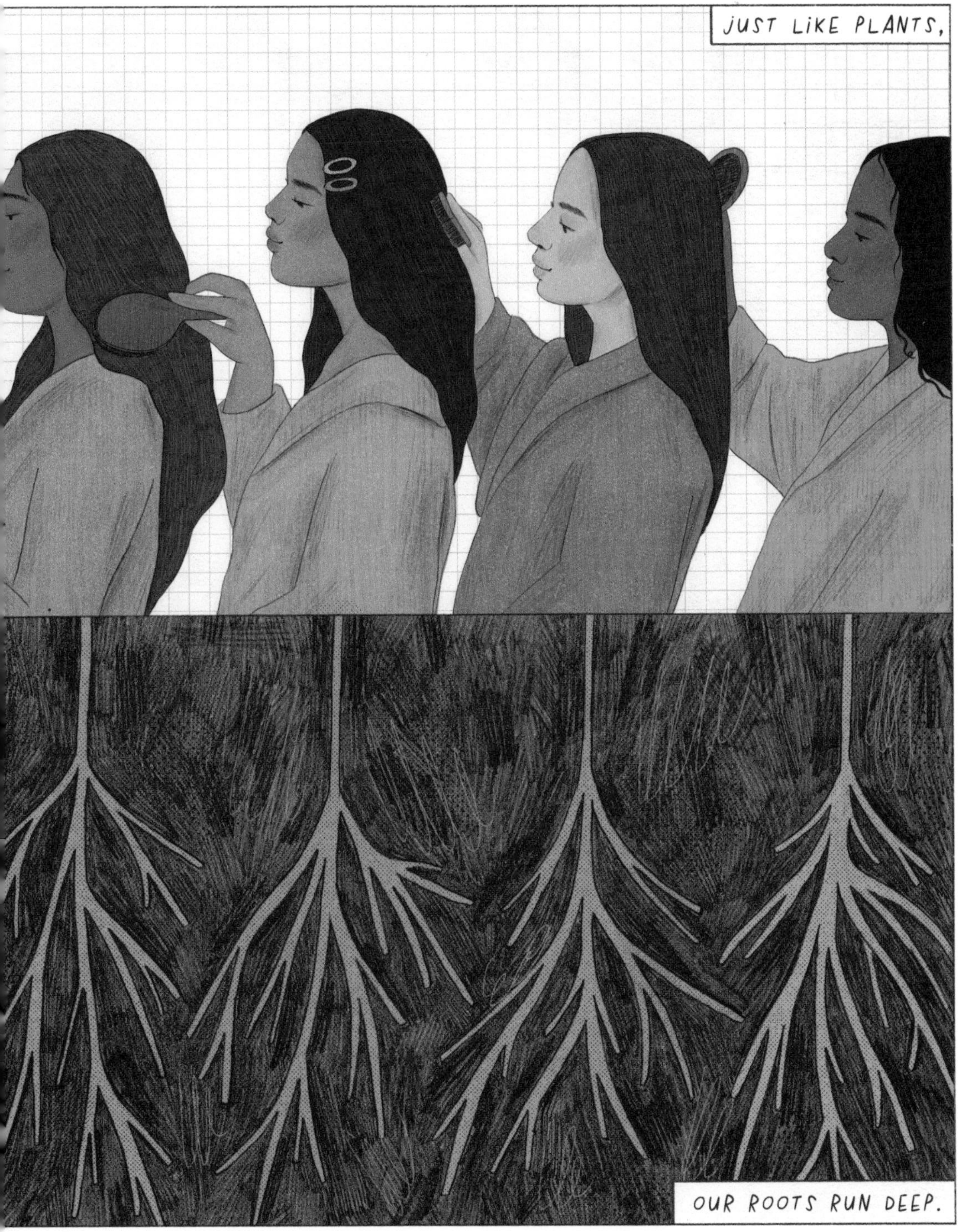
JUST LIKE PLANTS,
OUR ROOTS RUN DEEP.

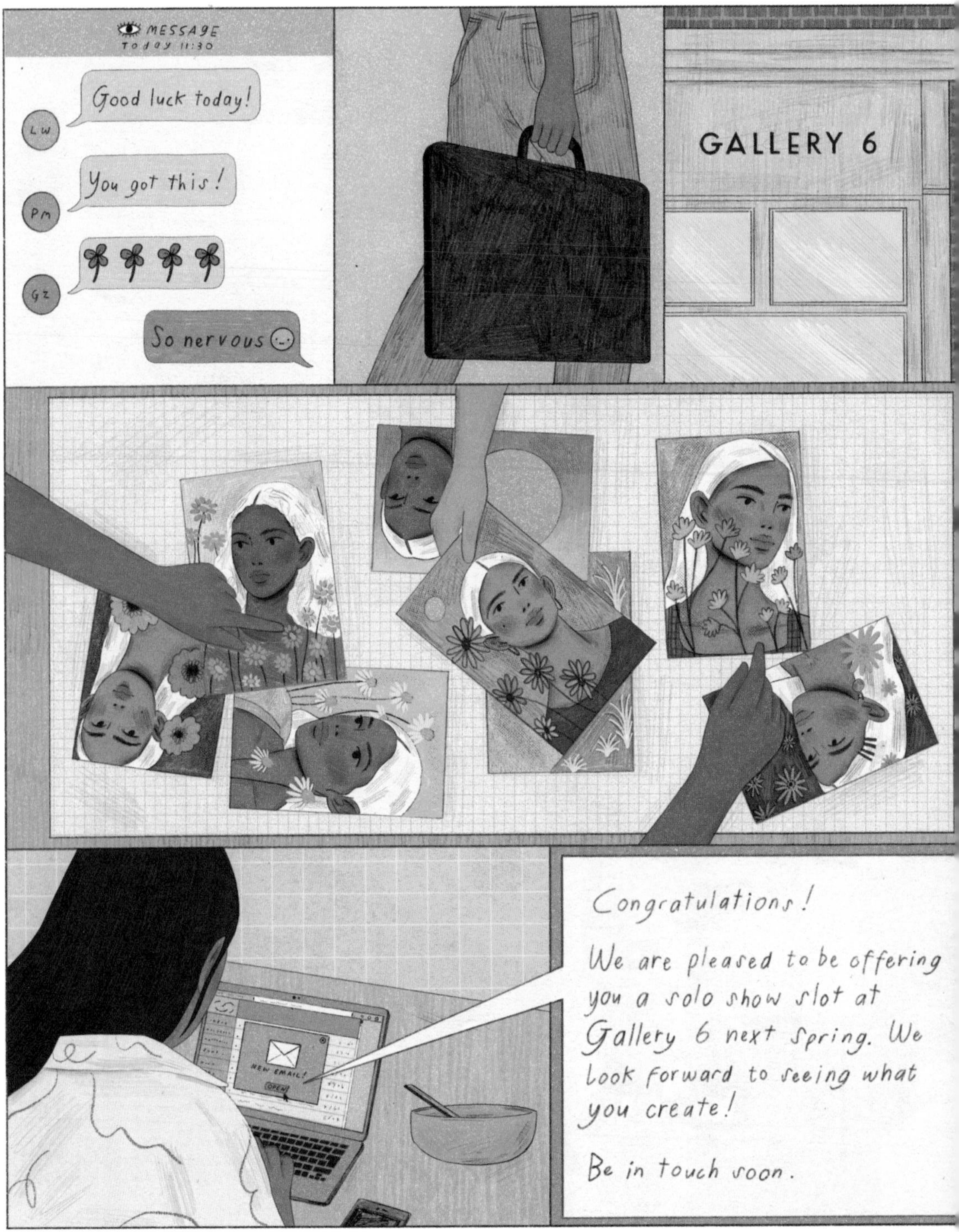
MESSAGE
Today 11:30
Good luck today!
LW
You got this!
PM
GZ
So nervous
GALLERY 6
NEW EMAIL!
OPEN
Congratulations!
We are pleased to be offering you a solo show slot at Gallery 6 next Spring. We look forward to seeing what you create!
Be in touch soon.

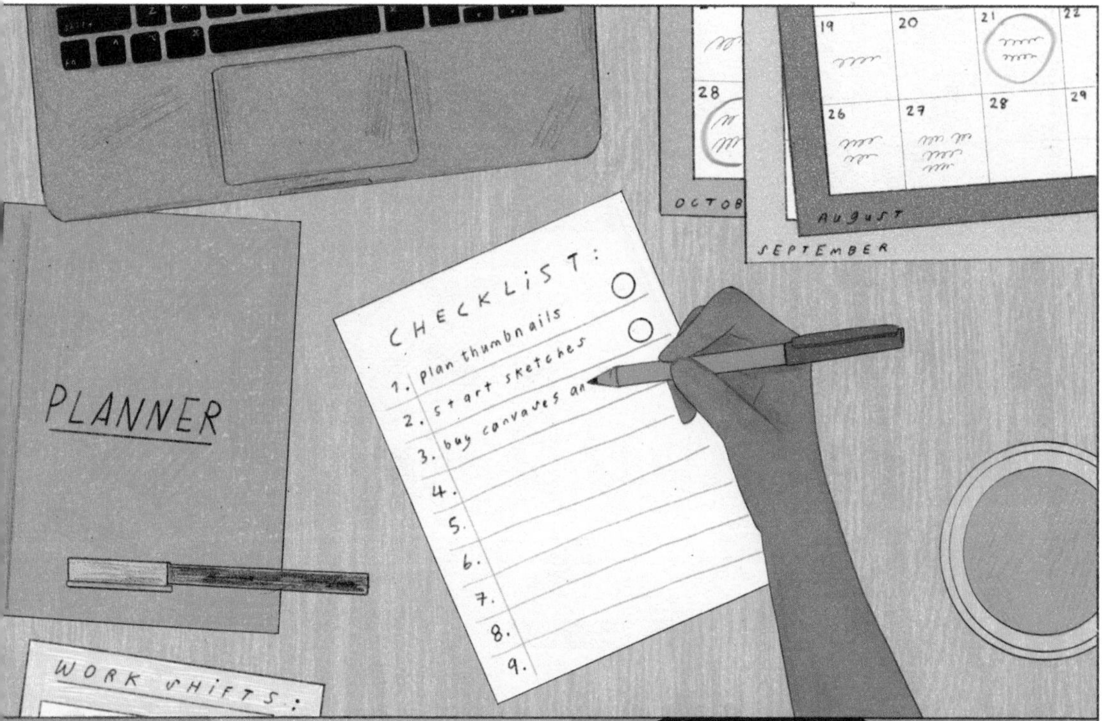
CHECKLIST:
1. plan thumbnails
2. start sketches
3. buy canvases an
4.
5.
6.
7.
8.
9.
PLANNER
WORK SHIFTS:
OCTOB
AUGUST
SEPTEMBER

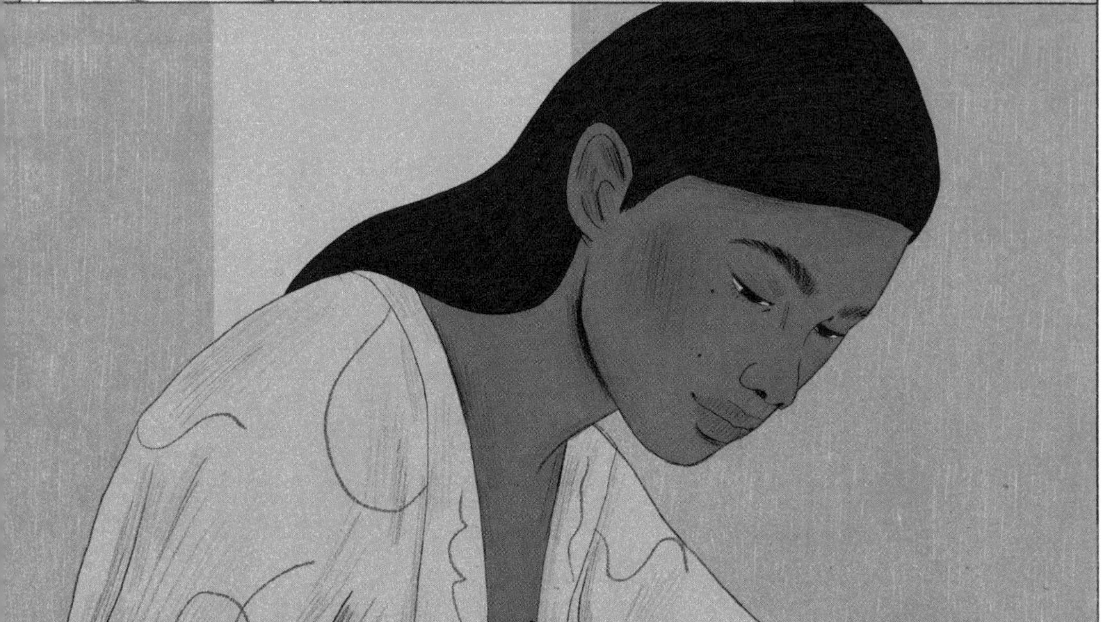

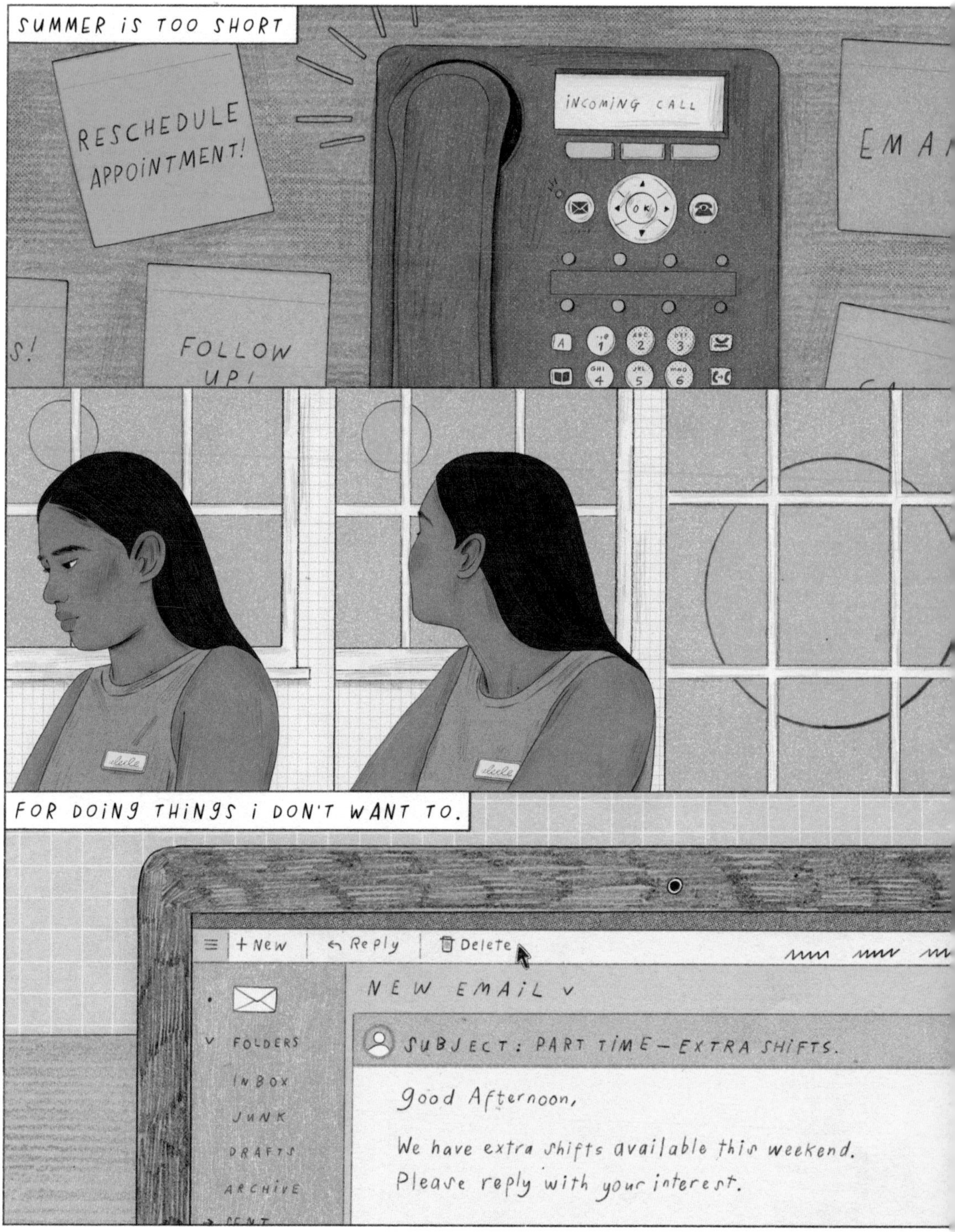
SUMMER IS TOO SHORT
RESCHEDULE APPOINTMENT!
INCOMING CALL
FOLLOW UP!
FOR DOING THINGS I DON'T WANT TO.
+ New
Reply
Delete
NEW EMAIL
FOLDERS
INBOX
JUNK
DRAFTS
ARCHIVE
SUBJECT: PART TIME—EXTRA SHIFTS.
Good Afternoon,
We have extra shifts available this weekend.
Please reply with your interest.

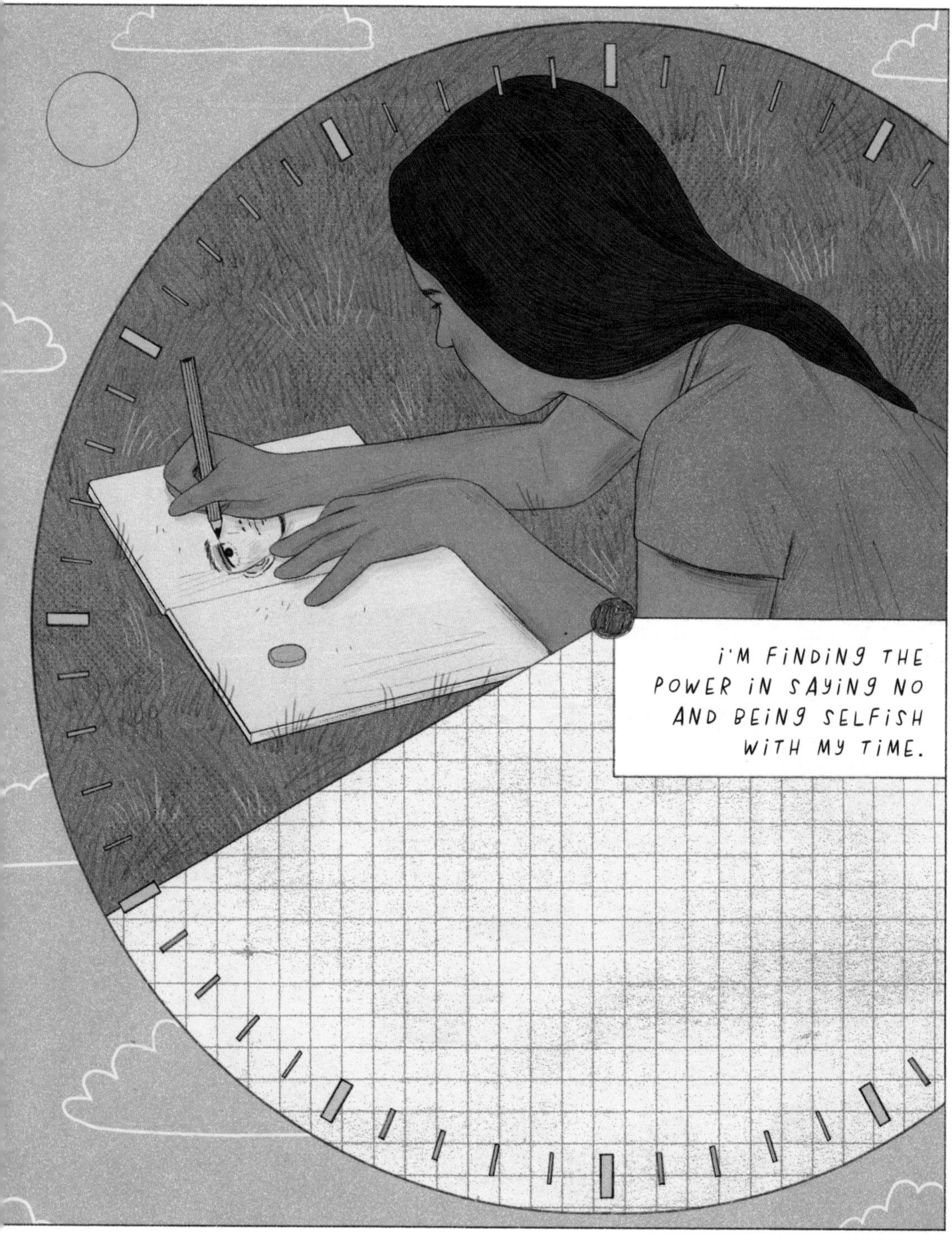
I'M FINDING THE POWER IN SAYING NO AND BEING SELFISH WITH MY TIME.

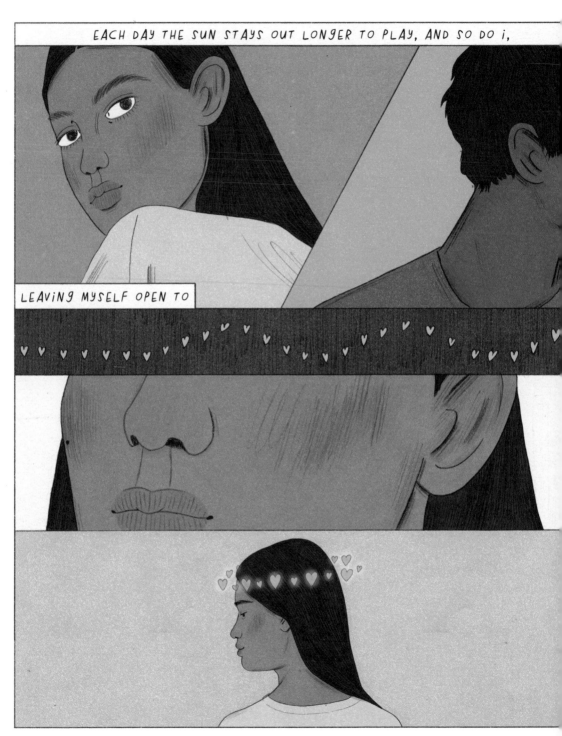

EACH DAY THE SUN STAYS OUT LONGER TO PLAY, AND SO DO I,

LEAVING MYSELF OPEN TO

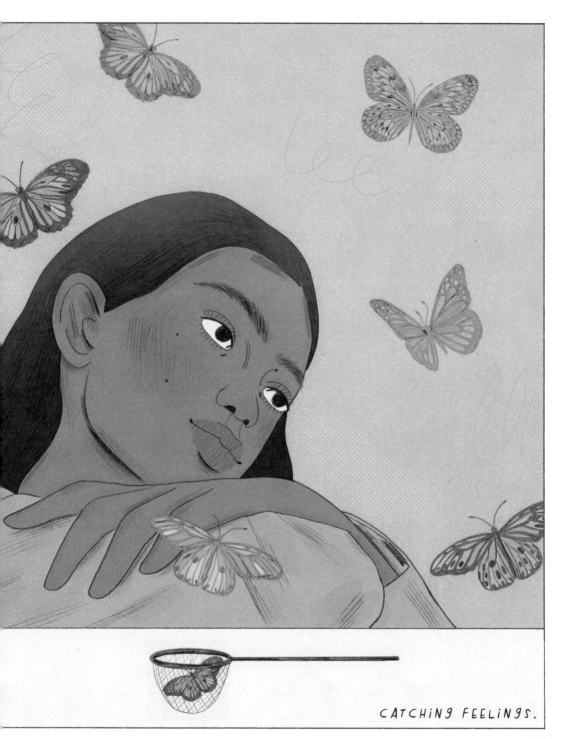

CATCHING FEELINGS.

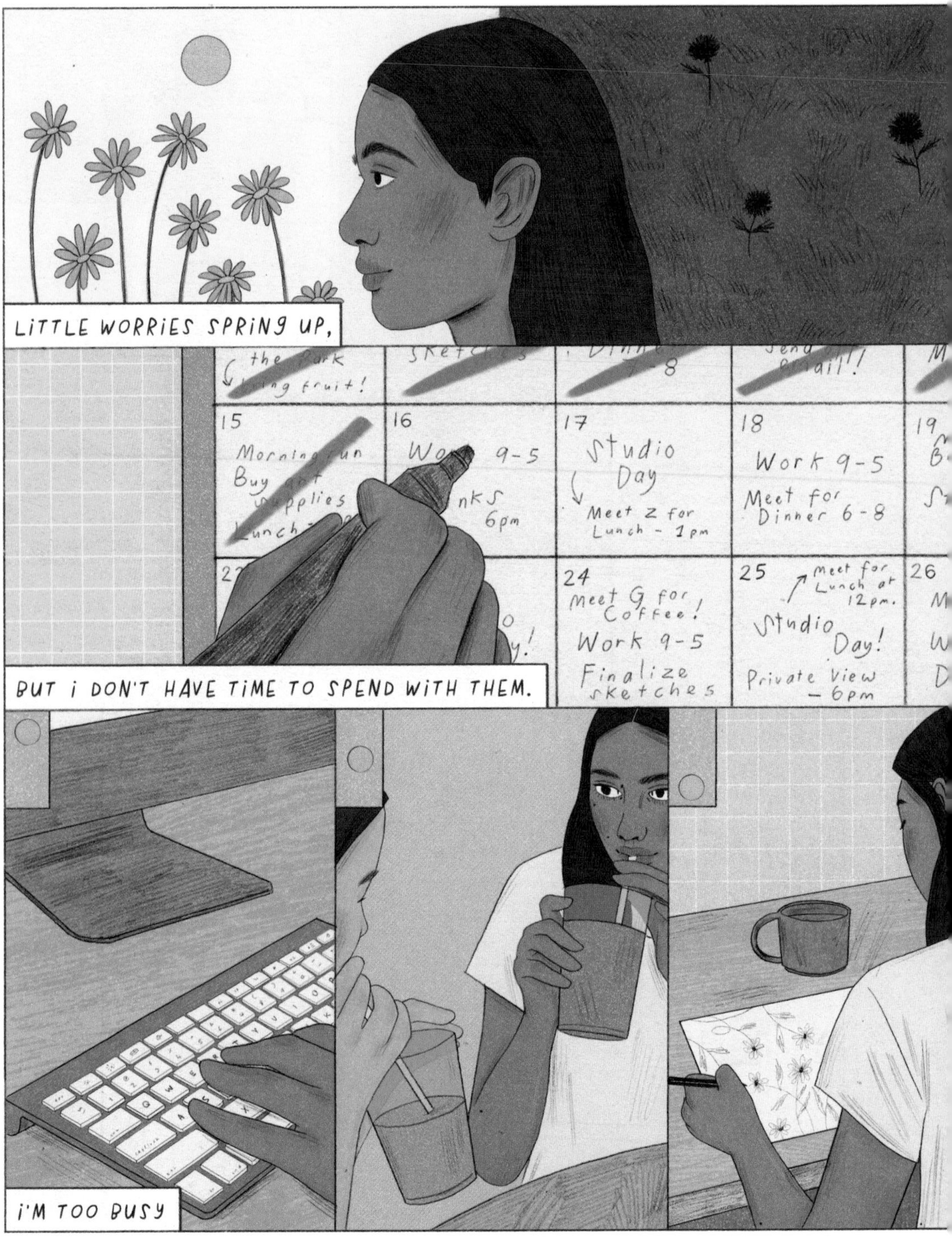
LiTTLE WORRiES SPRiNG UP,
15
16
Work 9-5
17
Studio Day
Meet Z for Lunch - 1pm
18
Work 9-5
Meet for Dinner 6-8
24
Meet G for Coffee!
Work 9-5
Finalize sketches
25
Meet for Lunch at 12pm.
Studio Day!
Private View - 6pm
26
BUT i DON'T HAVE TiME TO SPEND WiTH THEM.
i'M TOO BUSY

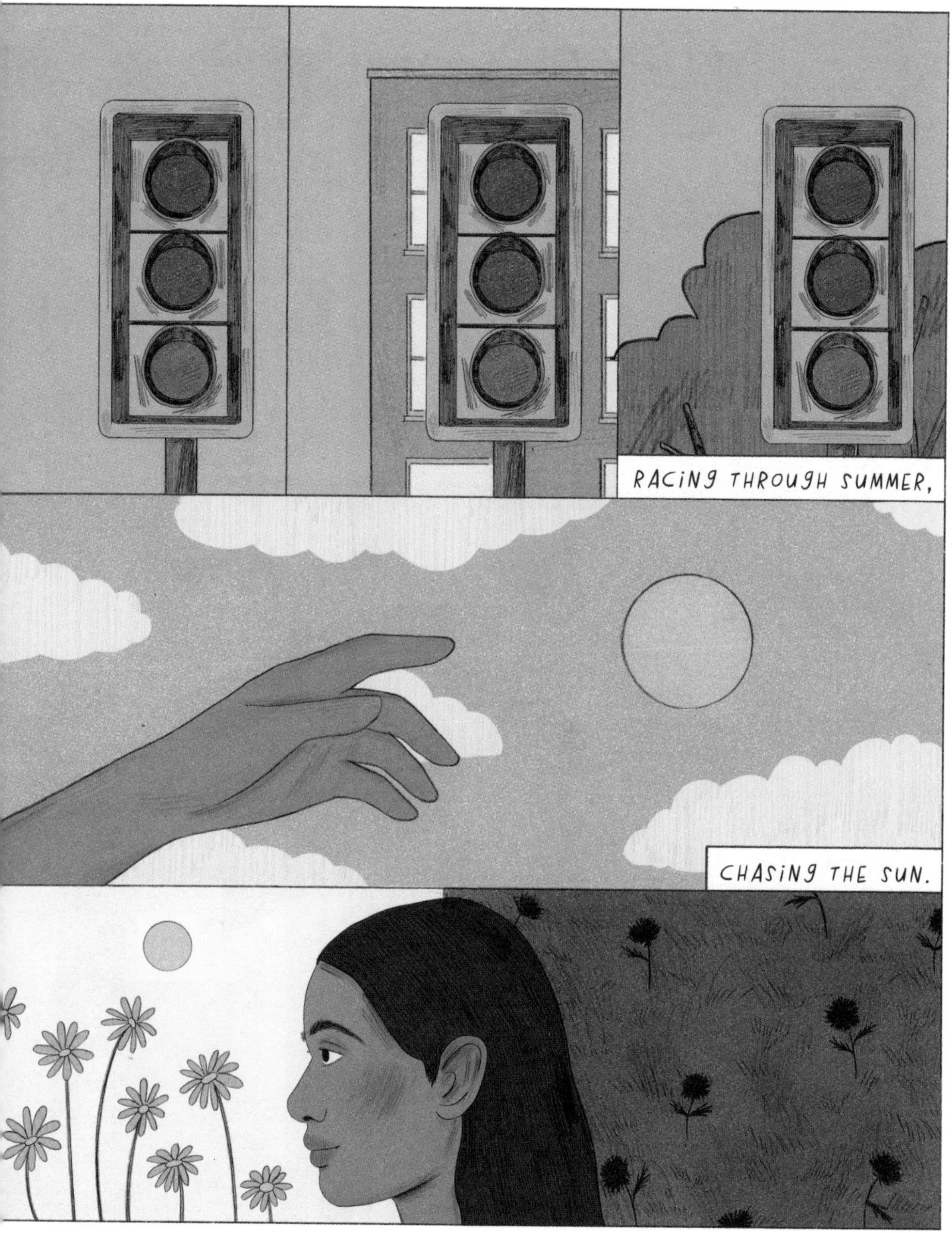
RACING THROUGH SUMMER,
CHASING THE SUN.

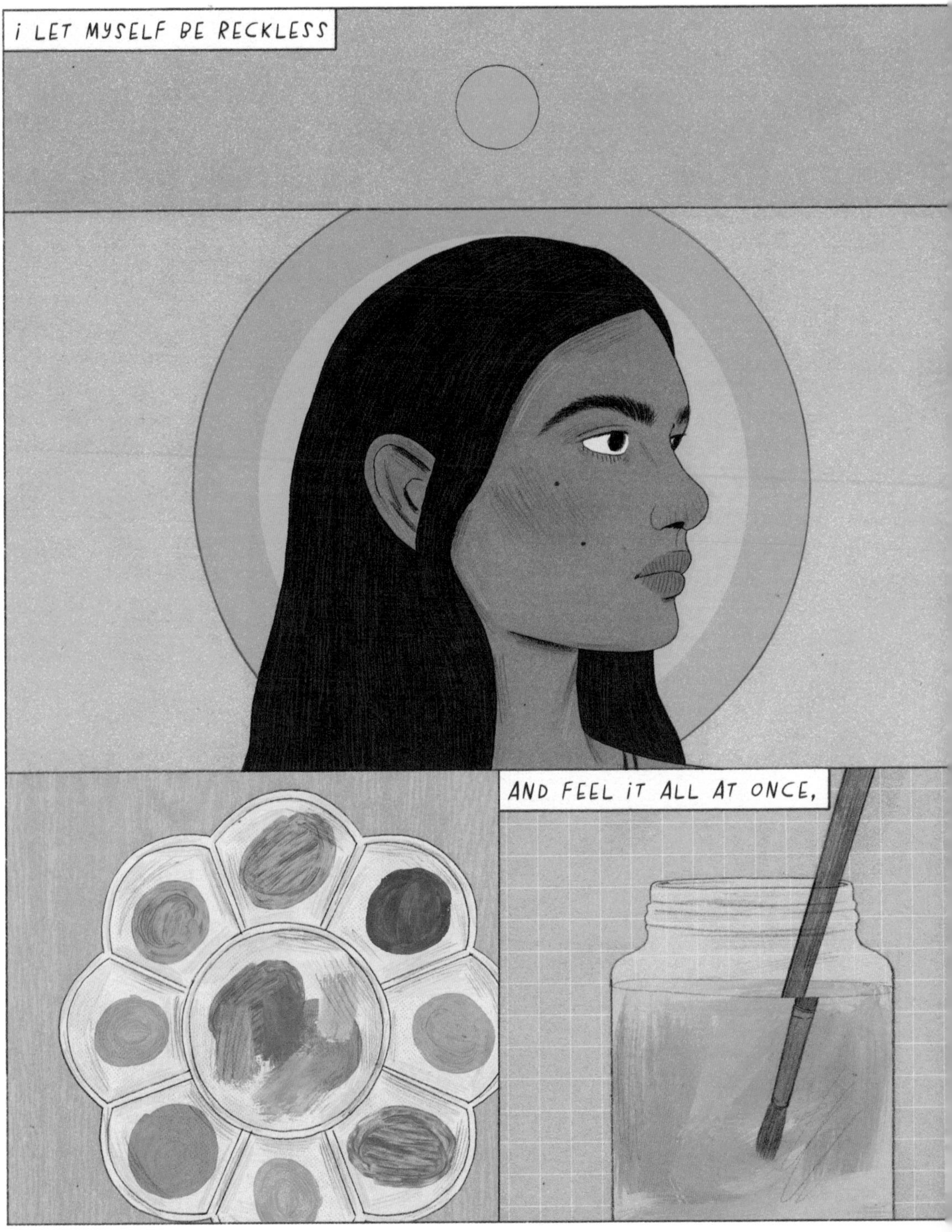
i LET MYSELF BE RECKLESS
AND FEEL iT ALL AT ONCE,

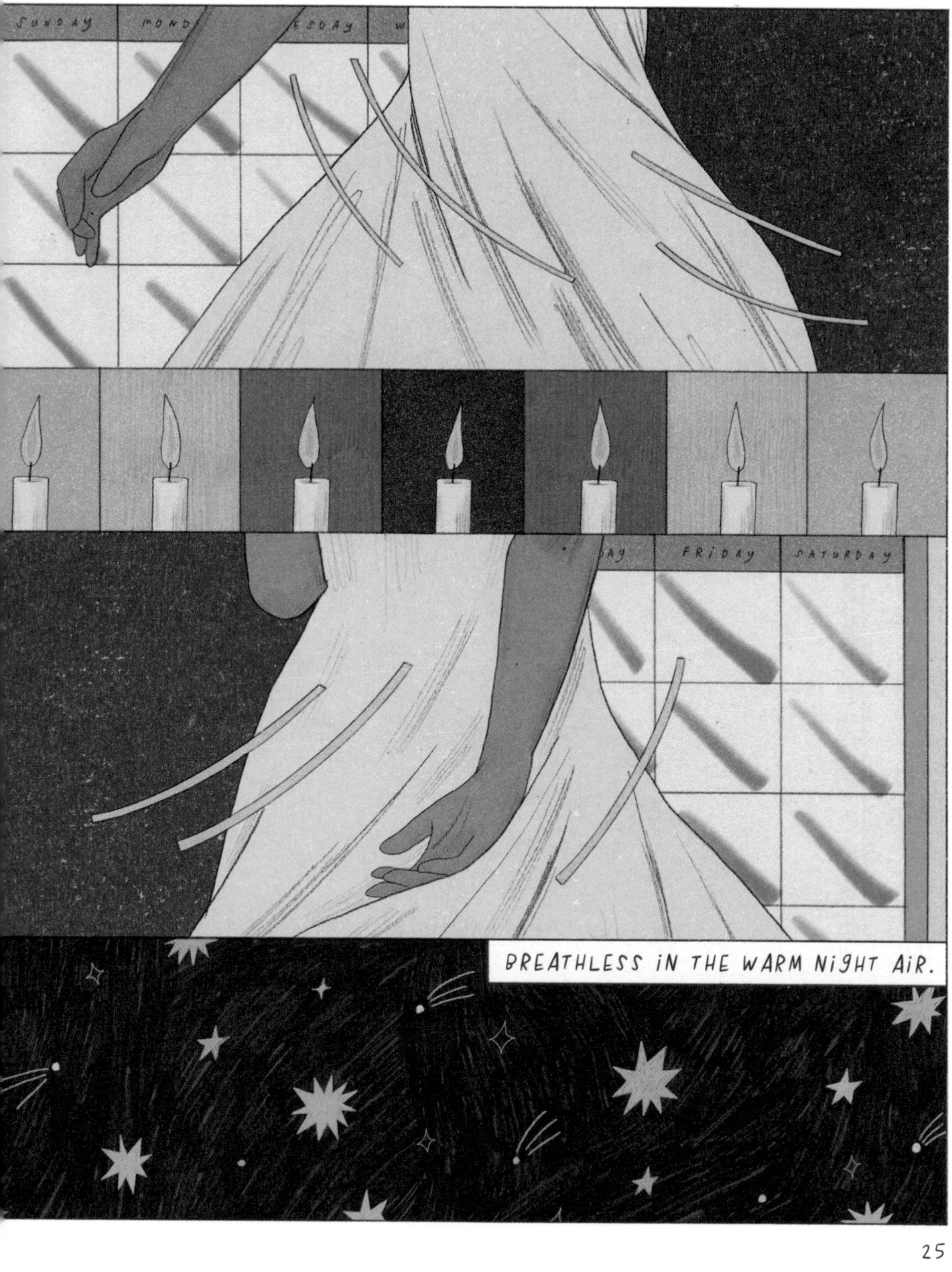
SUNDAY
FRIDAY
SATURDAY
BREATHLESS IN THE WARM NIGHT AIR.

CHAPTER TWO

LATE SUMMER

IN THE SECOND HALF OF SUMMER, TEMPERATURES RISE EVEN HIGHER.

AS THE PROLONGED PERIODS OF LIGHT PERSIST, SOME PLANTS BEGIN TO WILT, NO LONGER ABLE TO DANCE ABOUT IN THE BREEZE WITH THE OTHERS.

STRESS AND ANXIETY CREEP UP, SETTLING INTO THE SKIN AS SWEAT. THE HEAT OF SUMMER BECOMES UNCOMFORTABLE.

A WORRY OF NOT MAKING THE MOST OUT OF THE SEASON BUILDS ALONGSIDE THE SHAME OF NOT ENJOYING THE SUN AS MUCH AS EVERYONE ELSE.

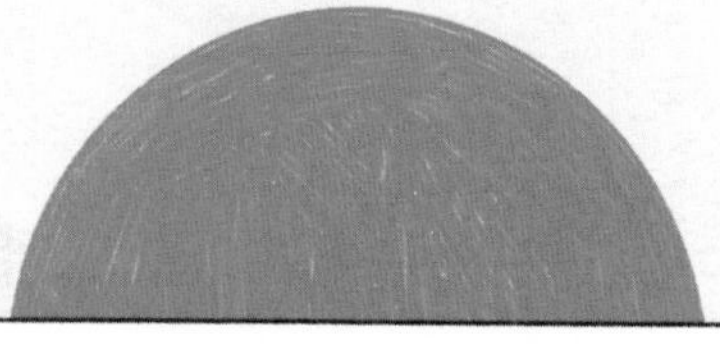

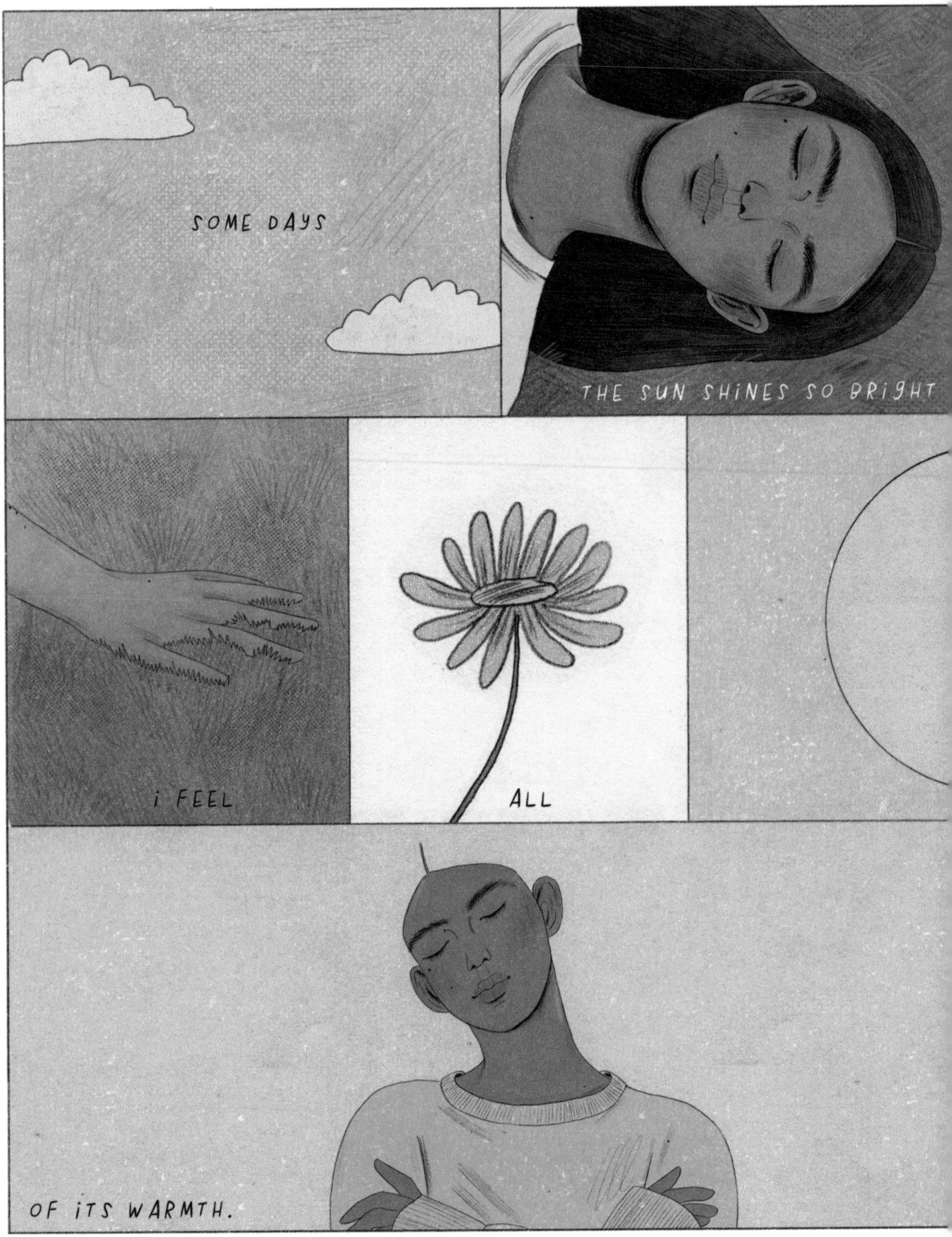
SOME DAYS
THE SUN SHINES SO BRIGHT
i FEEL
ALL
OF iTS WARMTH.

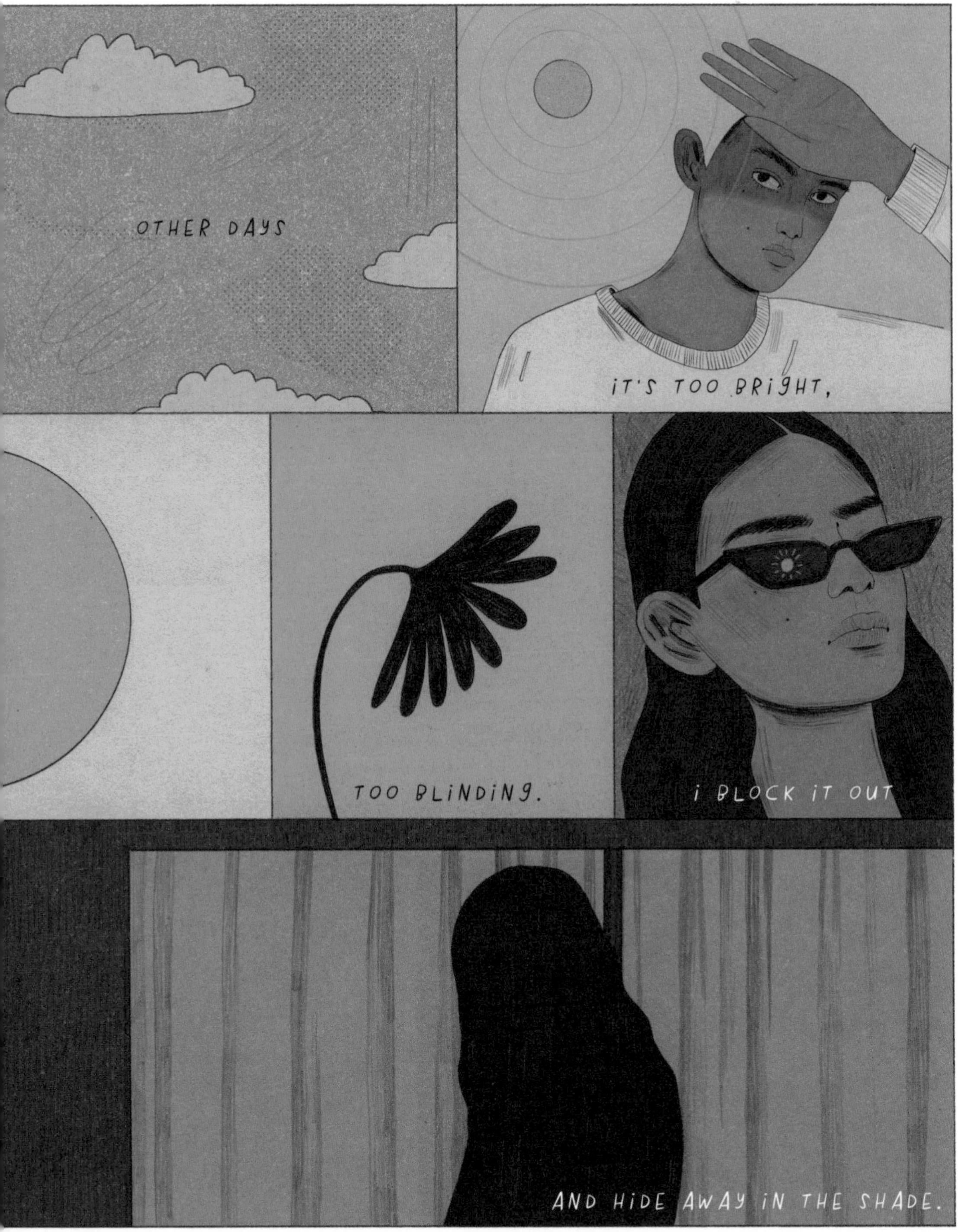
OTHER DAYS
IT'S TOO BRIGHT,
TOO BLINDING.
I BLOCK IT OUT
AND HIDE AWAY IN THE SHADE.

THERE'S A VOICE INSIDE MY HEAD.

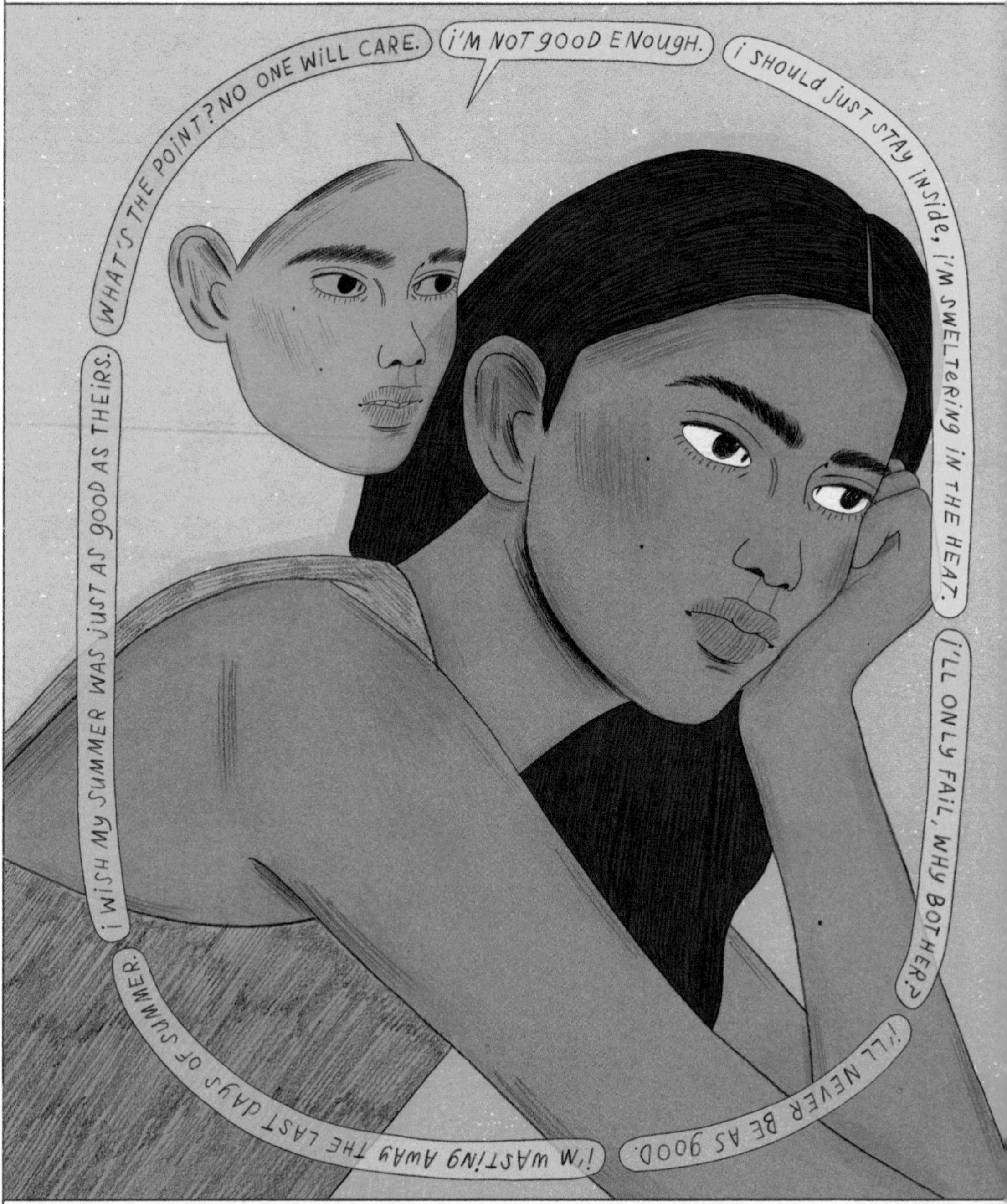
I'M NOT GOOD ENOUGH.
WHAT'S THE POINT? NO ONE WILL CARE.
I WISH MY SUMMER WAS JUST AS GOOD AS THEIRS.
I'M WASTING AWAY THE LAST DAYS OF SUMMER.
I'LL NEVER BE AS GOOD.
I'LL ONLY FAIL, WHY BOTHER?
I SHOULD JUST STAY INSIDE, I'M SWELTERING IN THE HEAT.

IT STARTED AS A WHISPER, BUT IT'S GOTTEN MUCH LOUDER.

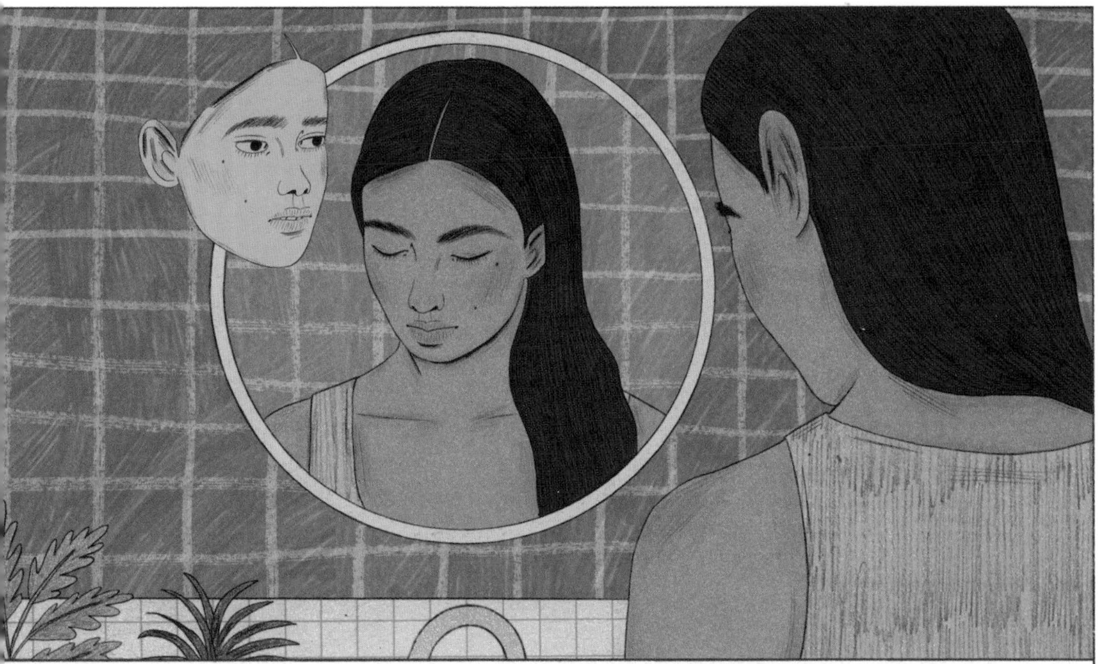

FIRST I CARRIED IT, NOW IT CARRIES ME.

DRAGGING ME AROUND, DRAGGING ME DOWN.

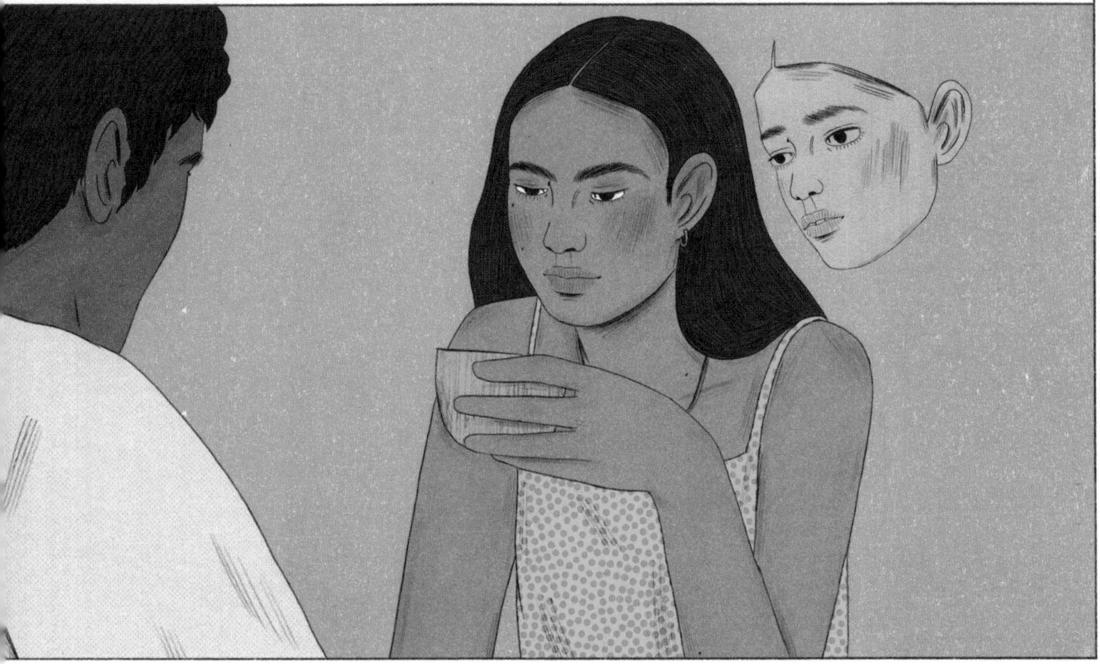

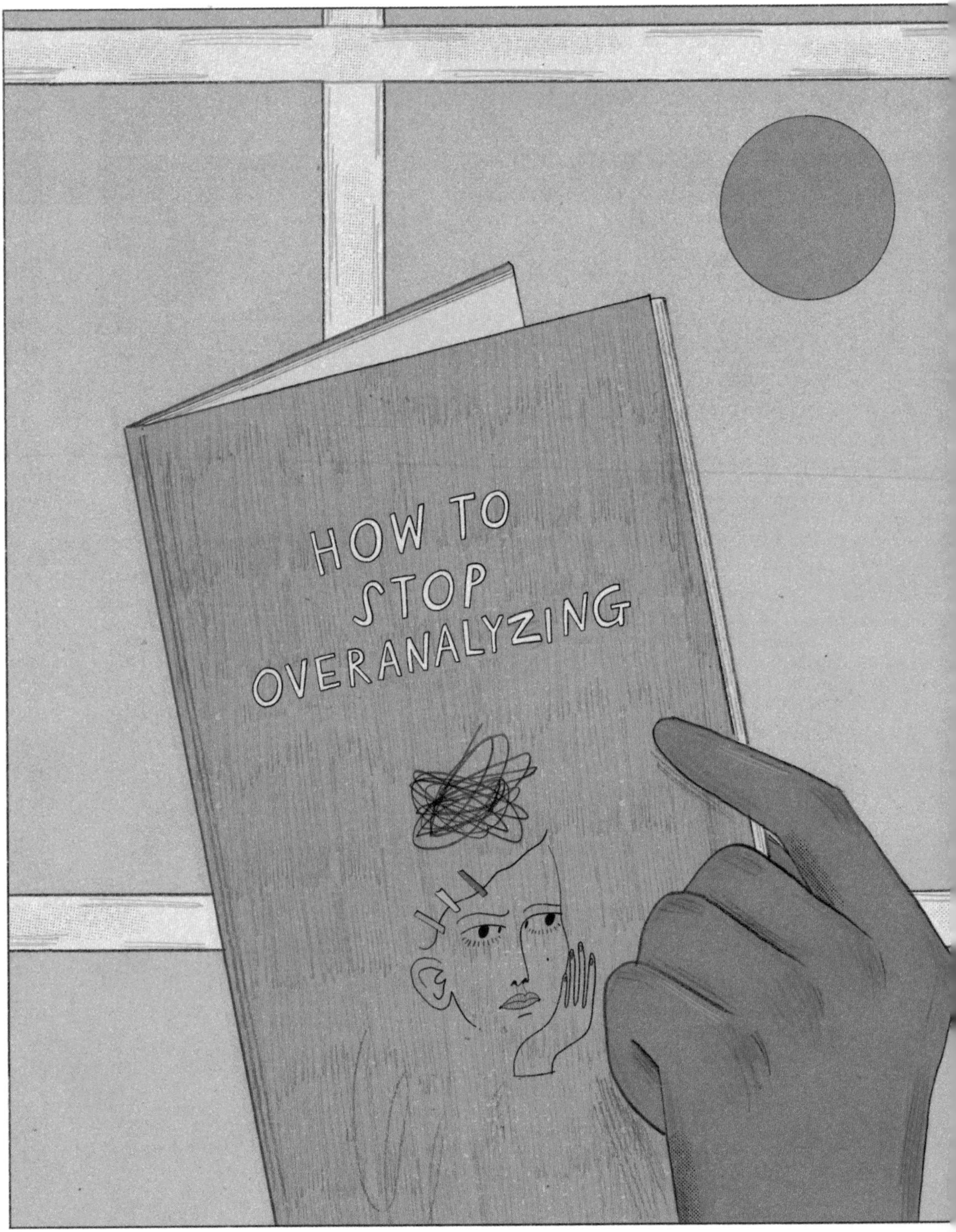
HOW TO
STOP
OVERANALYZING

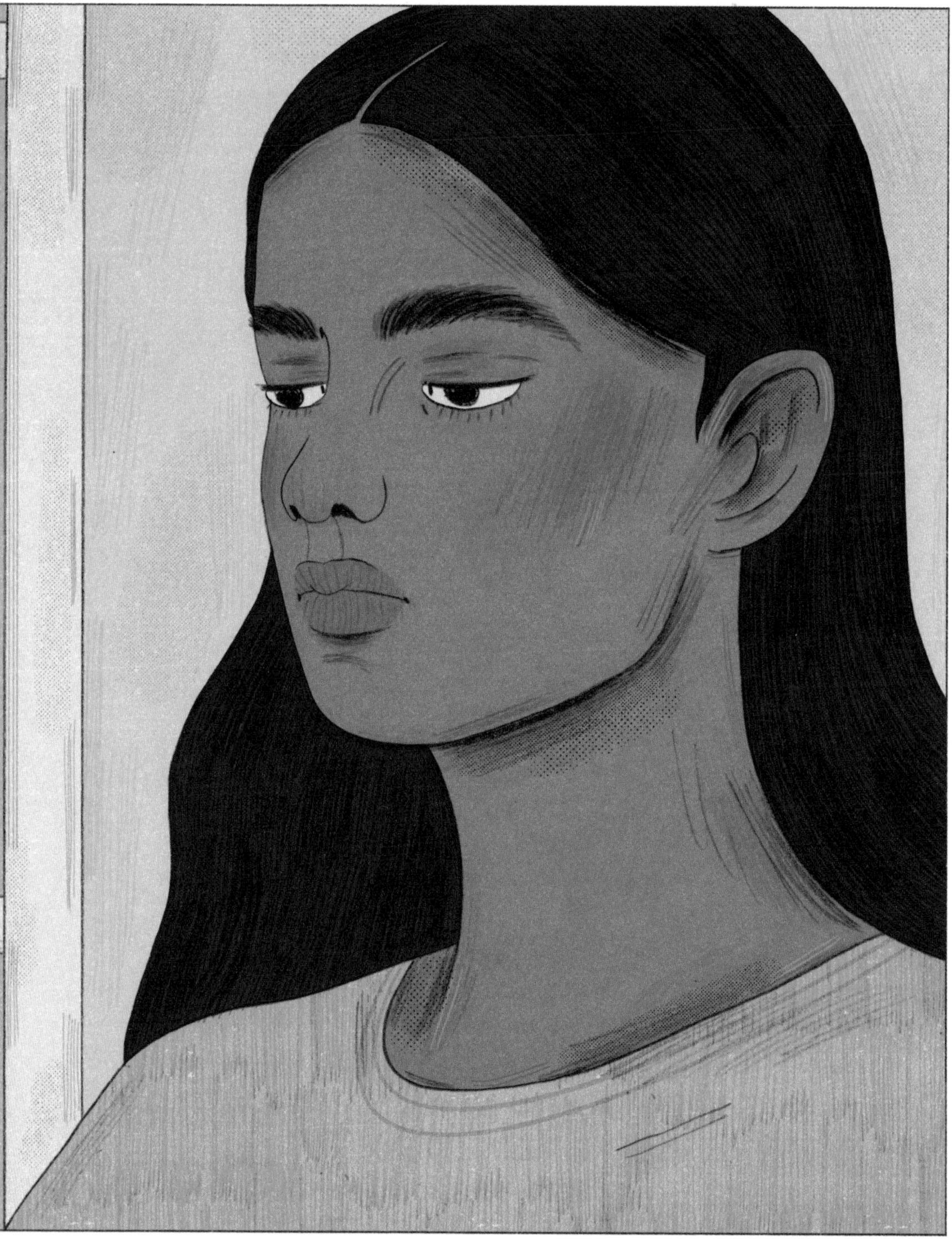

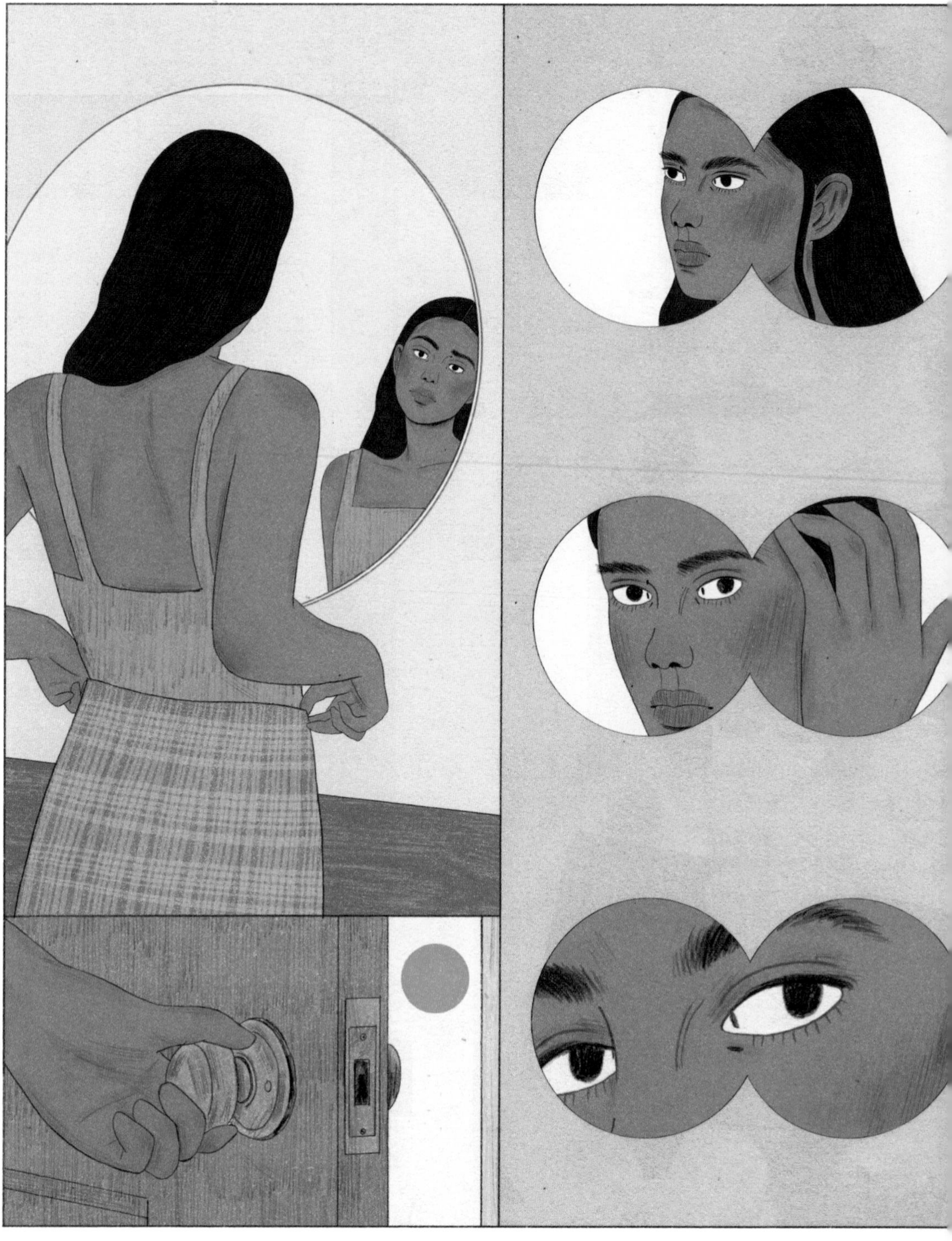

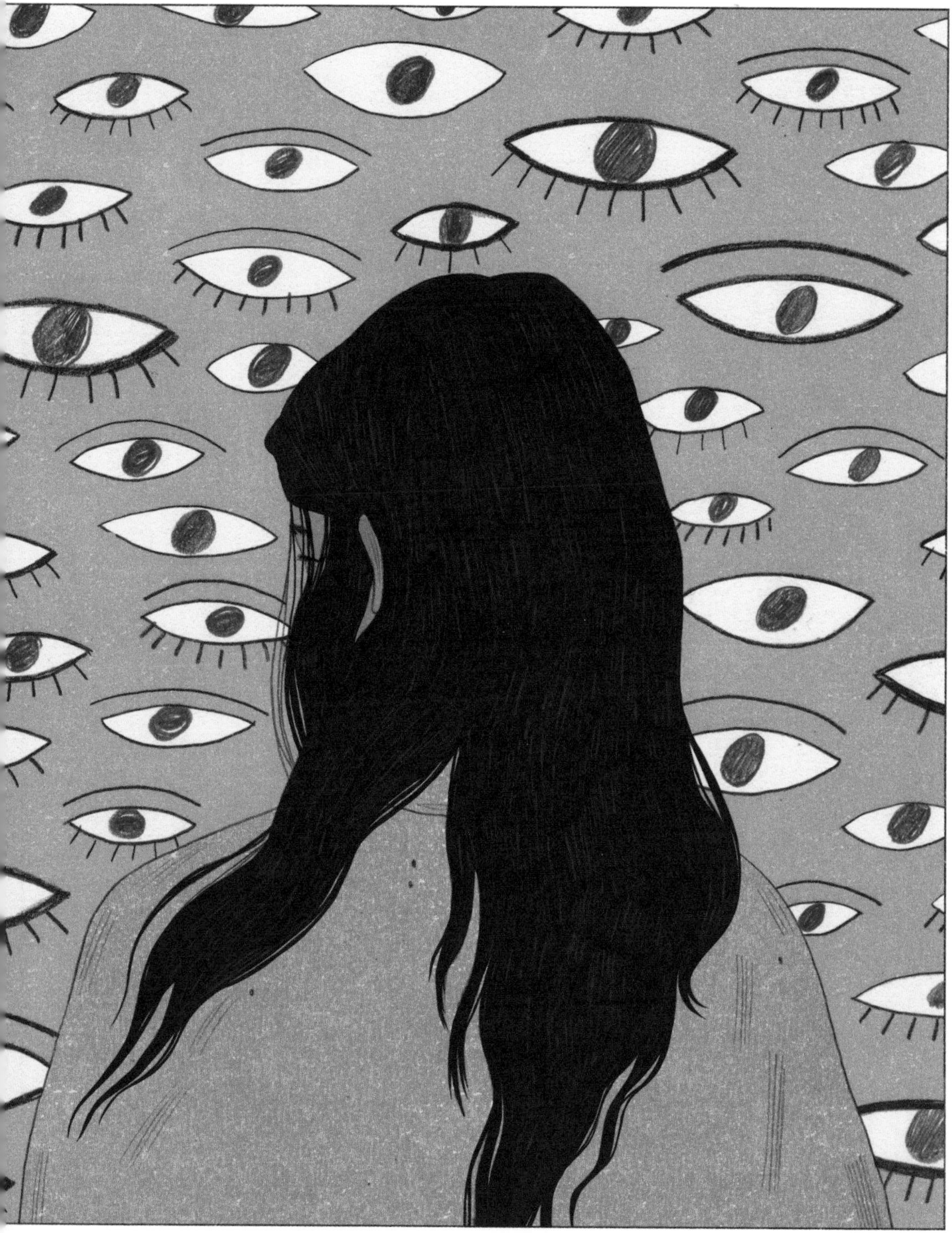

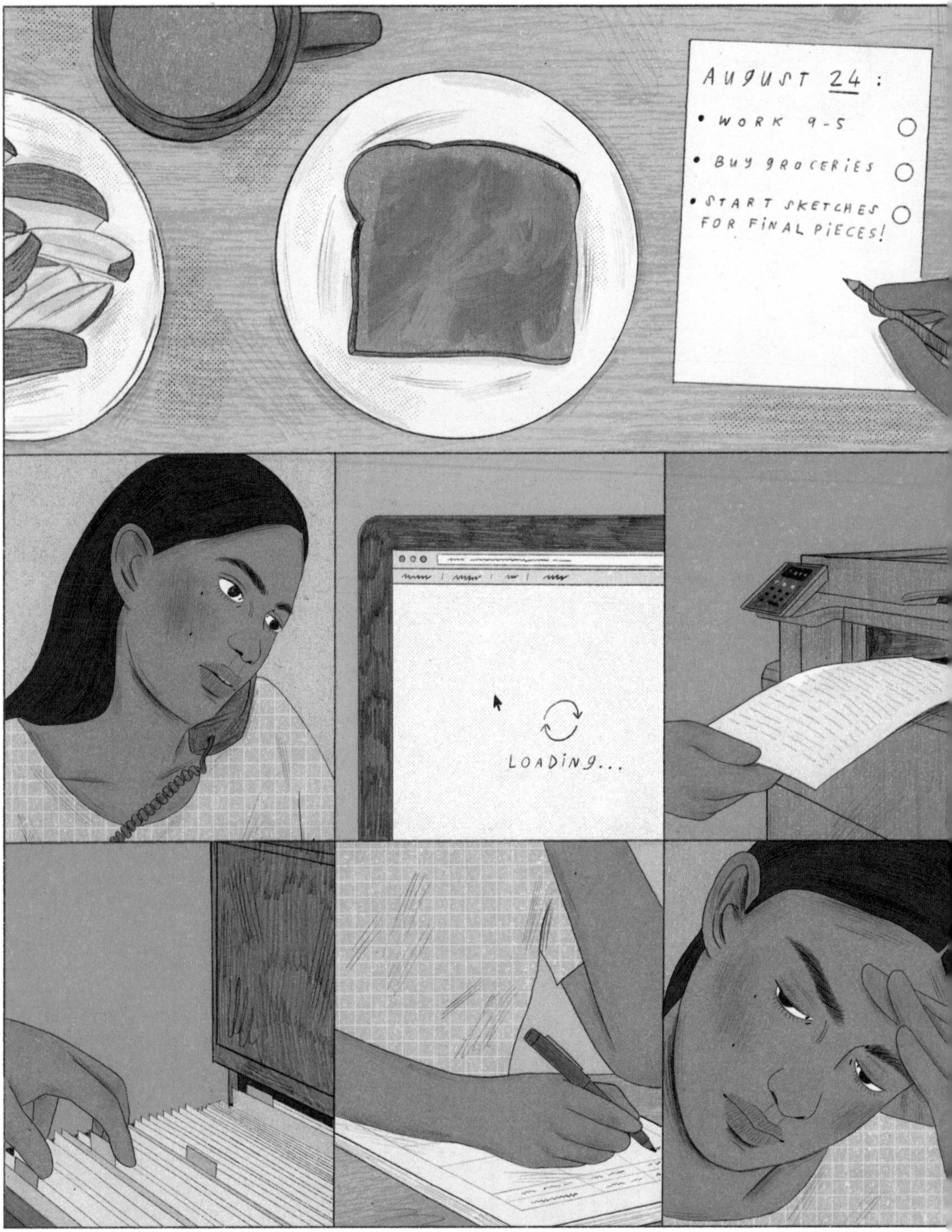
AUGUST 24:
• WORK 9-5
• BUY GROCERIES
• START SKETCHES FOR FINAL PIECES!
LOADING...

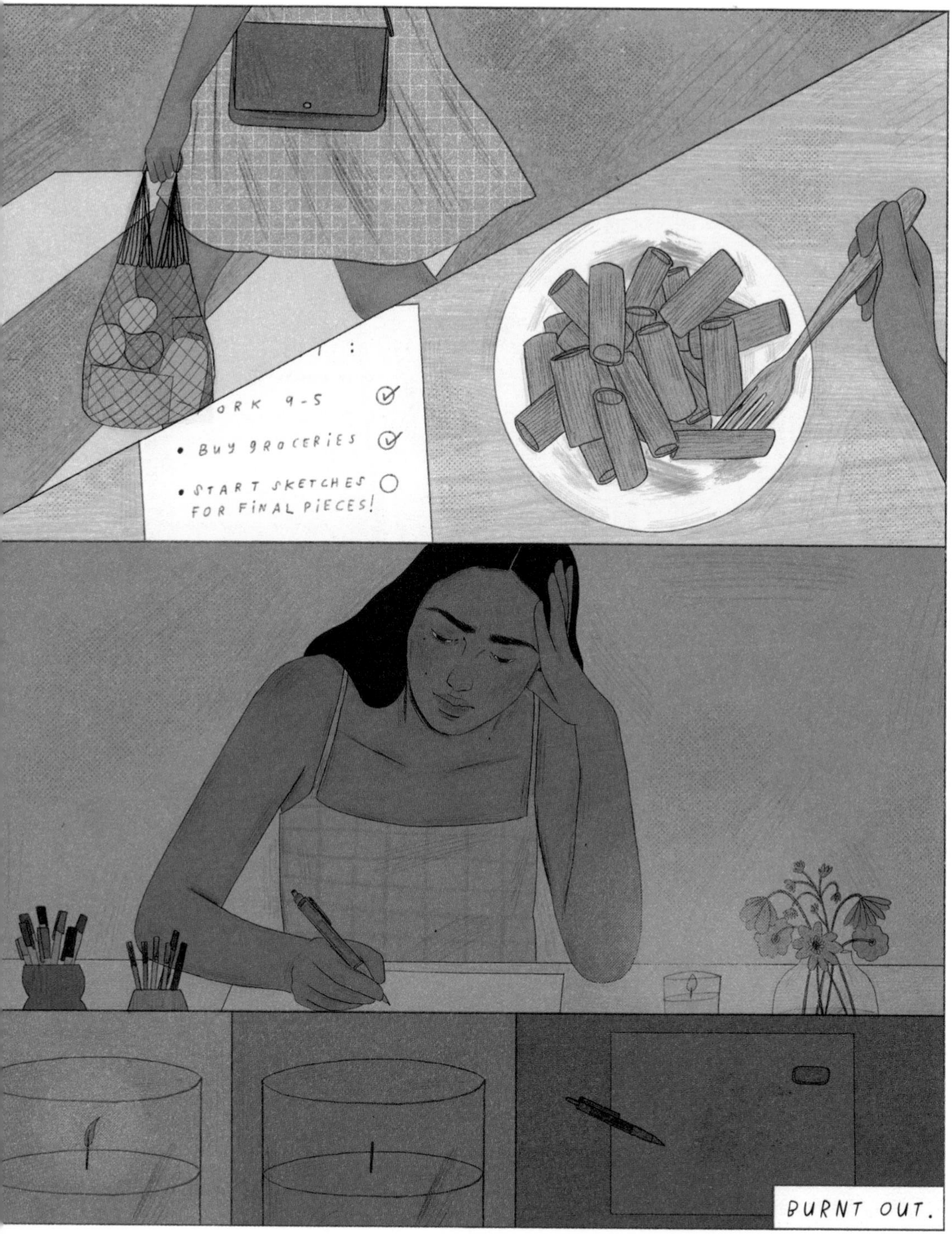
ORK 9-5
• BUY GROCERIES
• START SKETCHES FOR FINAL PIECES!
BURNT OUT.

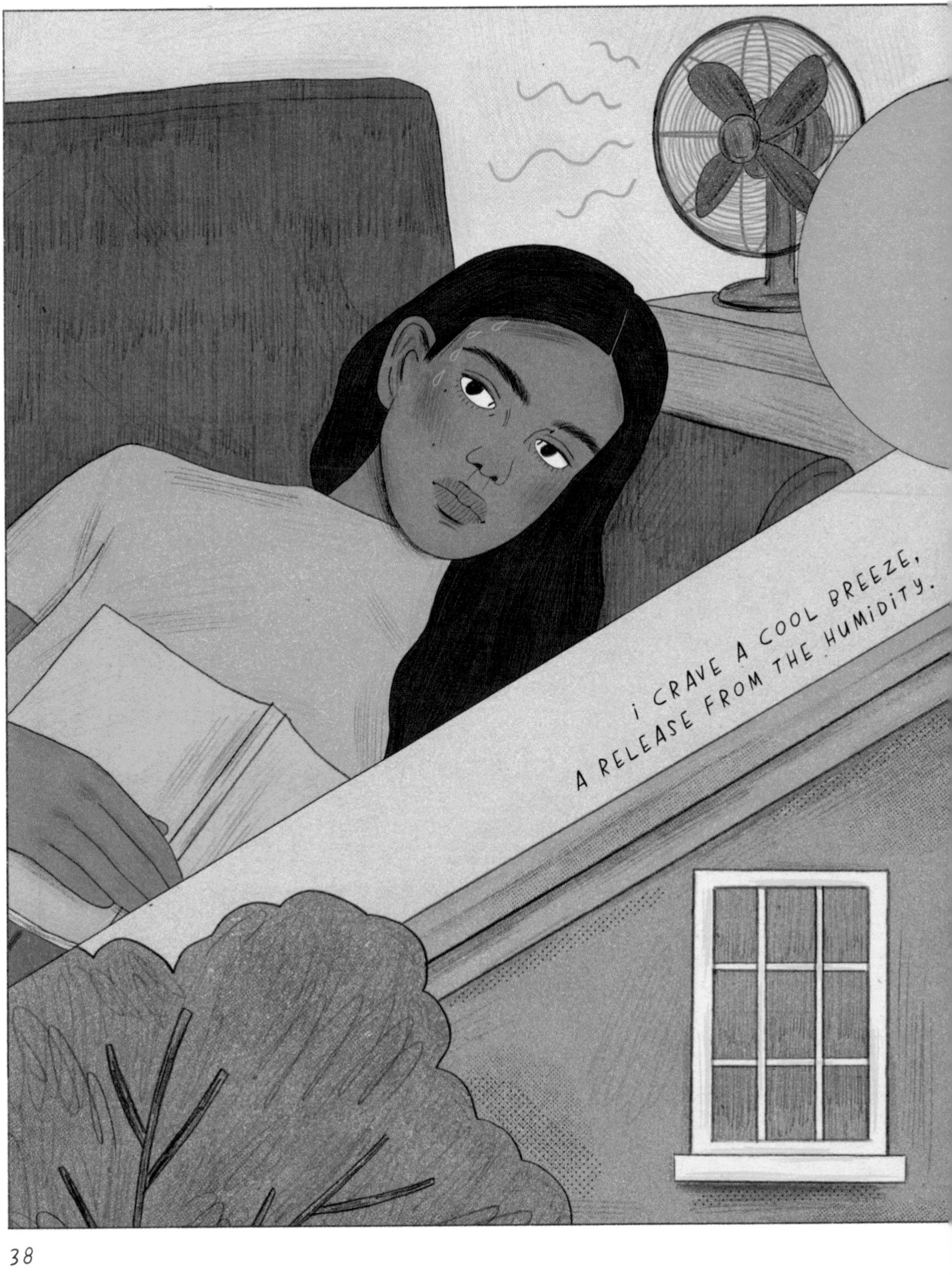
i CRAVE A COOL BREEZE,
A RELEASE FROM THE HUMIDITY.

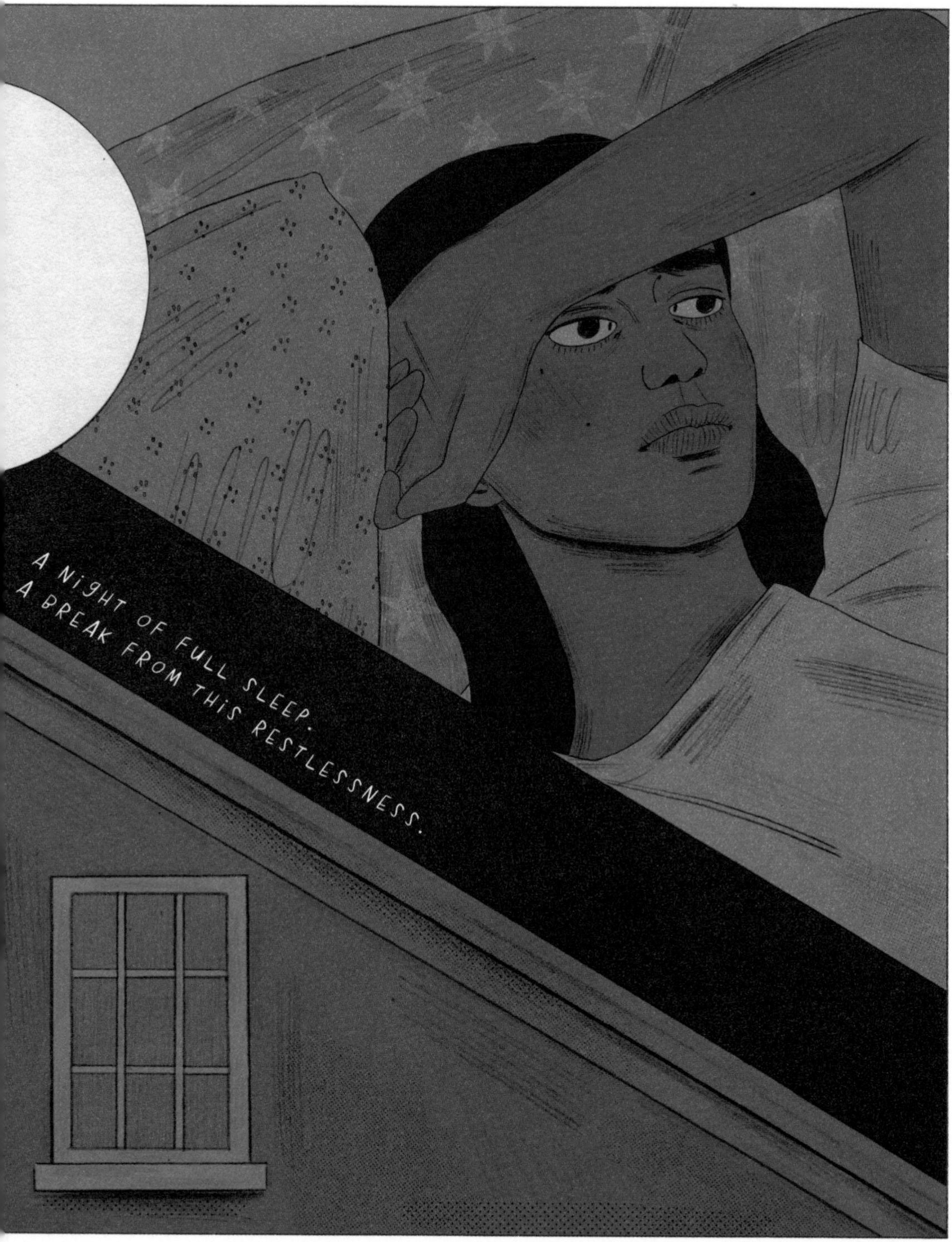
A NIGHT OF FULL SLEEP.
A BREAK FROM THIS RESTLESSNESS.

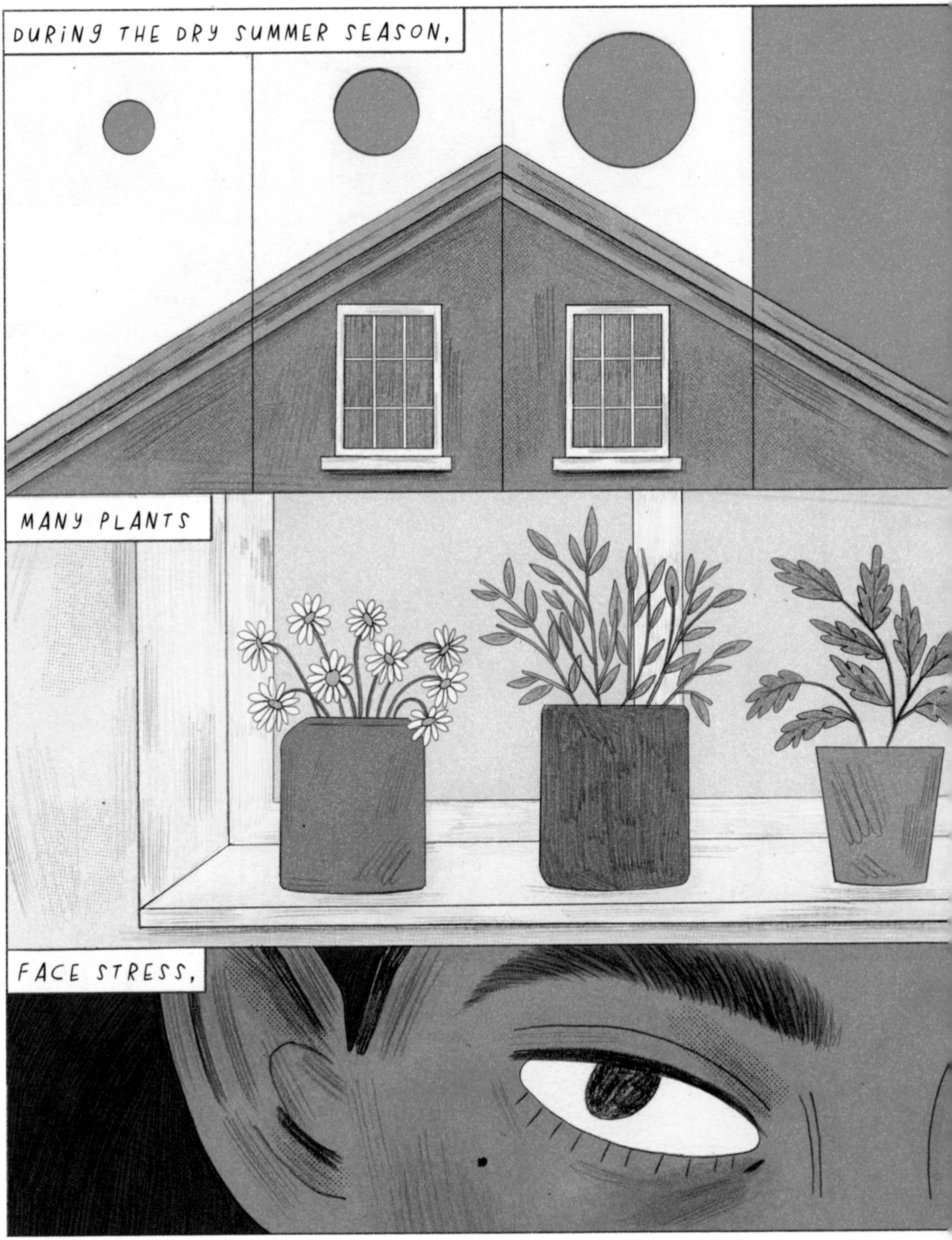
DURING THE DRY SUMMER SEASON,
MANY PLANTS
FACE STRESS,

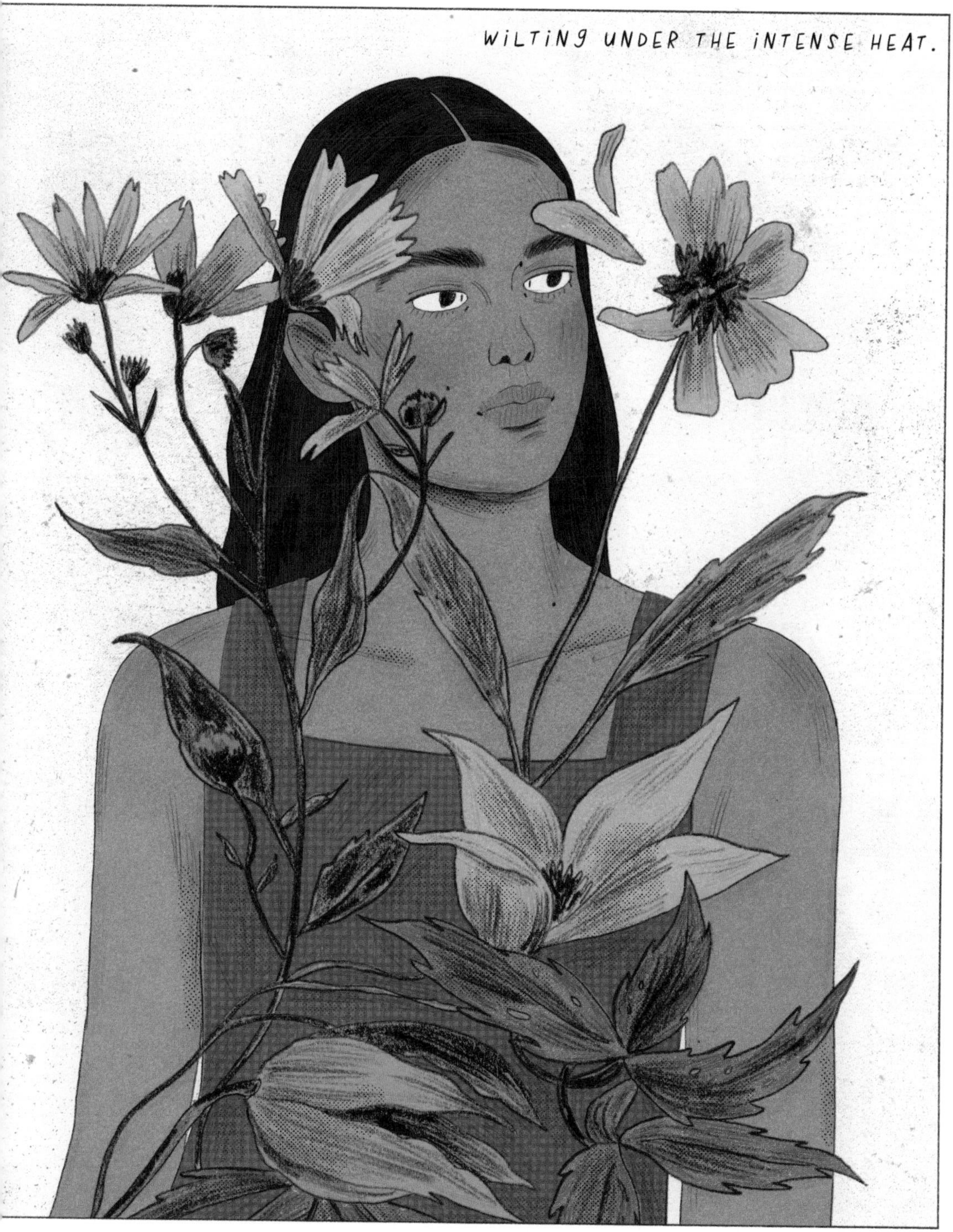
WILTING UNDER THE INTENSE HEAT.

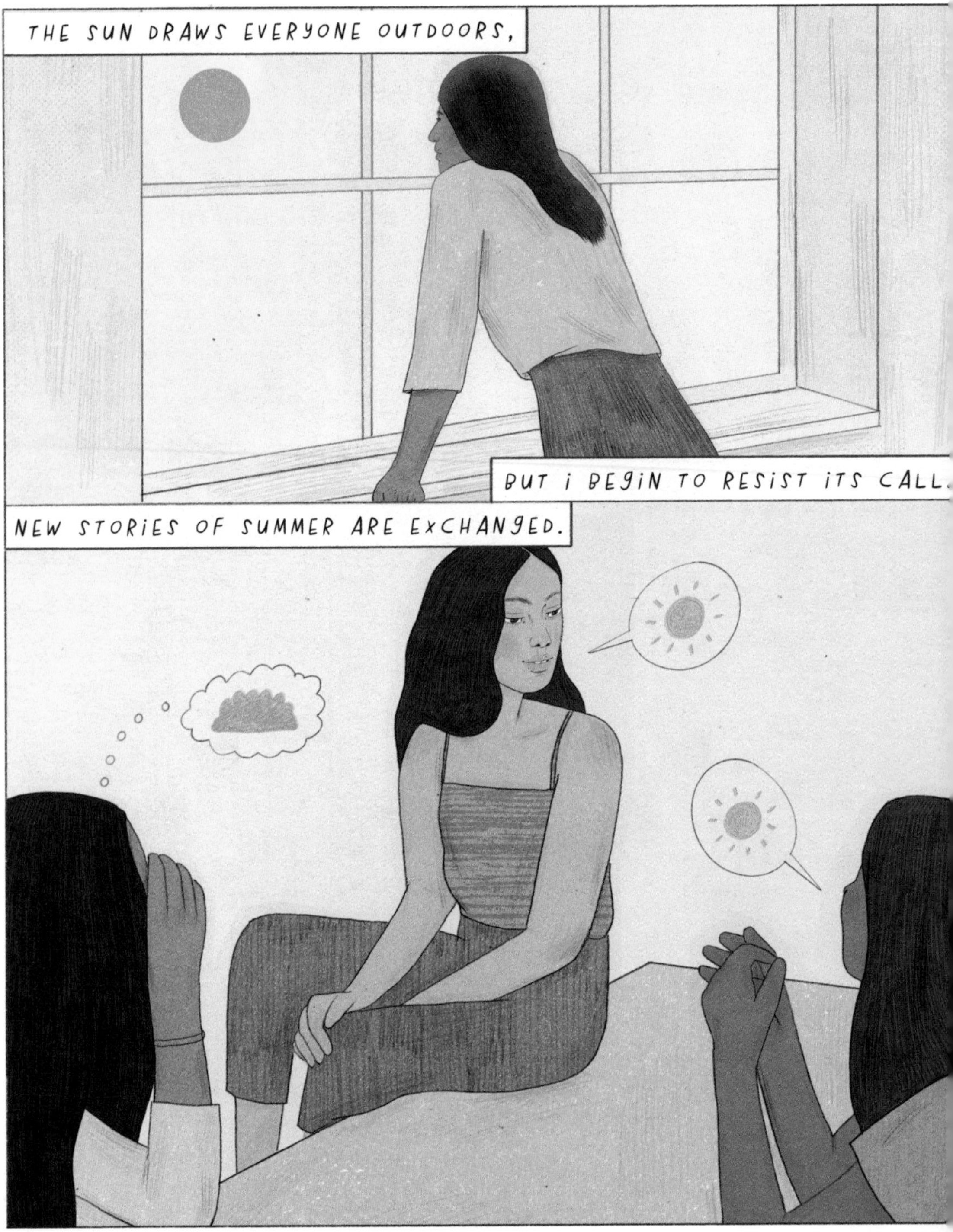
THE SUN DRAWS EVERYONE OUTDOORS,
BUT I BEGIN TO RESIST ITS CALL.
NEW STORIES OF SUMMER ARE EXCHANGED.

THE END OF THE SEASON IS LOOMING,

AND I KNOW I'LL REGRET WASTING THESE LAST FEW DAYS

HOT AND BOTHERED,

WAITING TO COOL DOWN.

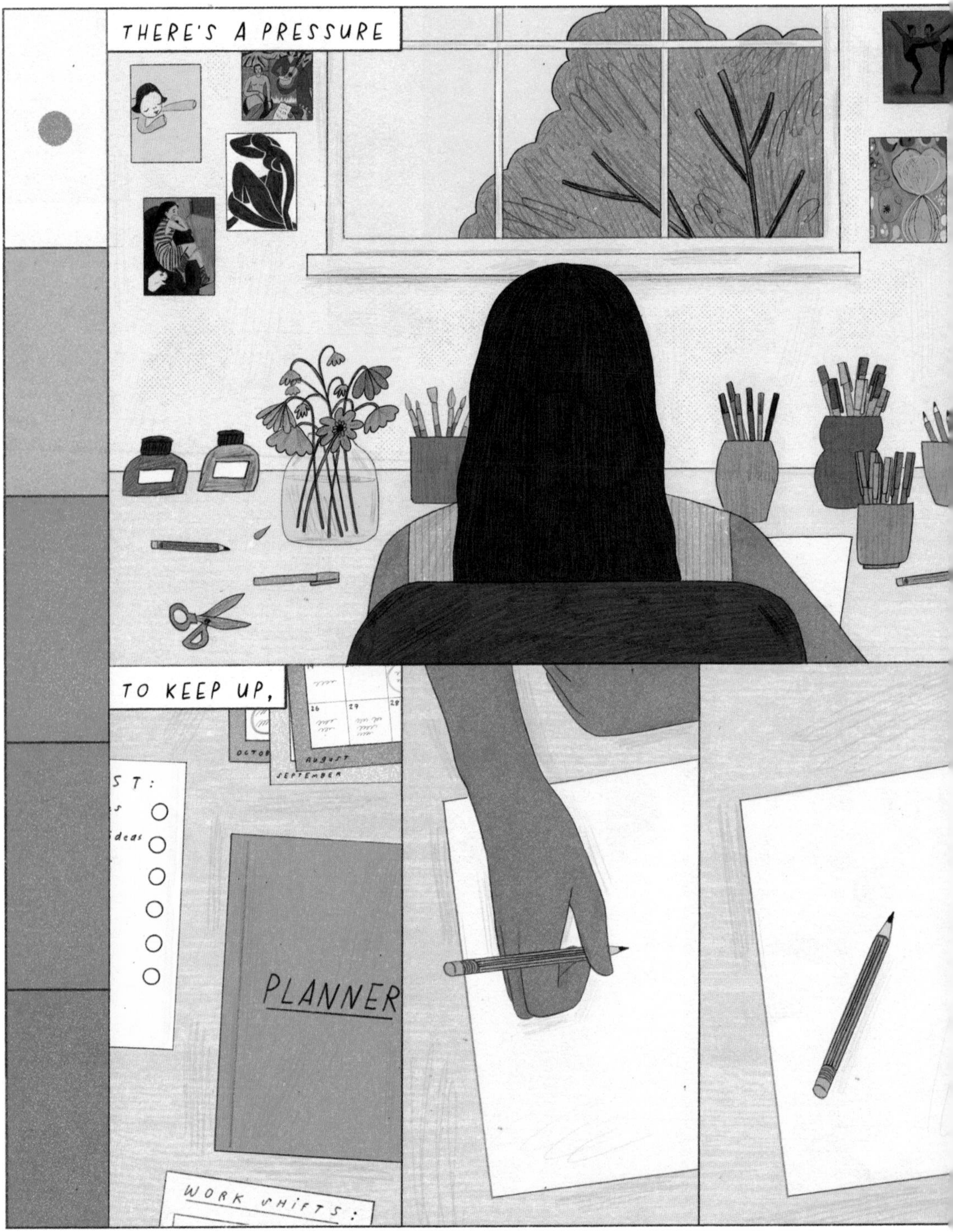
THERE'S A PRESSURE
TO KEEP UP,
PLANNER
WORK SHIFTS:

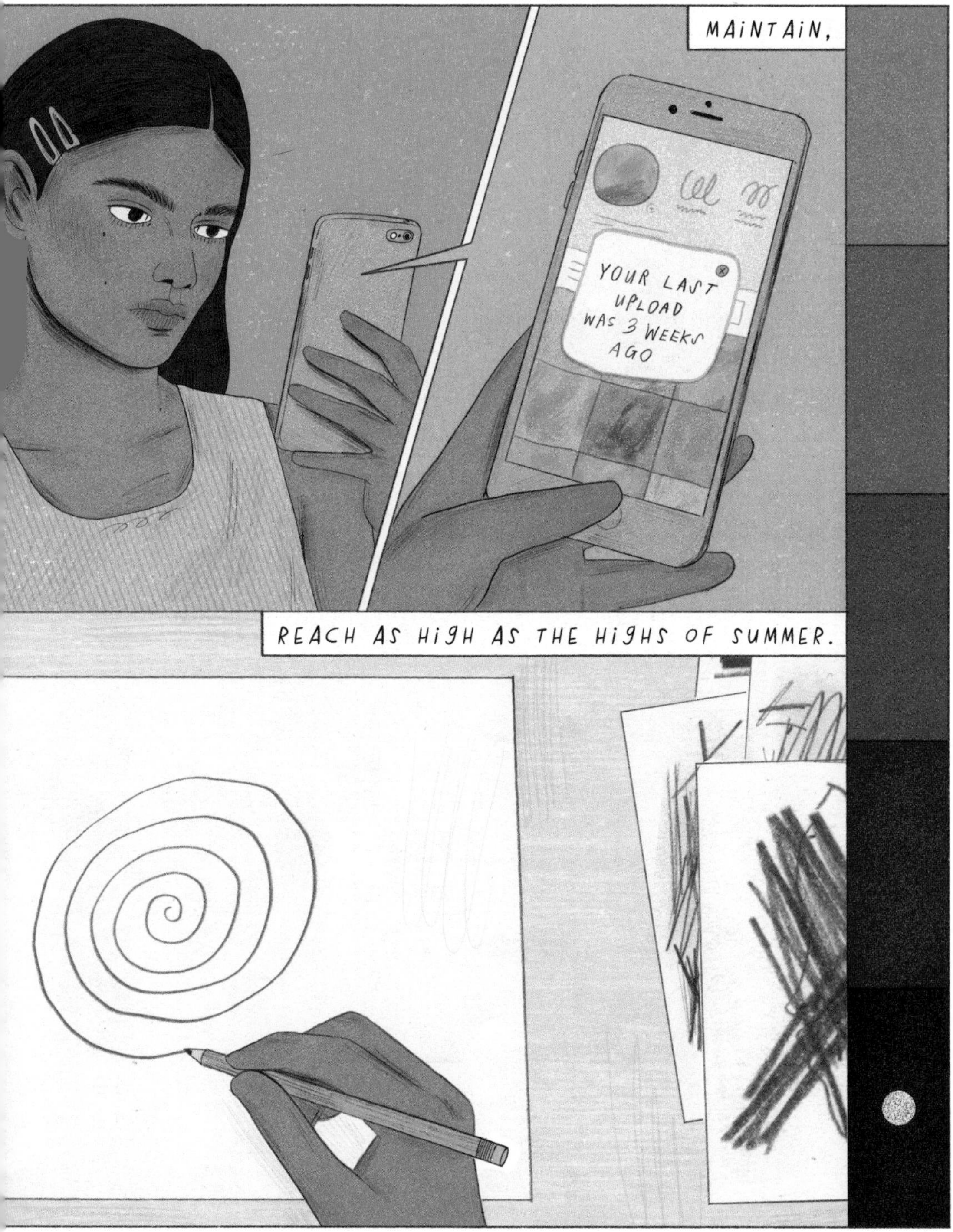
MAINTAIN,
YOUR LAST UPLOAD WAS 3 WEEKS AGO
REACH AS HIGH AS THE HIGHS OF SUMMER.

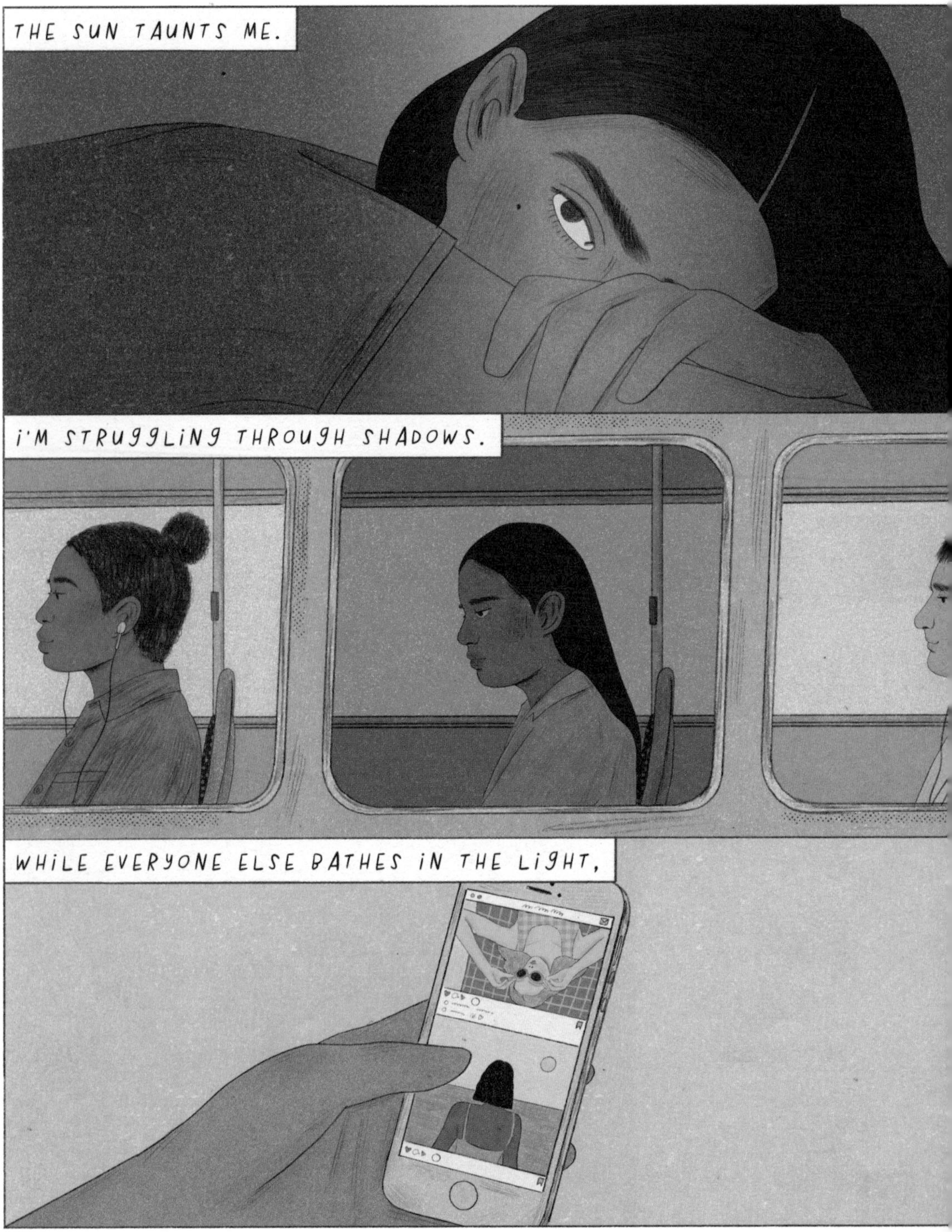
THE SUN TAUNTS ME.
I'M STRUGGLING THROUGH SHADOWS.
WHILE EVERYONE ELSE BATHES IN THE LIGHT,

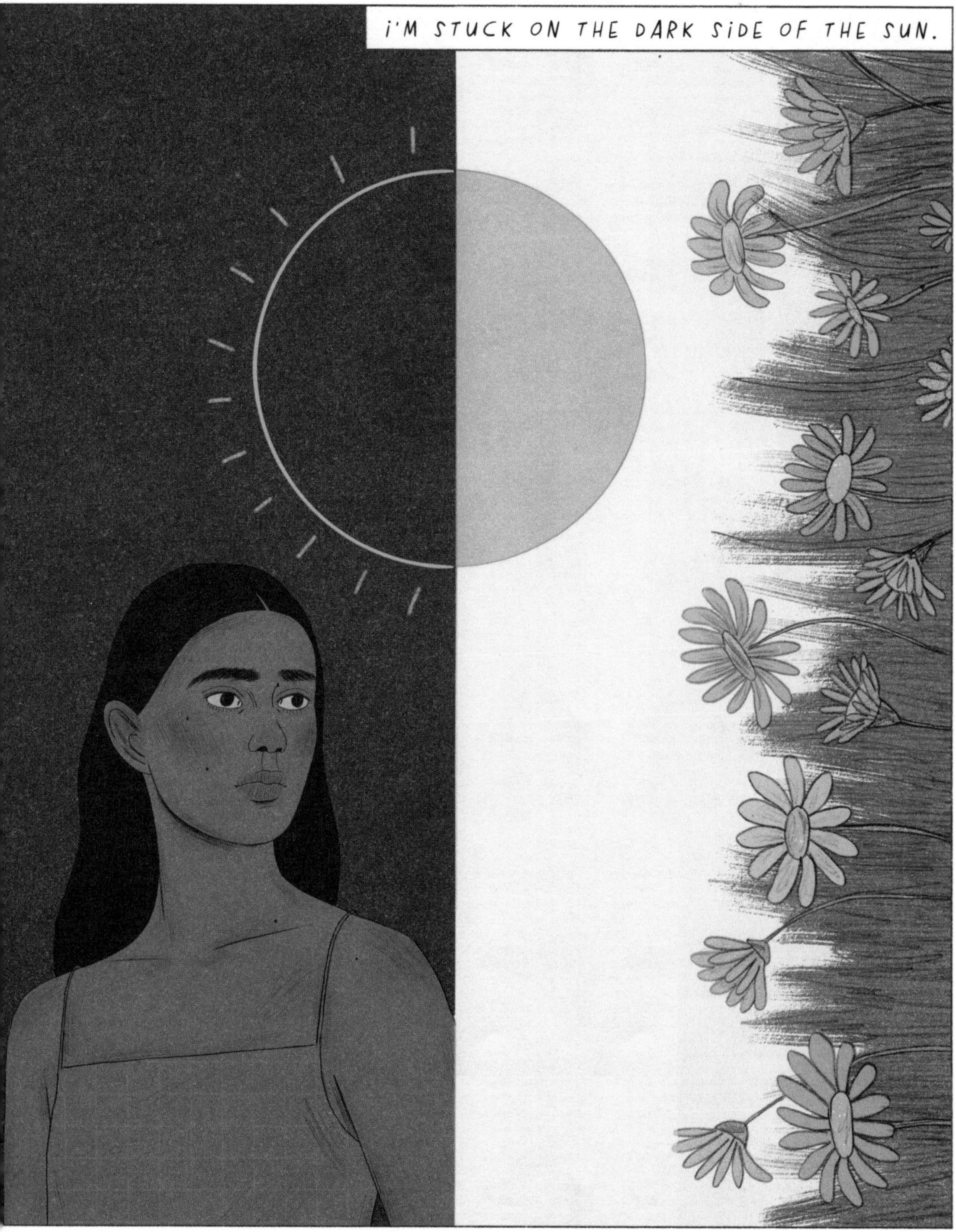
I'M STUCK ON THE DARK SIDE OF THE SUN.

CHAPTER THREE

MONSOON

THE PENT-UP FEELINGS OF ANxiETY THAT
HAVE BEEN SiMMERiNG UNDER THE SUN
REACH THEIR BOILING POINT.

THERE IS A DESPERATE NEED FOR
RAINFALL AS THE SUMMER SEASON
COMES TO A CLOSE. CLOUDS HUDDLE
TOGETHER iN A HUMiD SKY, WEiGHiNG
HEAVY, READY TO RELEASE.

AT LAST, THE RAiN PAiNTS THE SKiES iN
A GLOOMY BLUE, AND ALTHOUGH iT CAN
CAUSE MiNOR DAMAGE, iT'S ViTAL iN
HELPiNG PLANTS GROW.

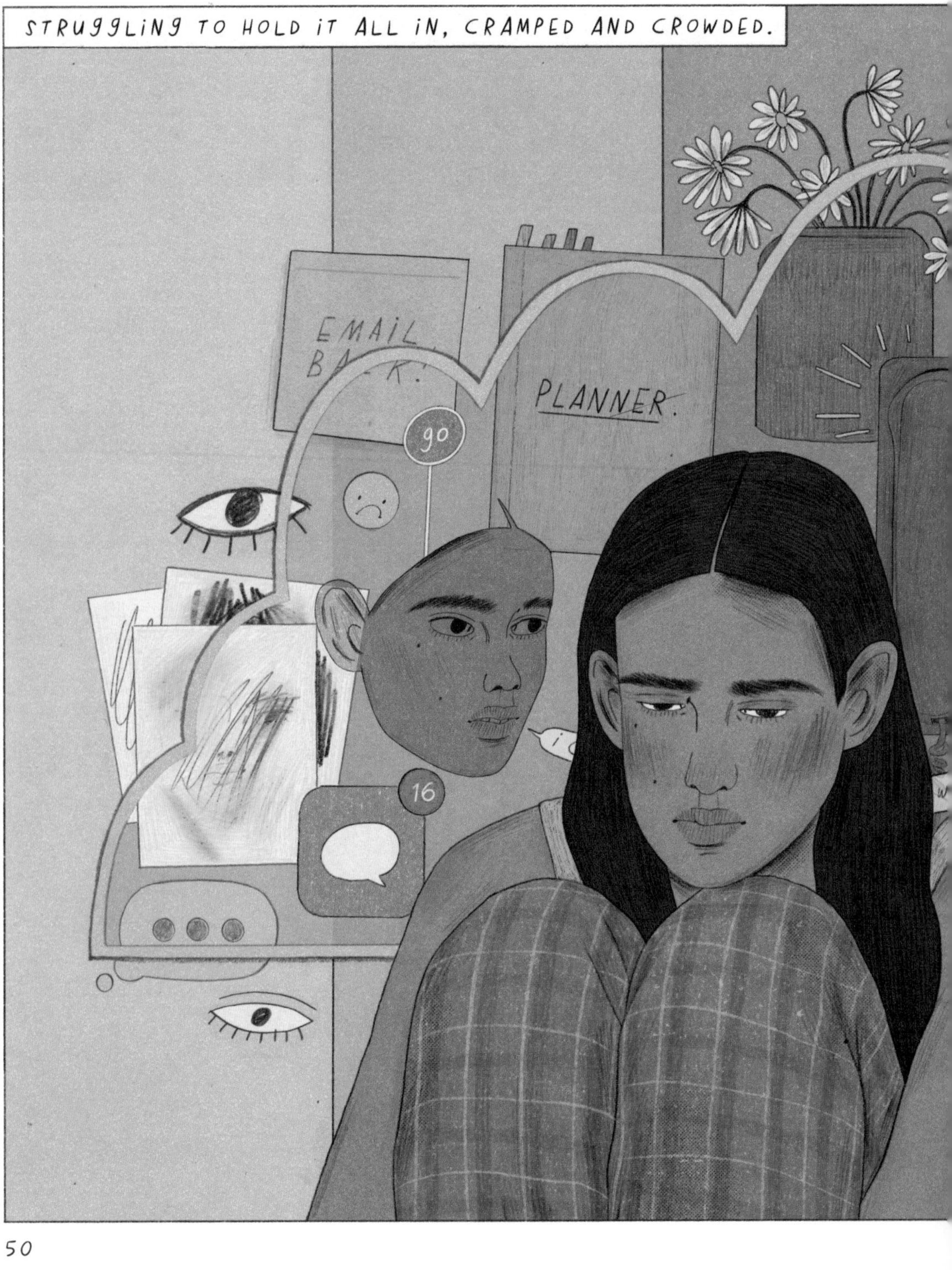
STRUGGLING TO HOLD IT ALL IN, CRAMPED AND CROWDED.
EMAIL BACK!
PLANNER
go
16

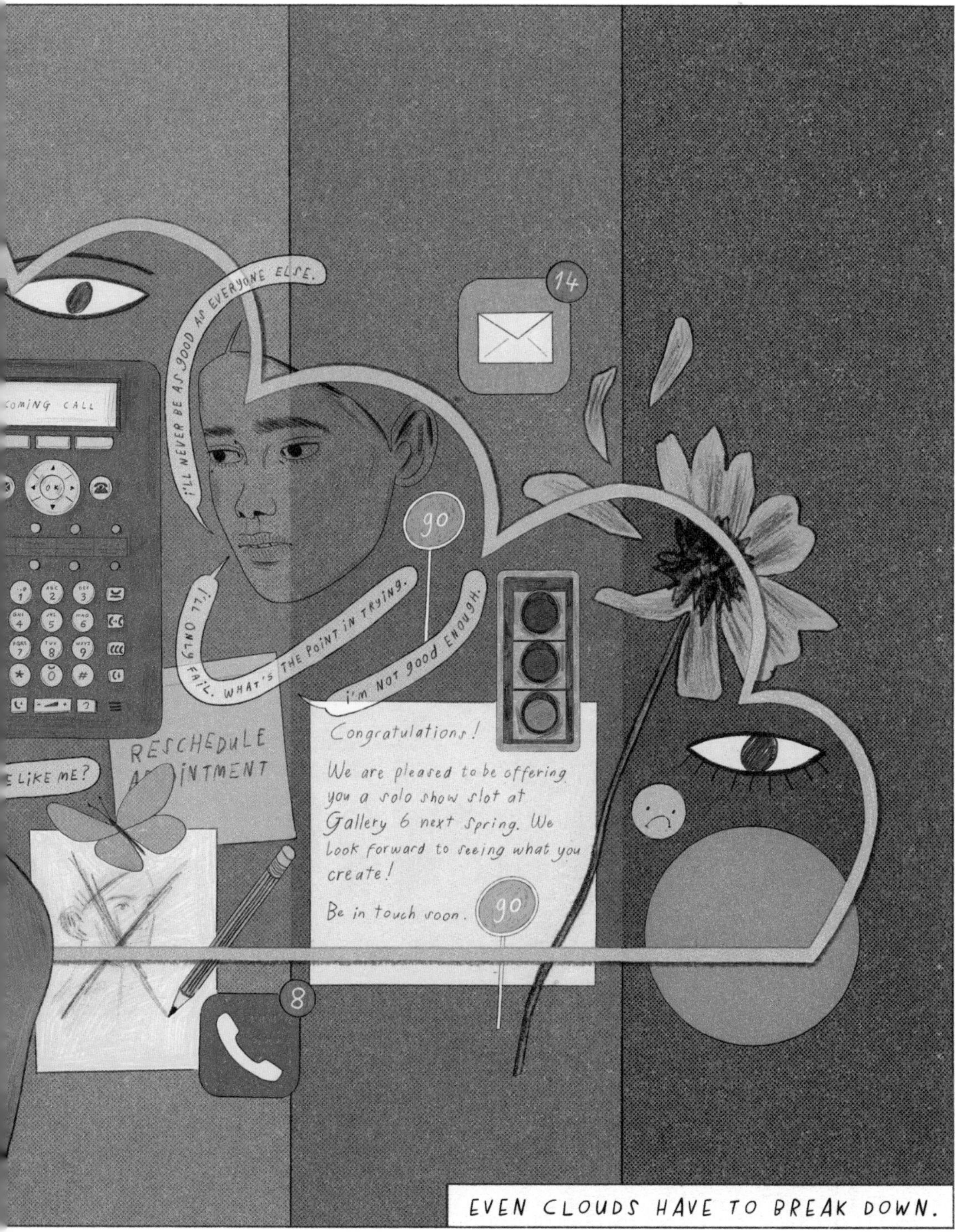

I'LL NEVER BE AS GOOD AS EVERYONE ELSE.
COMING CALL
I'LL ONLY FAIL. WHAT'S THE POINT IN TRYING.
I'M NOT GOOD ENOUGH.
go
14
RESCHEDULE
INTMENT
E LIKE ME?
Congratulations!
We are pleased to be offering you a solo show slot at Gallery 6 next Spring. We look forward to seeing what you create!
Be in touch soon.
go
8
EVEN CLOUDS HAVE TO BREAK DOWN.

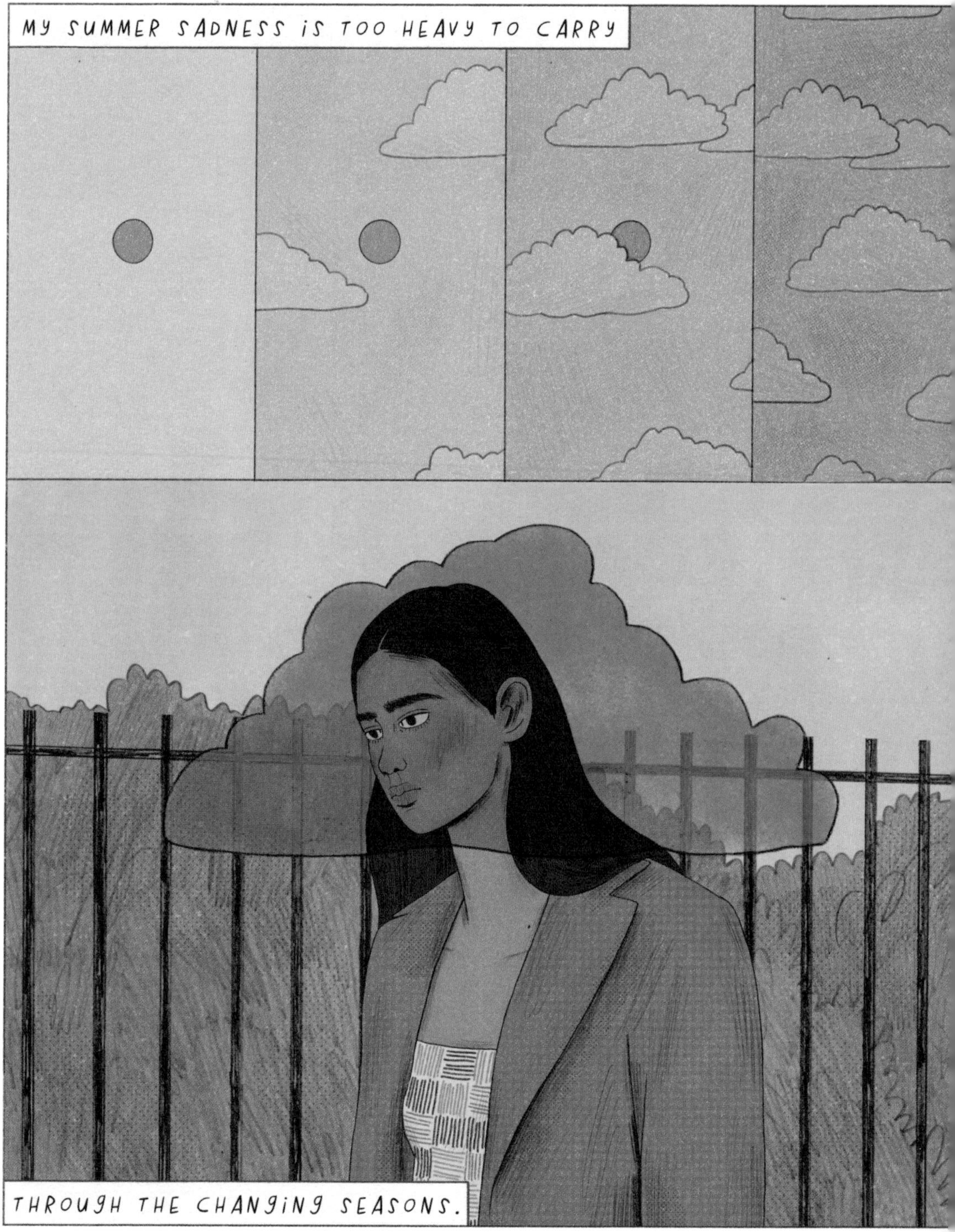
MY SUMMER SADNESS iS TOO HEAVY TO CARRY
THROUGH THE CHANGiNG SEASONS.

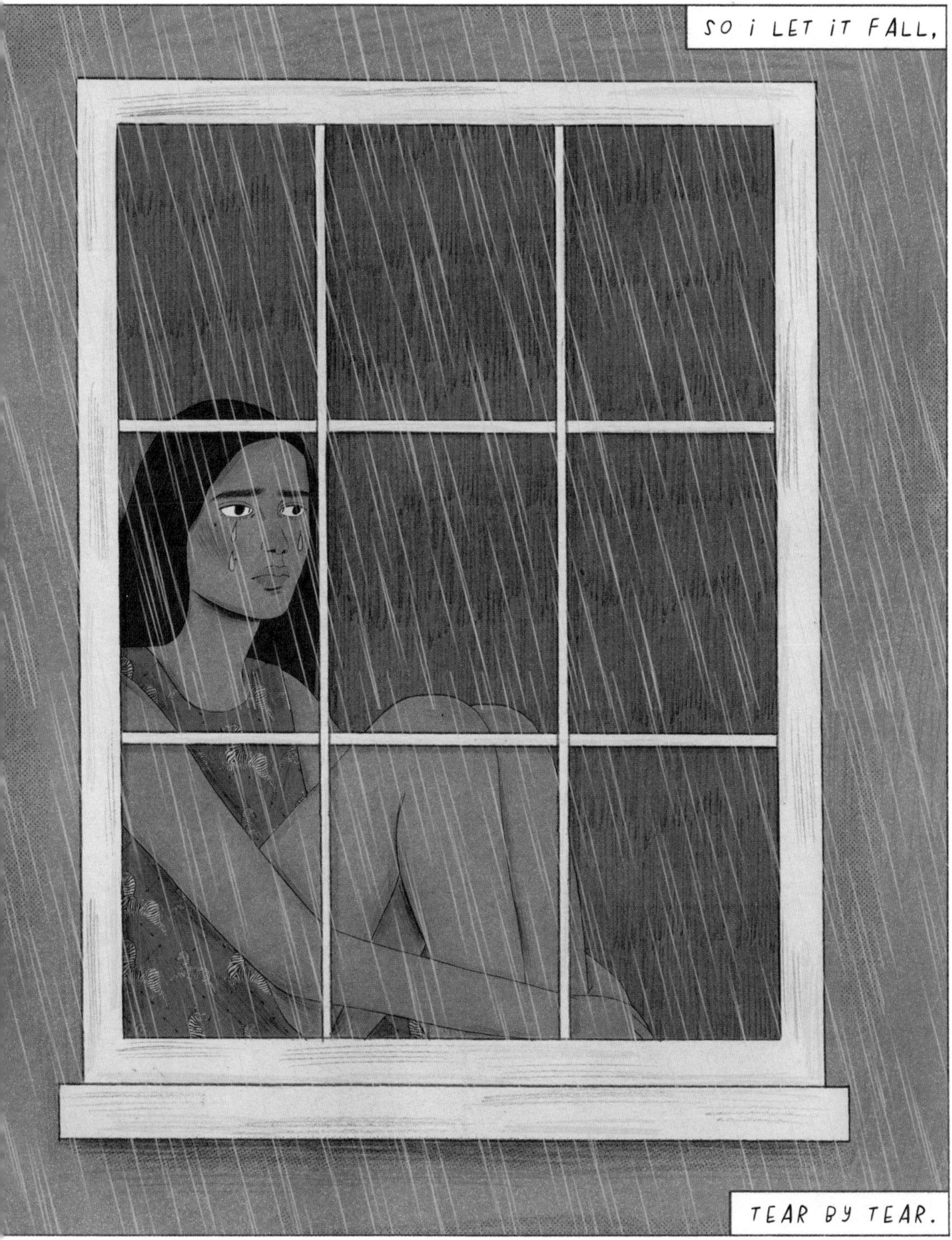
SO I LET IT FALL,
TEAR BY TEAR.

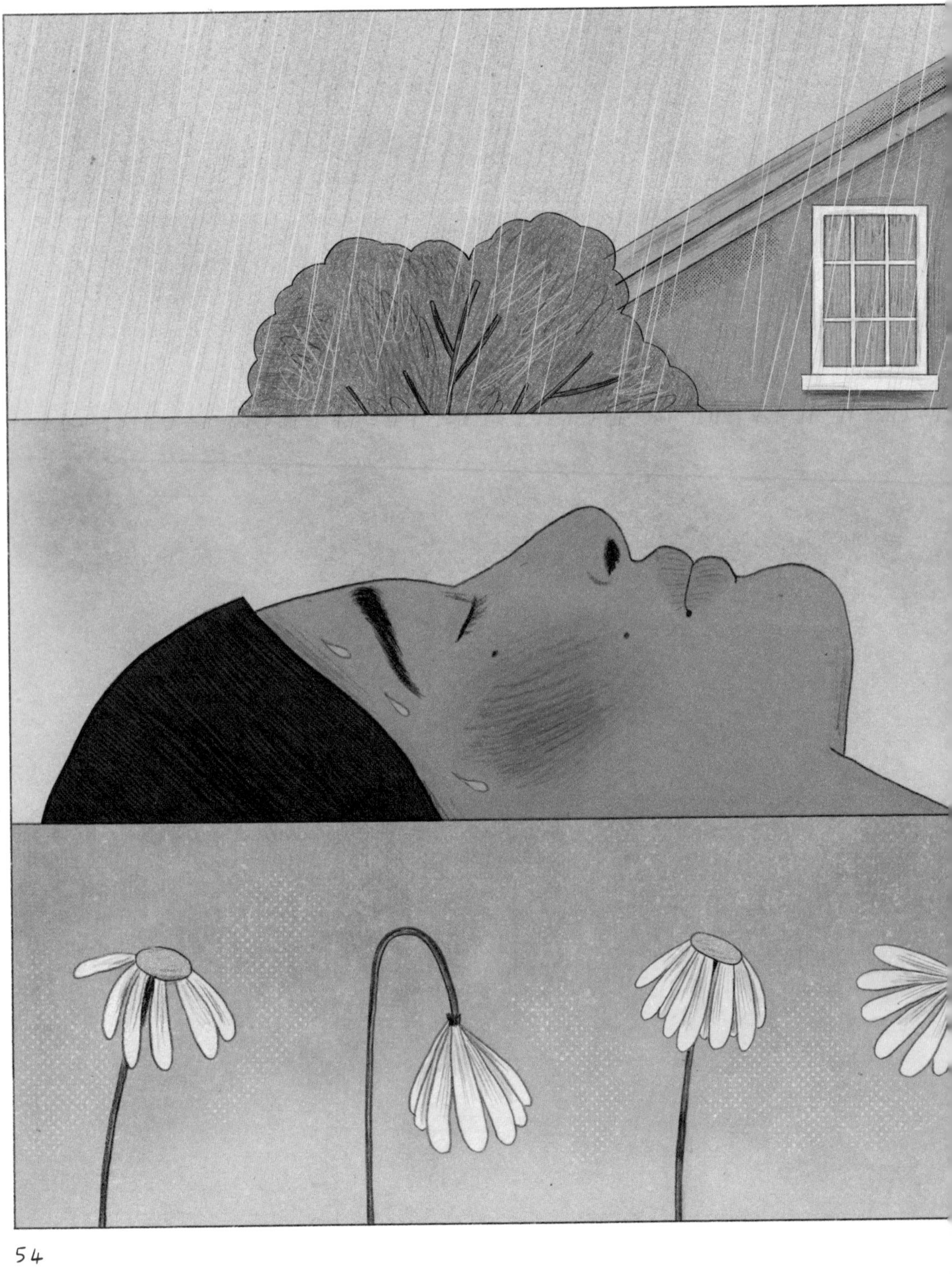

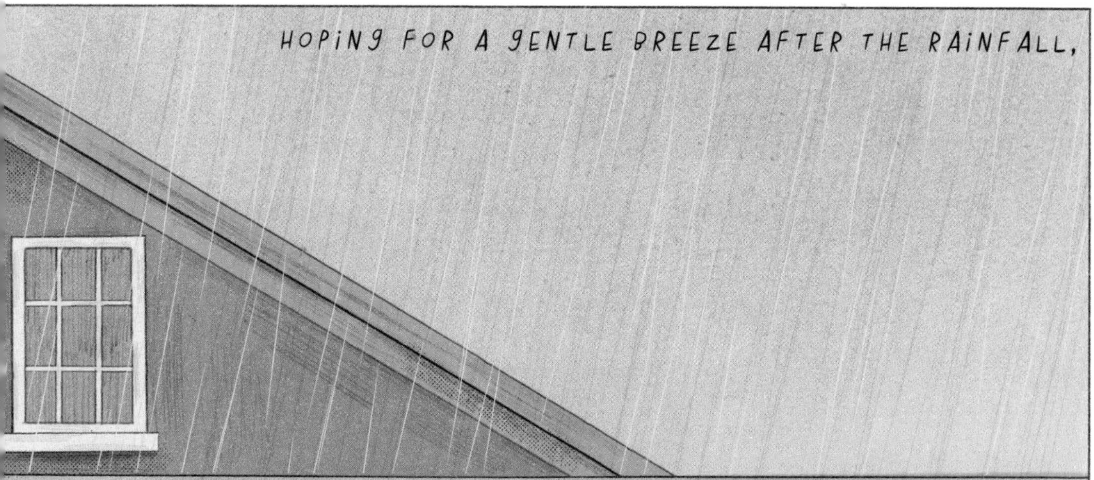
HOPING FOR A GENTLE BREEZE AFTER THE RAINFALL,

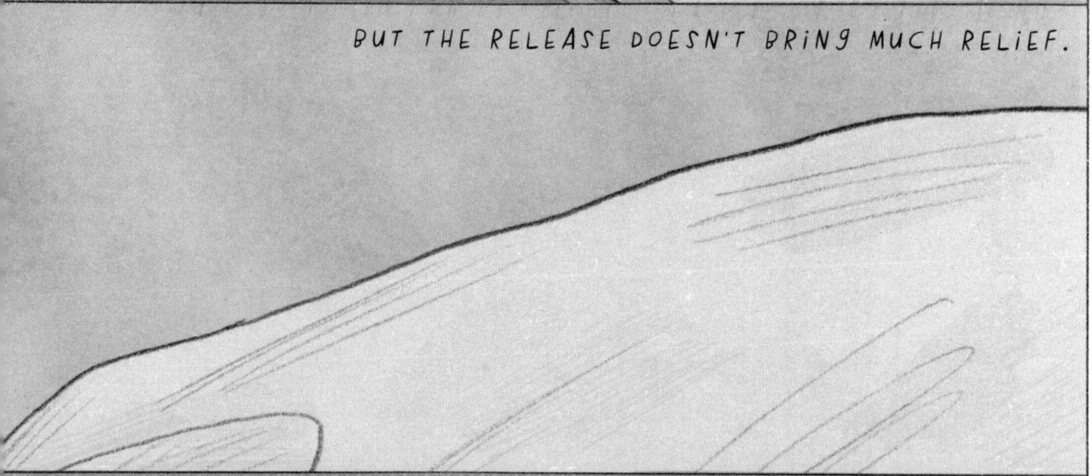
BUT THE RELEASE DOESN'T BRING MUCH RELIEF.

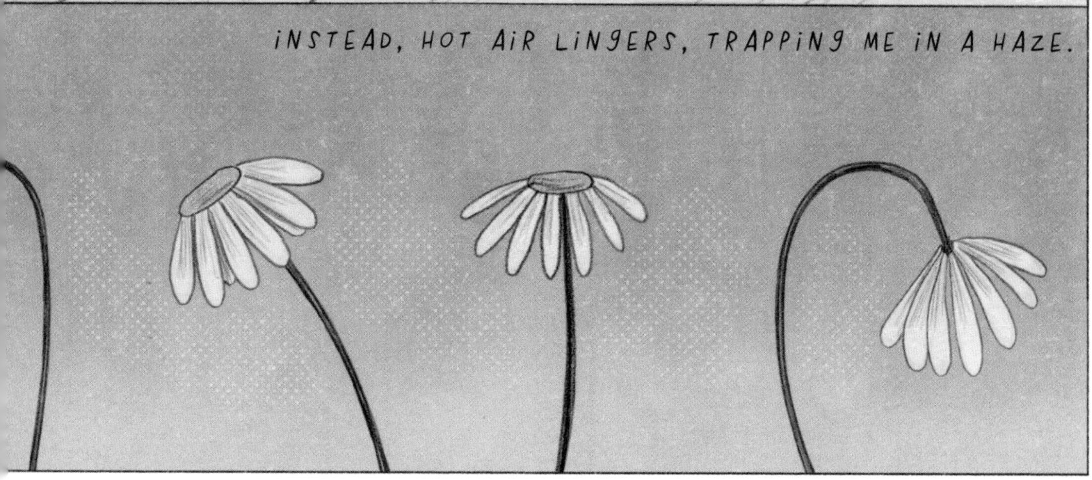
INSTEAD, HOT AIR LINGERS, TRAPPING ME IN A HAZE.

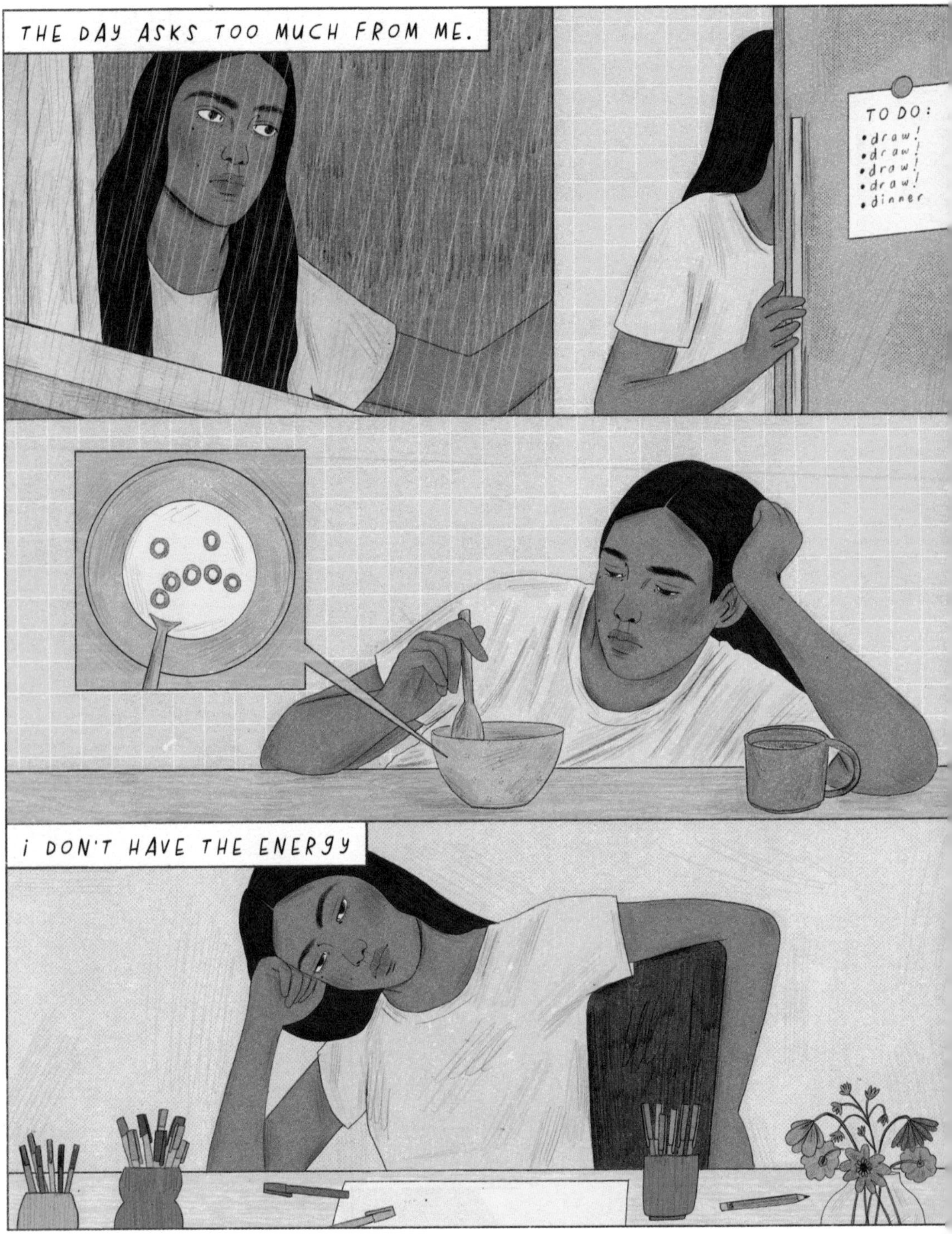
THE DAY ASKS TOO MUCH FROM ME.
TO DO:
•draw!
•draw!
•draw!
•draw!
•dinner
i DON'T HAVE THE ENERGY

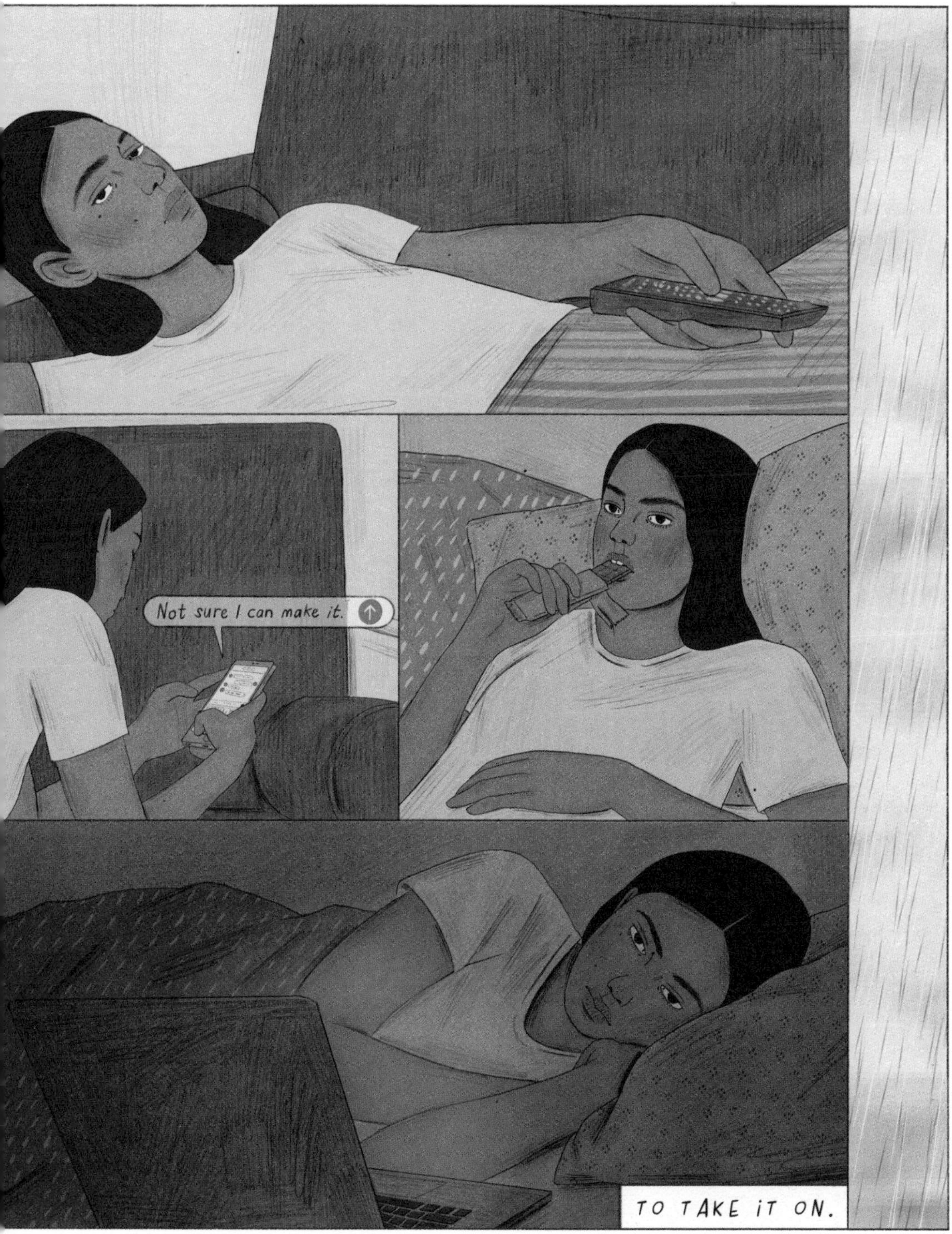
Not sure I can make it.
TO TAKE IT ON.

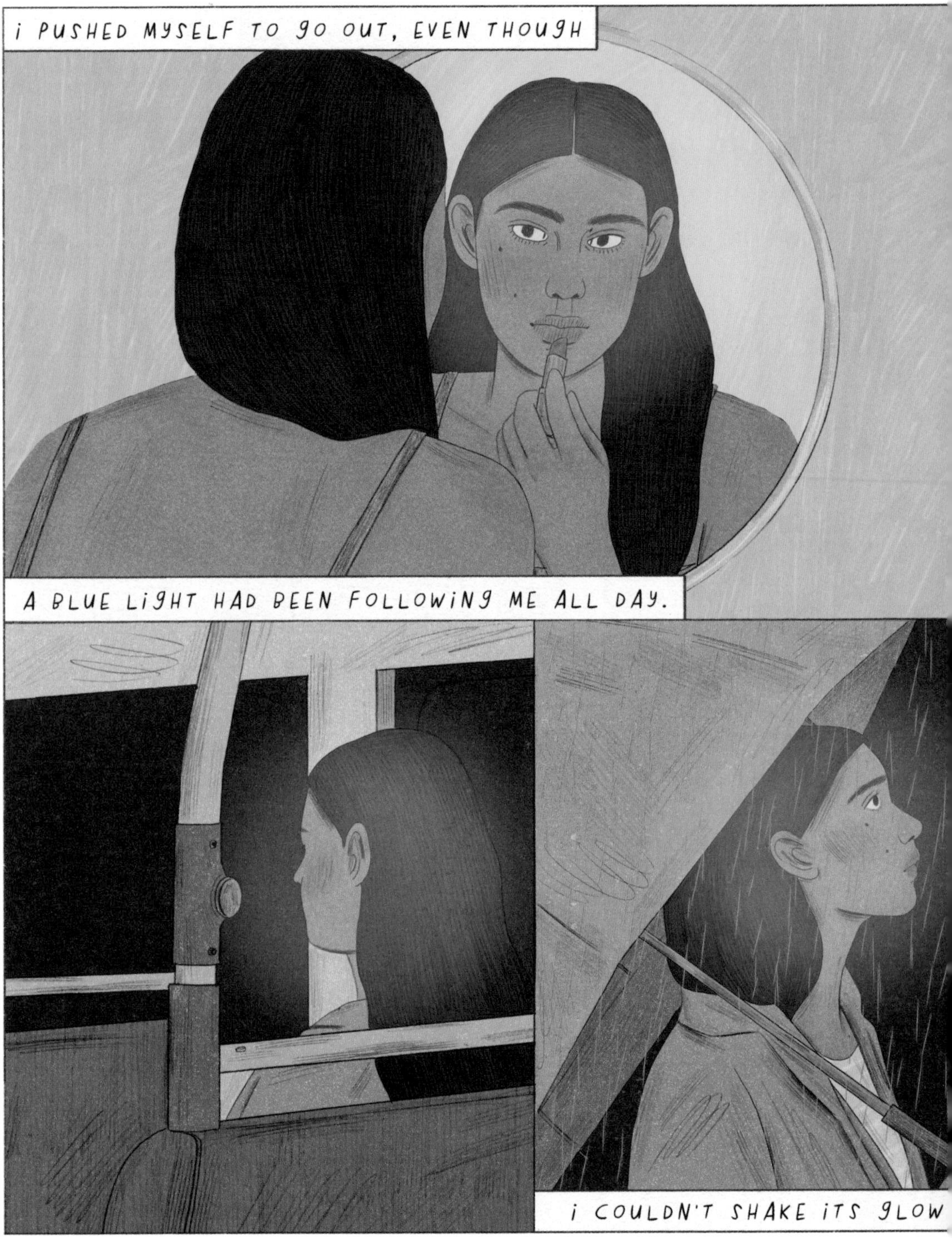
i PUSHED MYSELF TO go OUT, EVEN THOUgH
A BLUE LigHT HAD BEEN FOLLOWiNg ME ALL DAY.
i COULDN'T SHAKE iTS gLOW

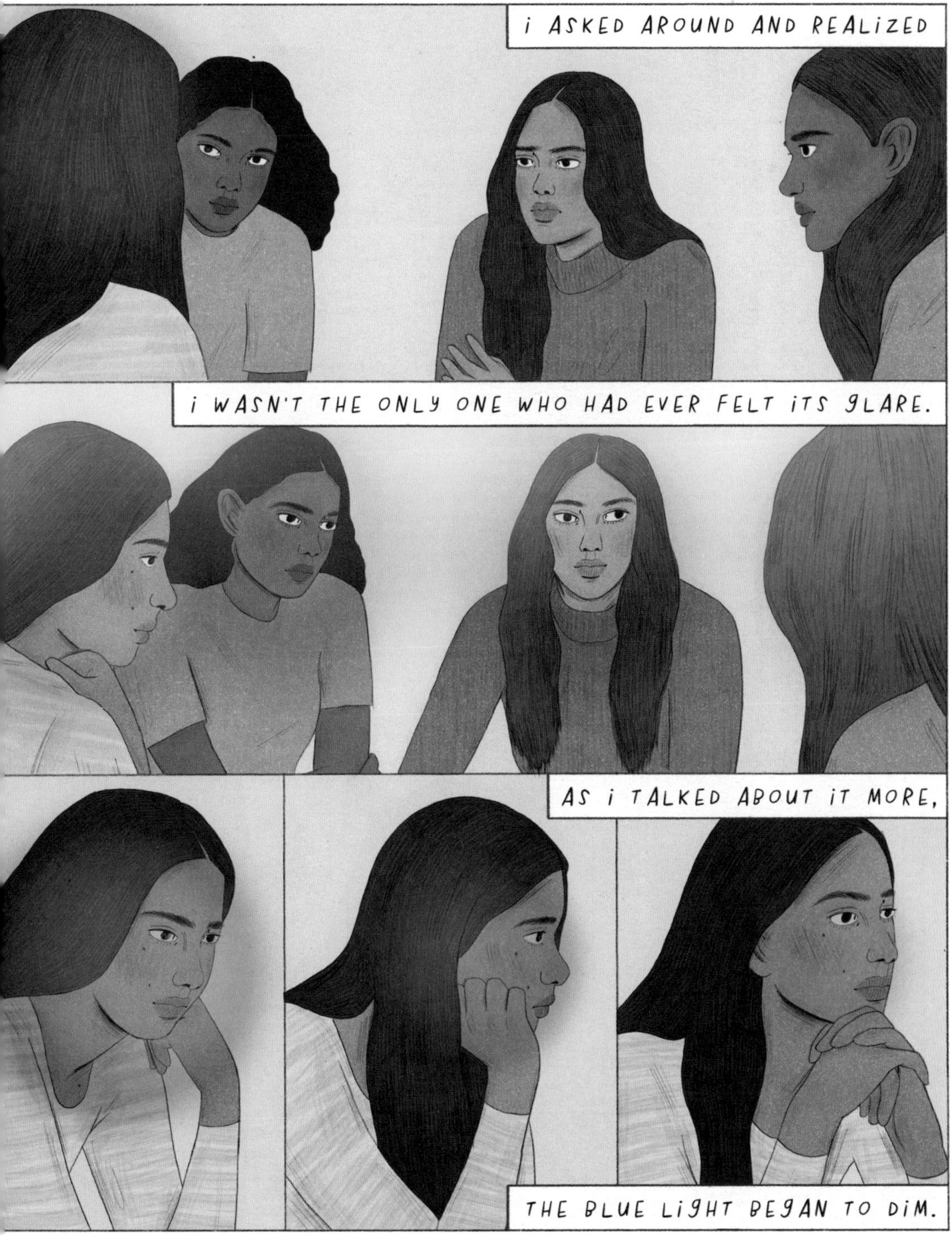
i ASKED AROUND AND REALiZED
i WASN'T THE ONLY ONE WHO HAD EVER FELT iTS gLARE.
AS i TALKED ABOUT iT MORE,
THE BLUE LigHT BEgAN TO DiM.

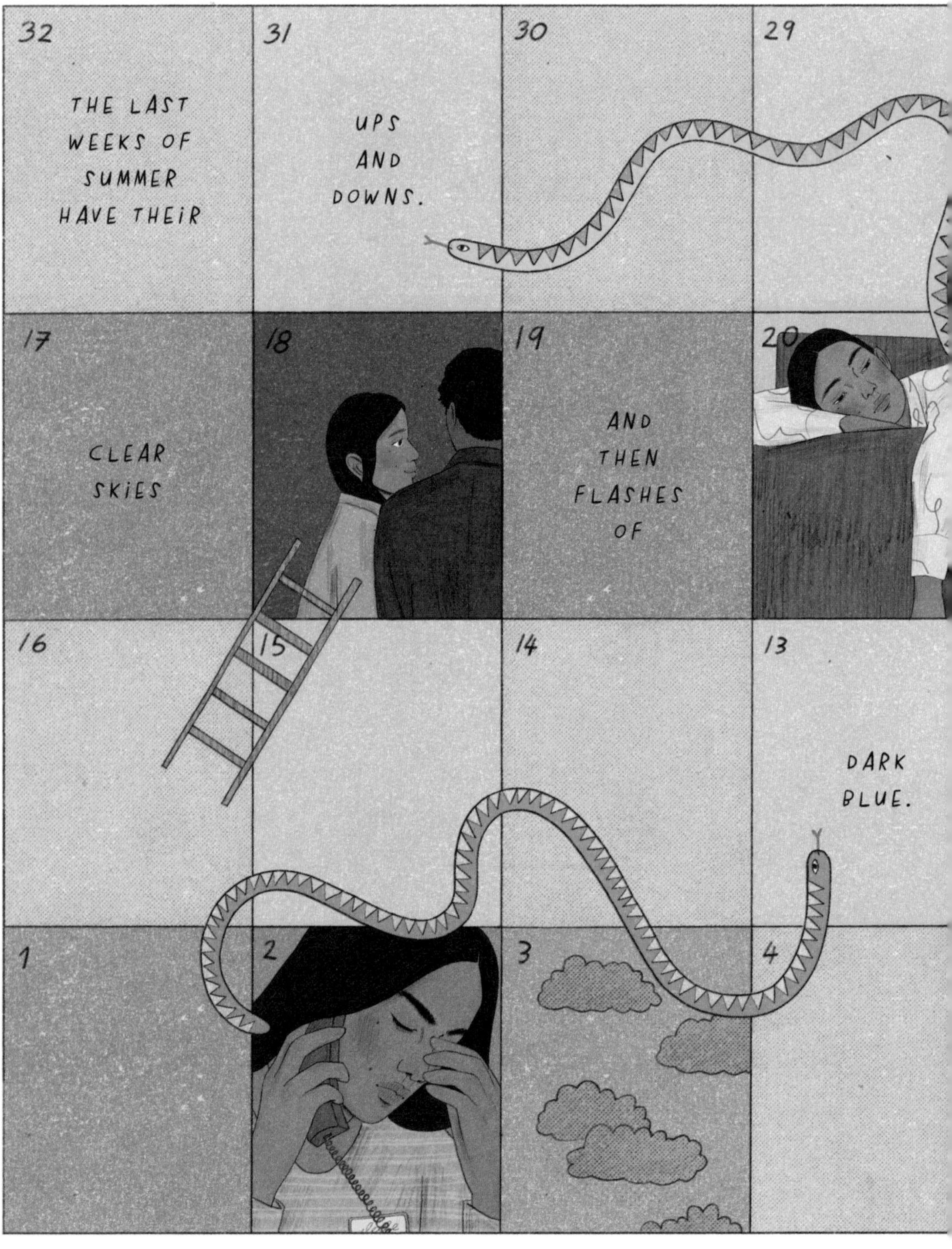
32
THE LAST WEEKS OF SUMMER HAVE THEIR
31
UPS AND DOWNS.
30
29
17
CLEAR SKIES
18
19
AND THEN FLASHES OF
20
16
15
14
13
DARK BLUE.
1
2
3
4

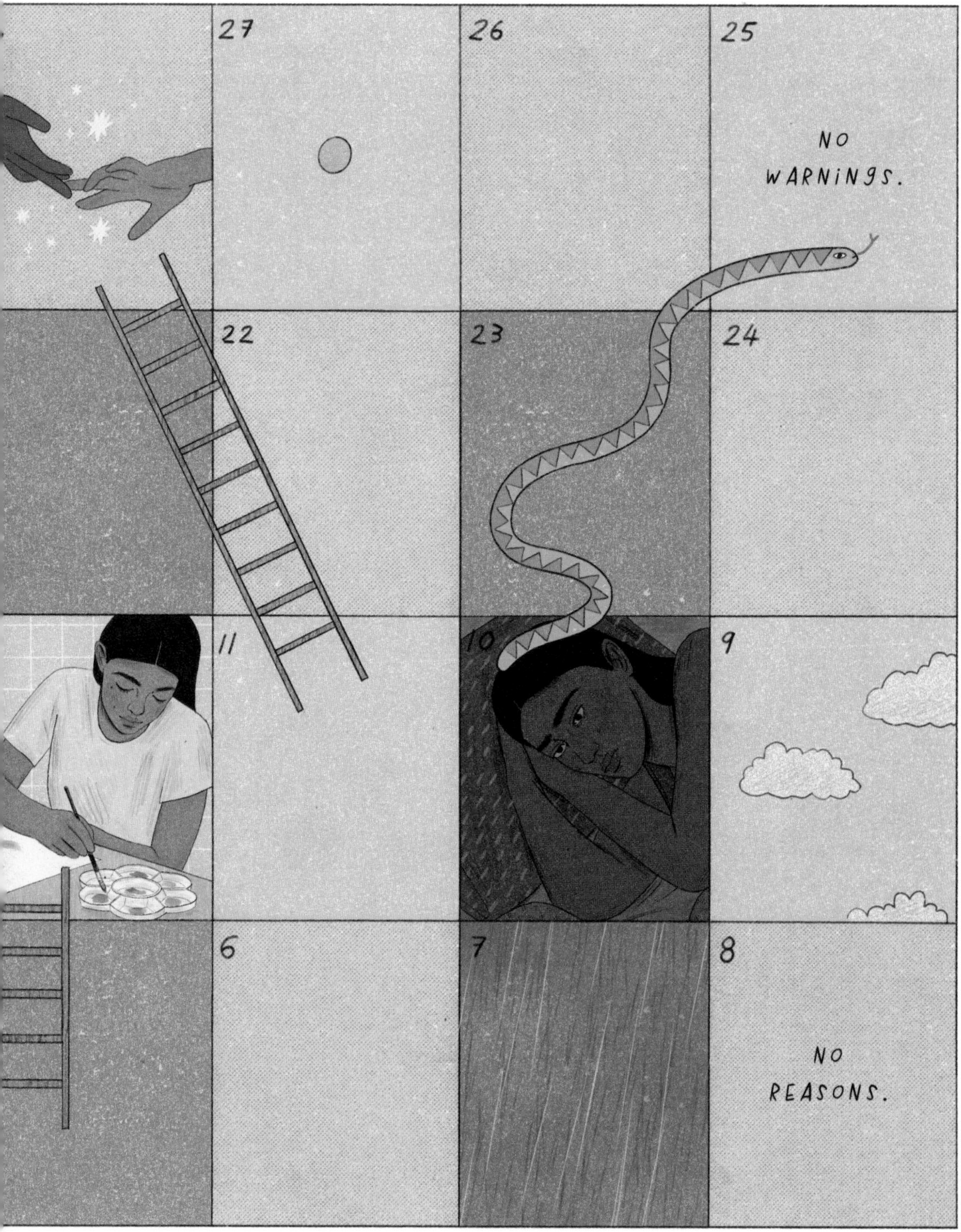
27
26
25
NO WARNINGS.
22
23
24
11
10
9
6
7
8
NO REASONS.

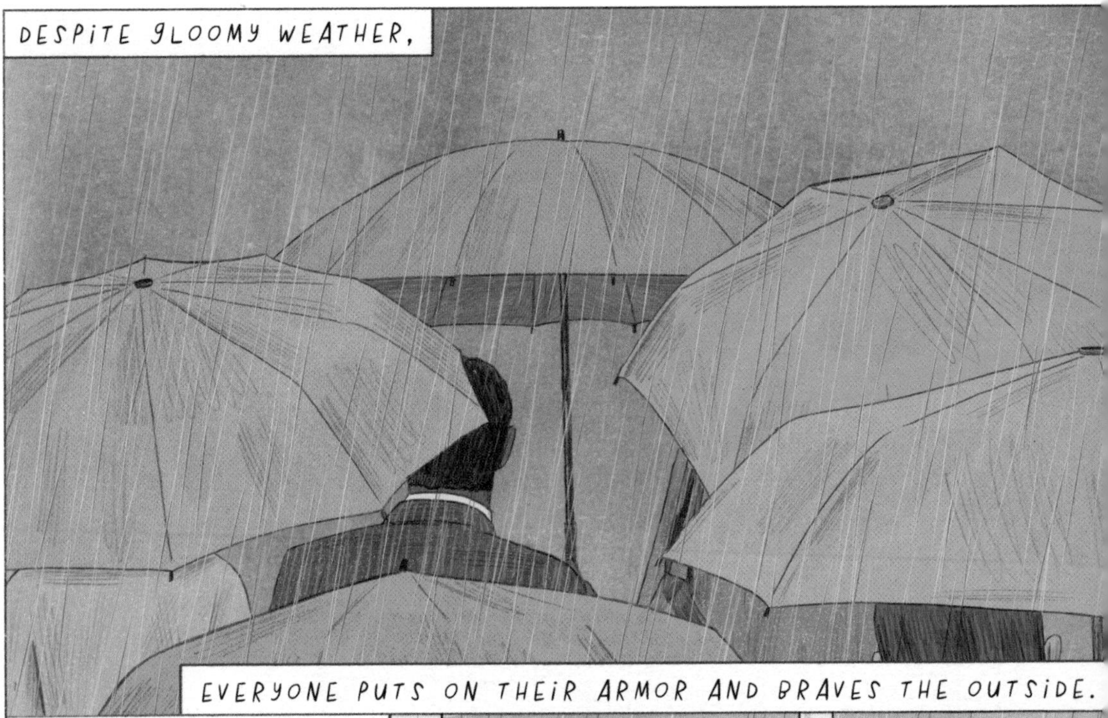
DESPITE GLOOMY WEATHER,
EVERYONE PUTS ON THEIR ARMOR AND BRAVES THE OUTSIDE.

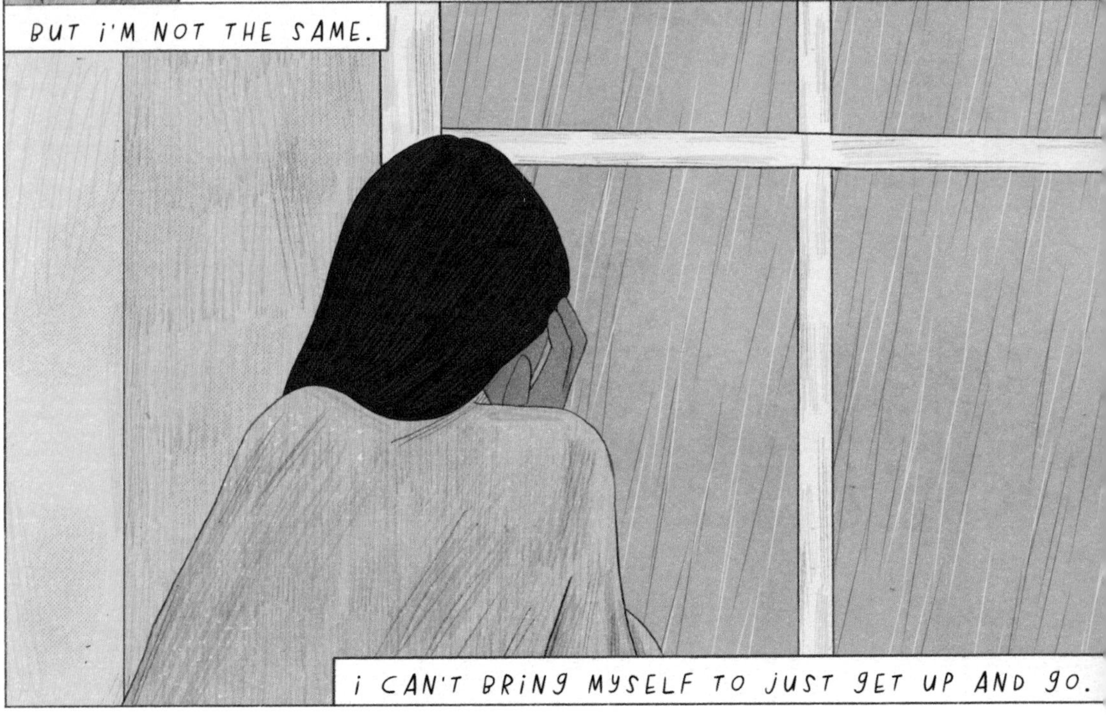
BUT I'M NOT THE SAME.
I CAN'T BRING MYSELF TO JUST GET UP AND GO.

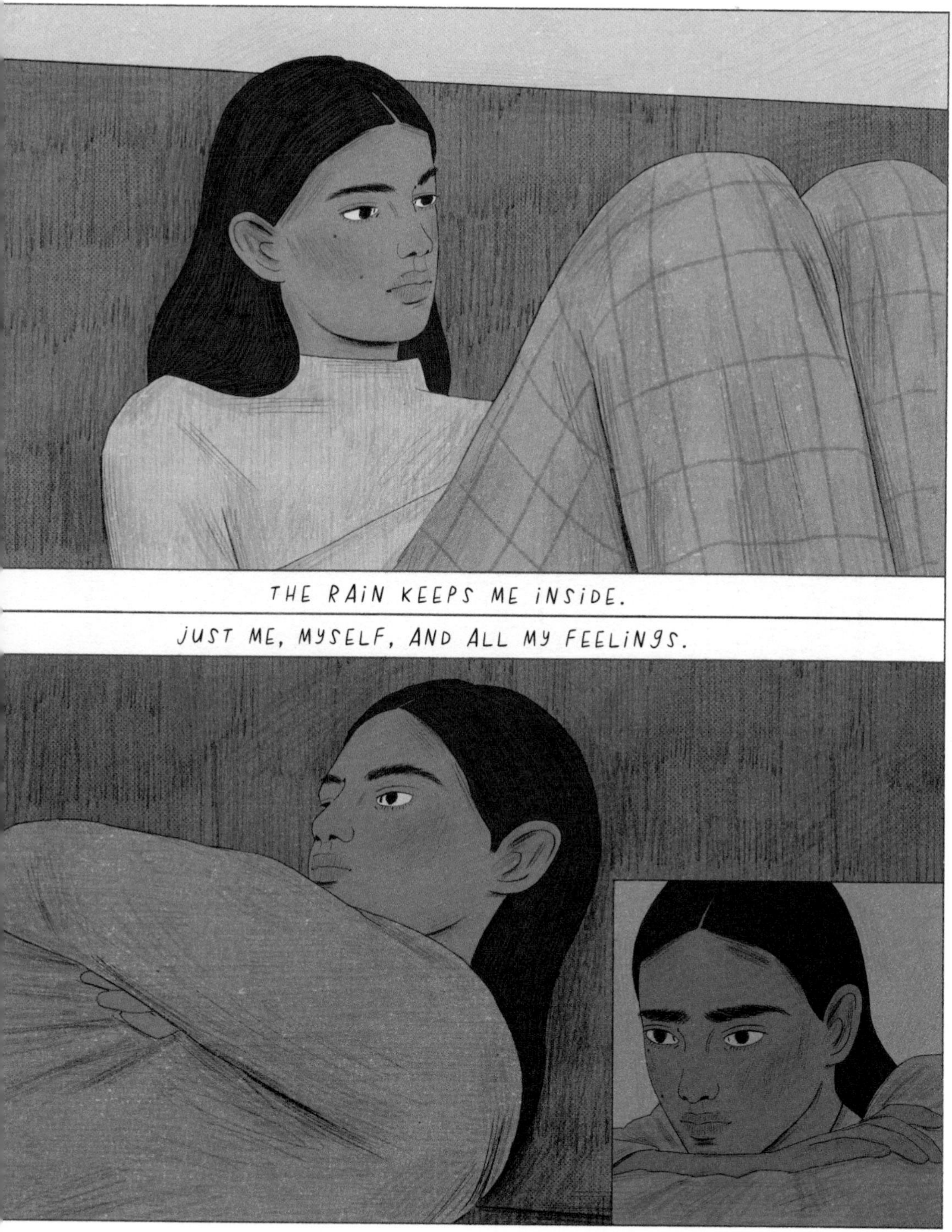
THE RAIN KEEPS ME INSIDE.
JUST ME, MYSELF, AND ALL MY FEELINGS.

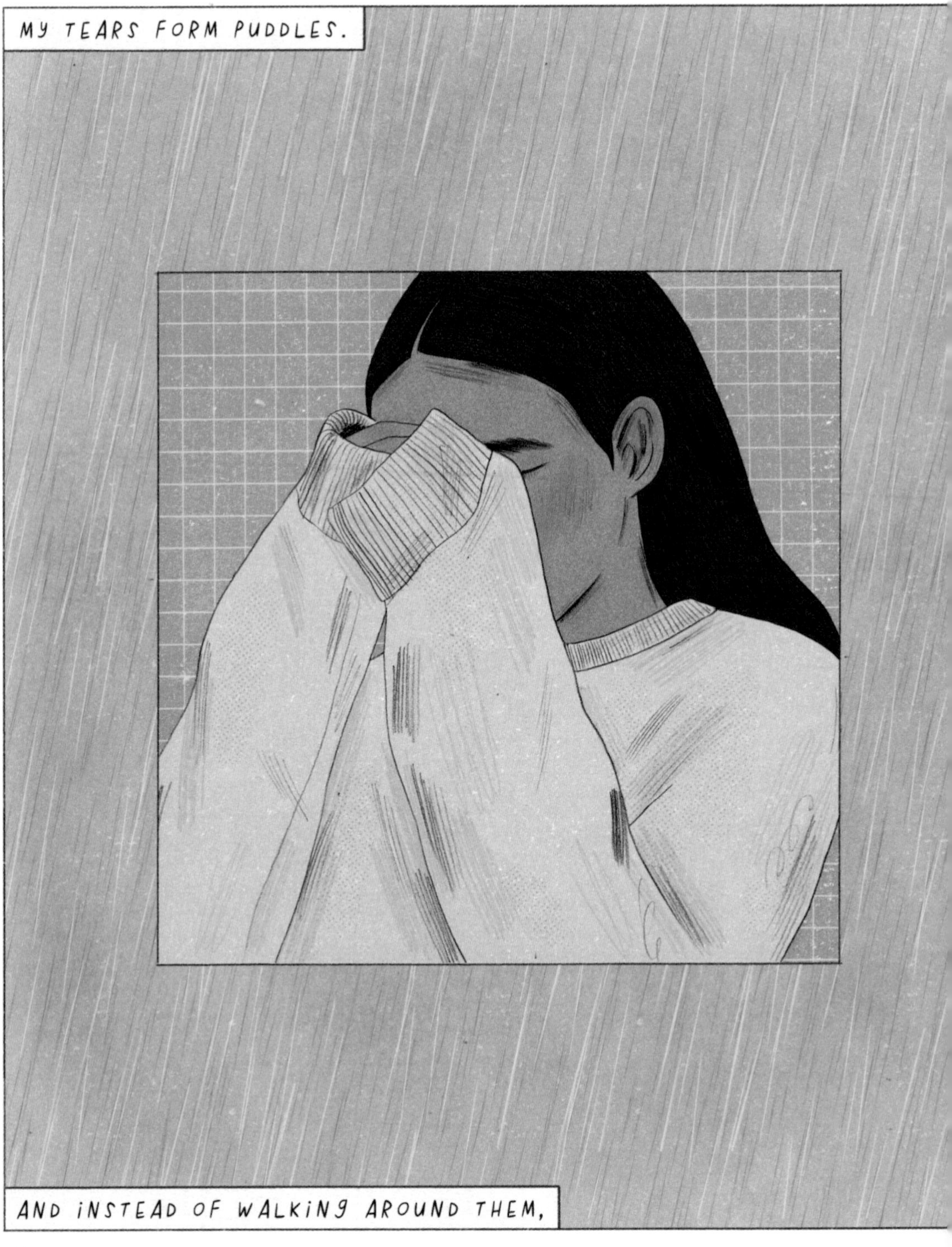
MY TEARS FORM PUDDLES.
AND INSTEAD OF WALKING AROUND THEM,

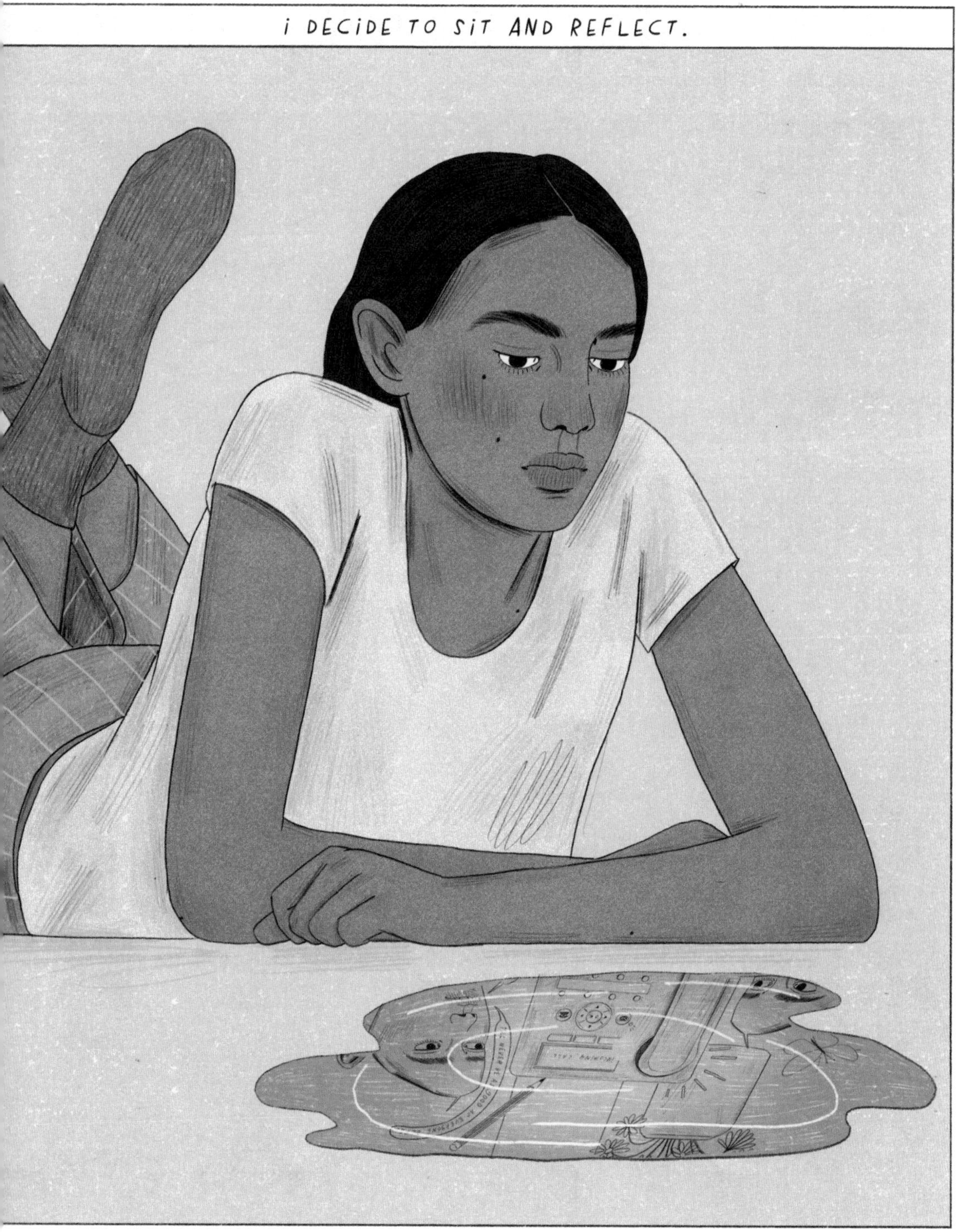
i DECIDE TO SIT AND REFLECT.

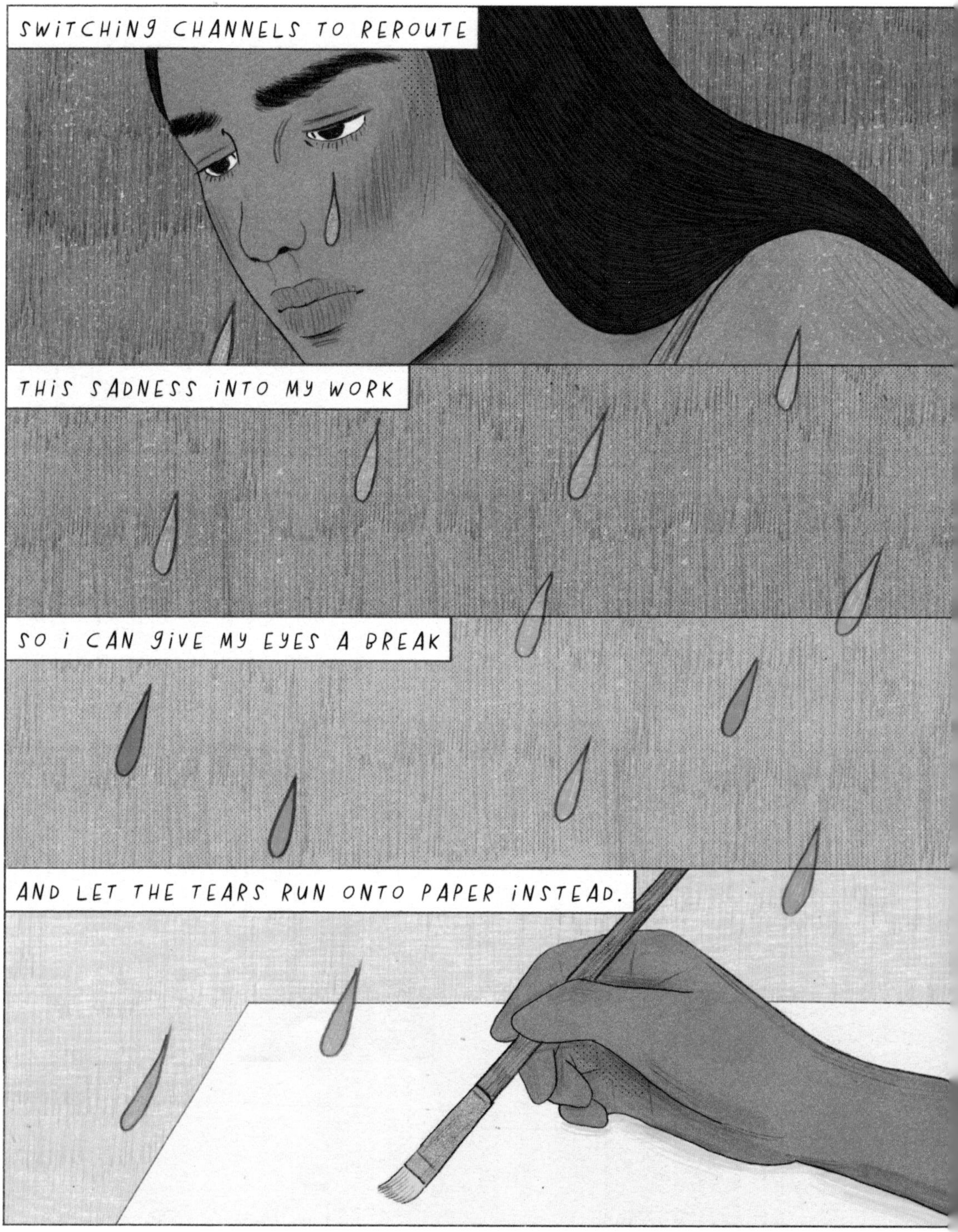
SWITCHING CHANNELS TO REROUTE
THIS SADNESS INTO MY WORK
SO I CAN GIVE MY EYES A BREAK
AND LET THE TEARS RUN ONTO PAPER INSTEAD.

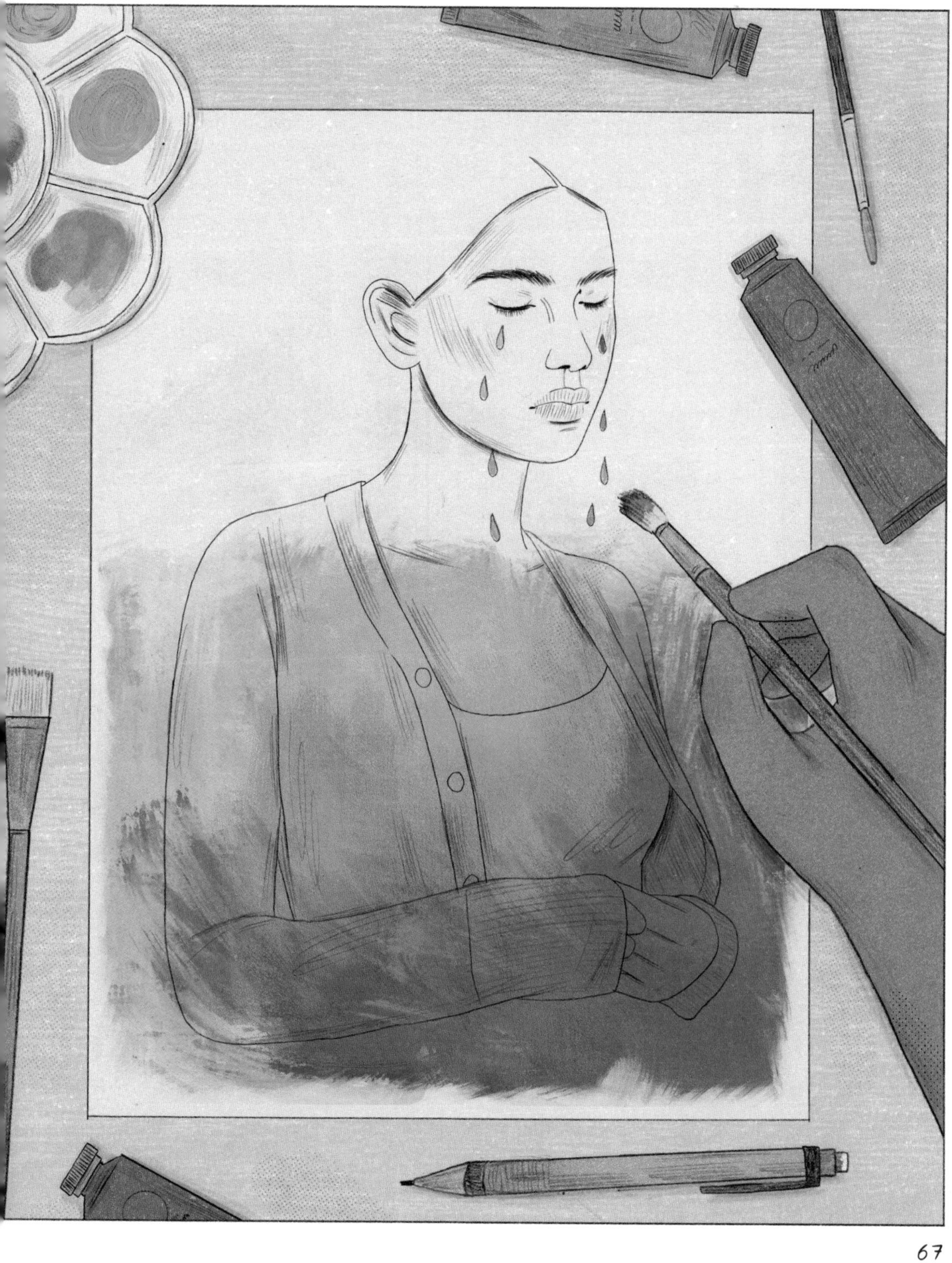

CHAPTER FOUR

AUTUMN

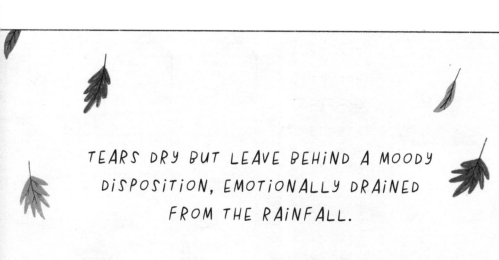

TEARS DRY BUT LEAVE BEHIND A MOODY
DISPOSITION, EMOTIONALLY DRAINED
FROM THE RAINFALL.

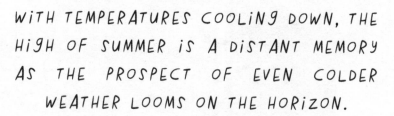

AUTUMN IS THE SEASON OF GRADUAL
TRANSITION, AND WHILE THE CLOCKS GO
BACK, THERE IS A STRUGGLE TO MOVE
FORWARD. EVEN THE SUN HIDES BEHIND
THE CLOUDS AS THE DAYS BECOME
SHORTER, REPLACING A PALETTE OF BLUE
WITH GRAY.

WITH TEMPERATURES COOLING DOWN, THE
HIGH OF SUMMER IS A DISTANT MEMORY
AS THE PROSPECT OF EVEN COLDER
WEATHER LOOMS ON THE HORIZON.

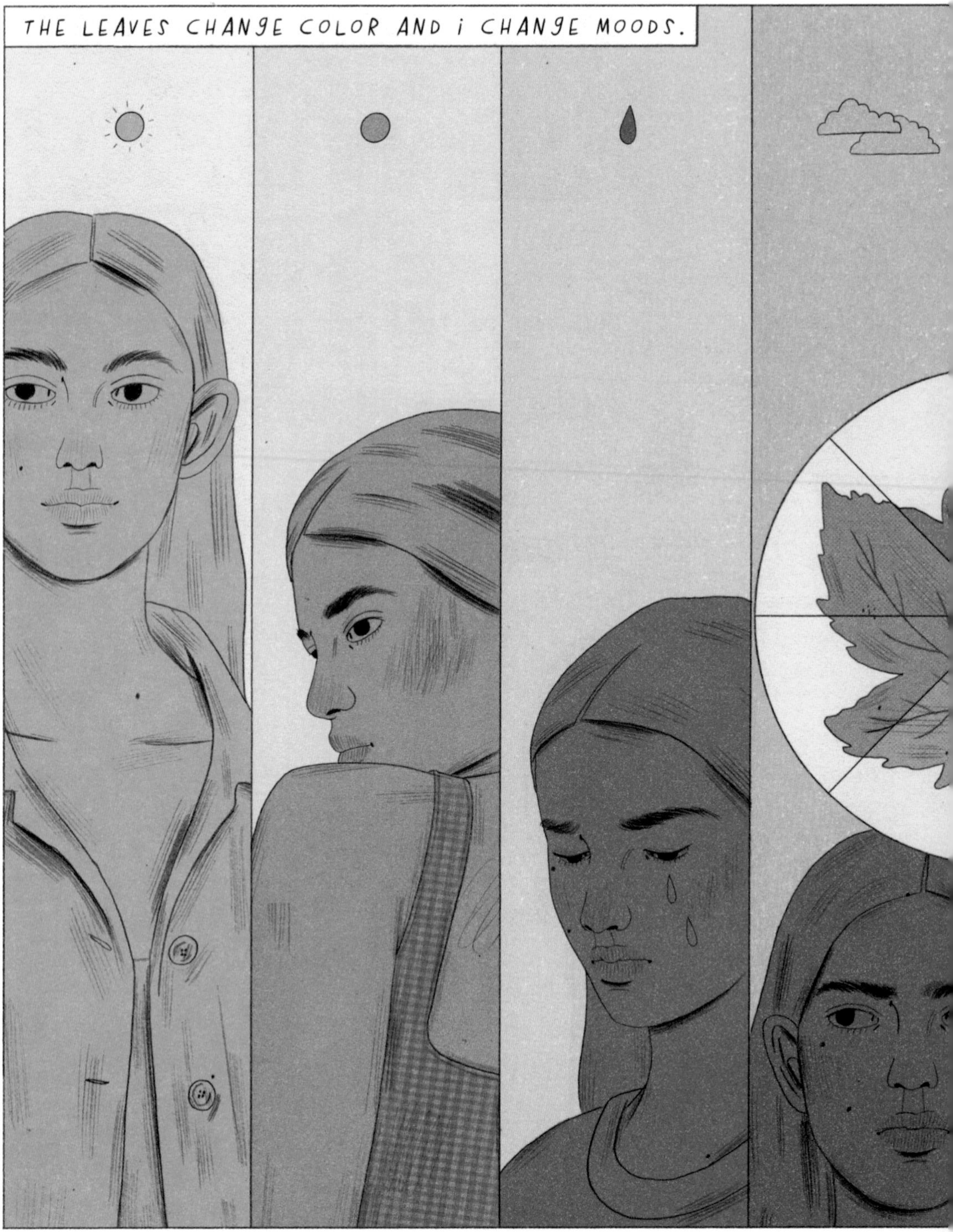
THE LEAVES CHANGE COLOR AND i CHANGE MOODS.

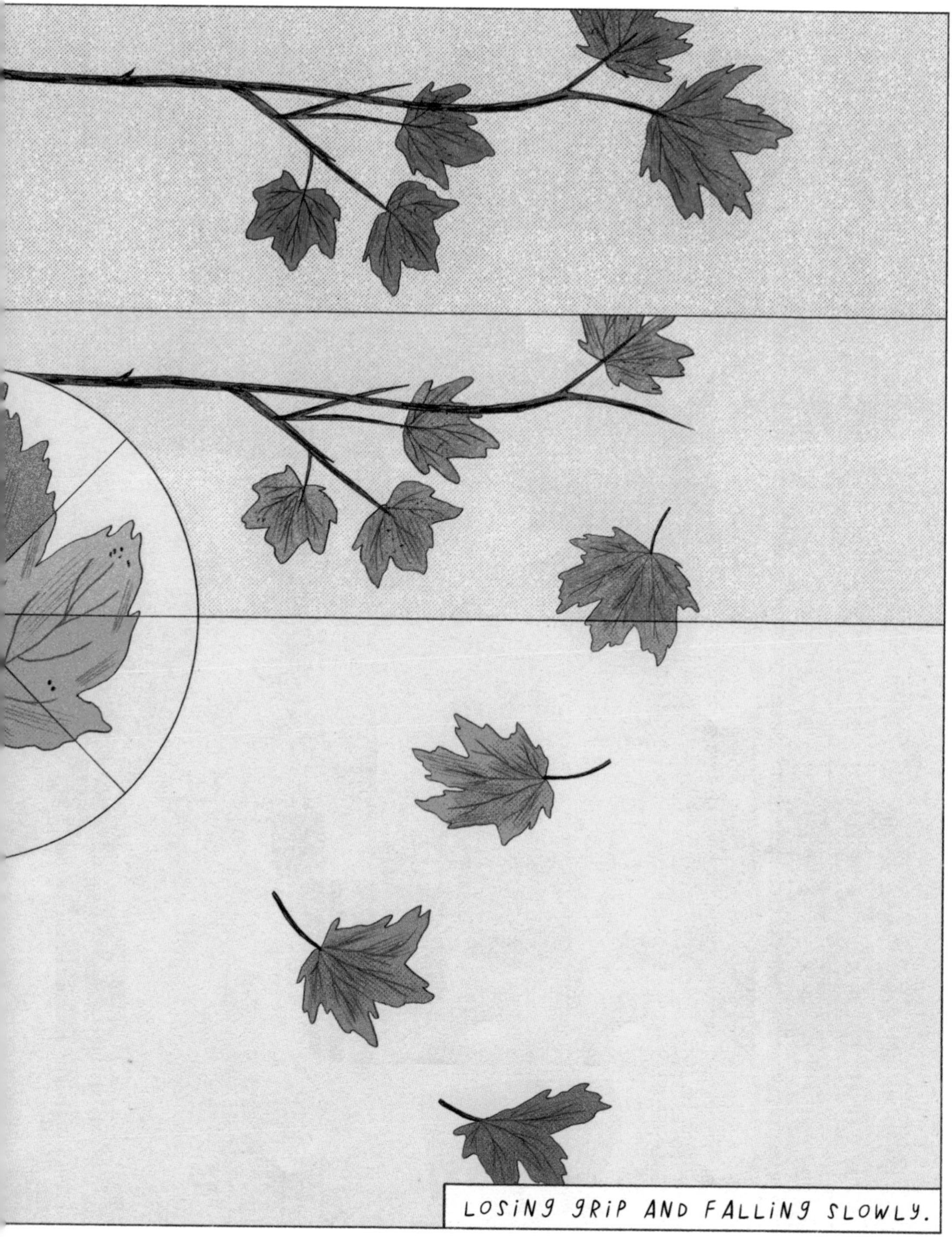

LOSING GRIP AND FALLING SLOWLY.

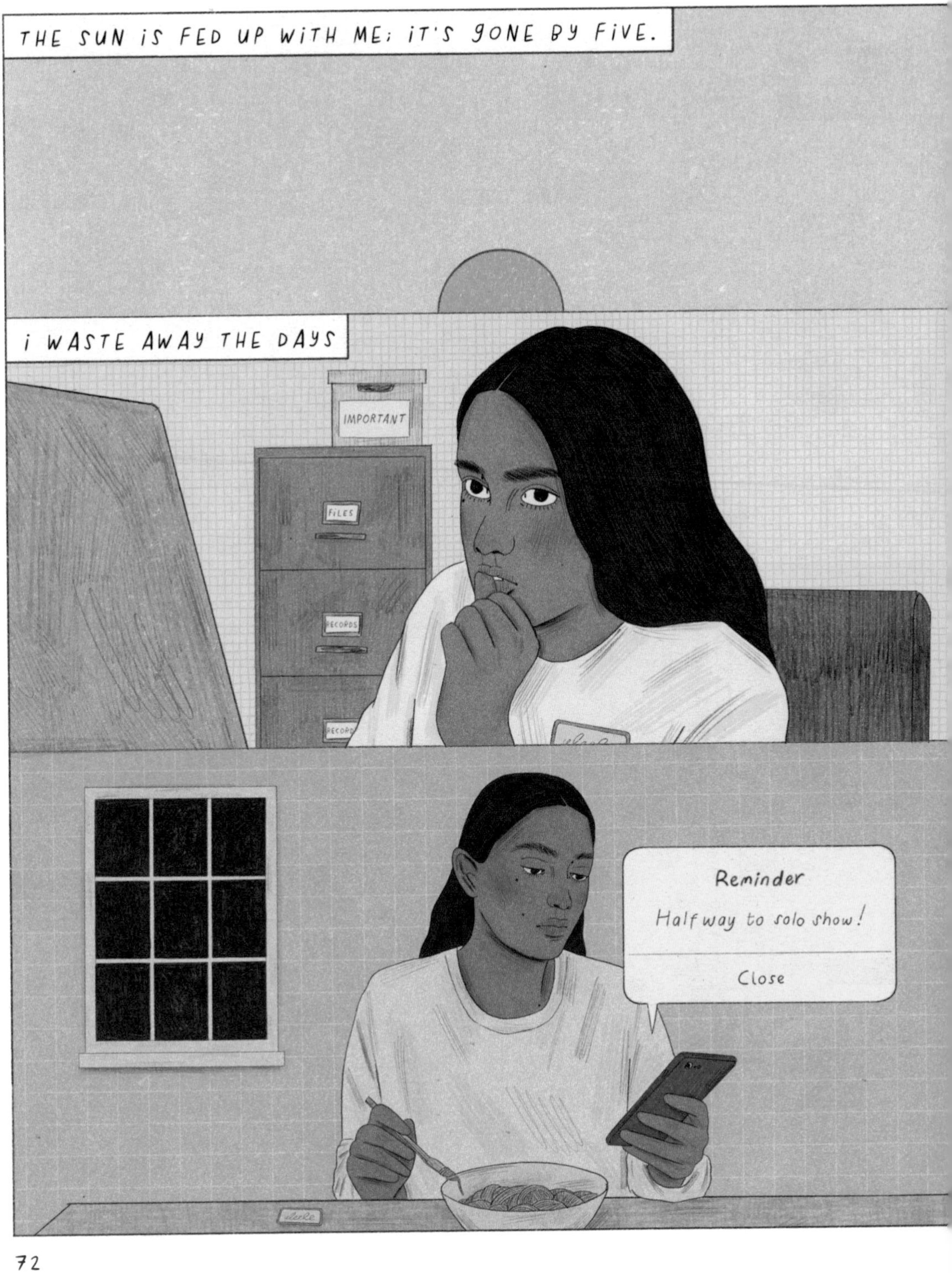
THE SUN IS FED UP WITH ME; IT'S GONE BY FIVE.
I WASTE AWAY THE DAYS
IMPORTANT
FILES
RECORDS
Reminder
Halfway to solo show!
Close

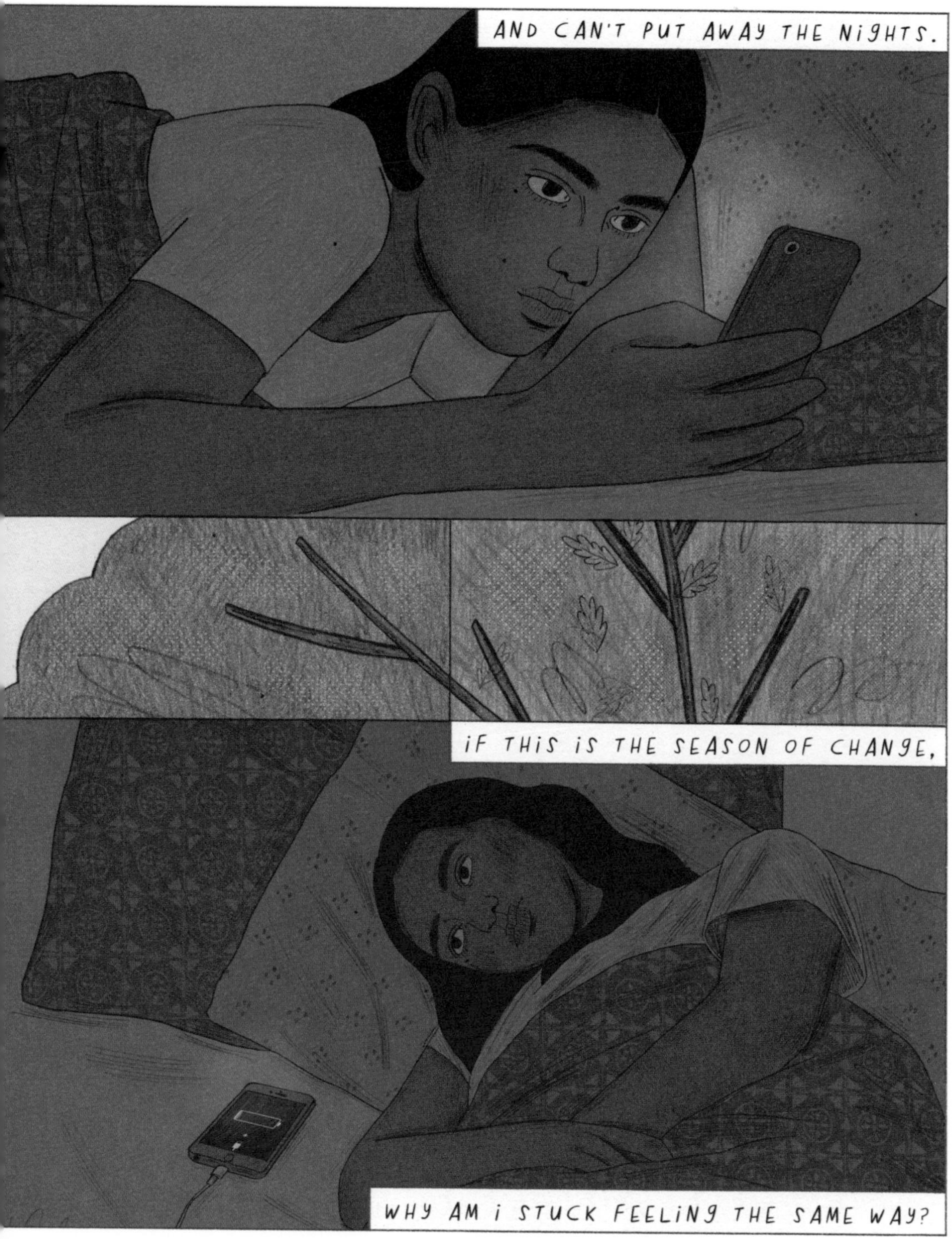
AND CAN'T PUT AWAY THE NIGHTS.
IF THIS IS THE SEASON OF CHANGE,
WHY AM I STUCK FEELING THE SAME WAY?

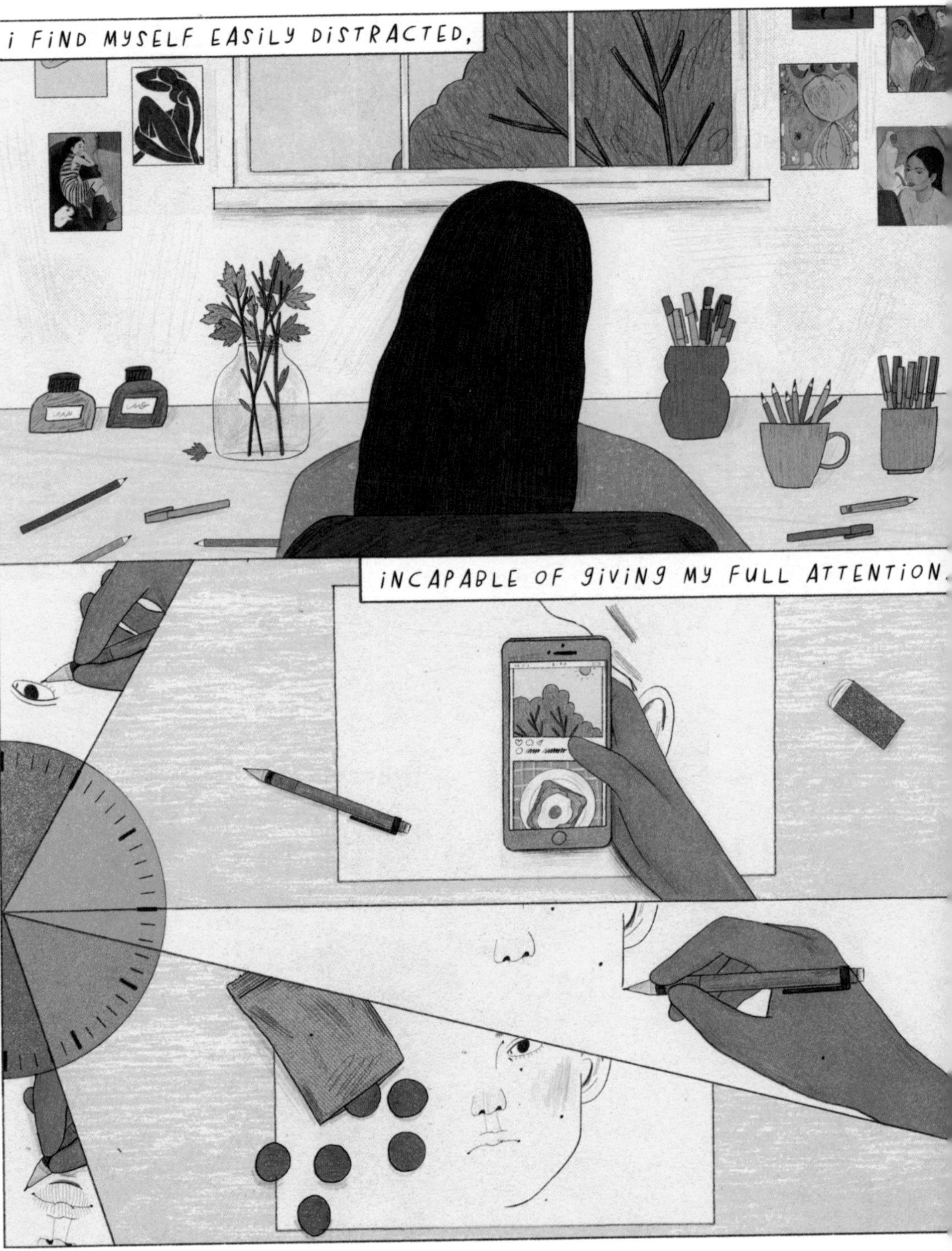
i FiND MYSELF EASiLY DiSTRACTED,
iNCAPABLE OF GiViNG MY FULL ATTENTiON.

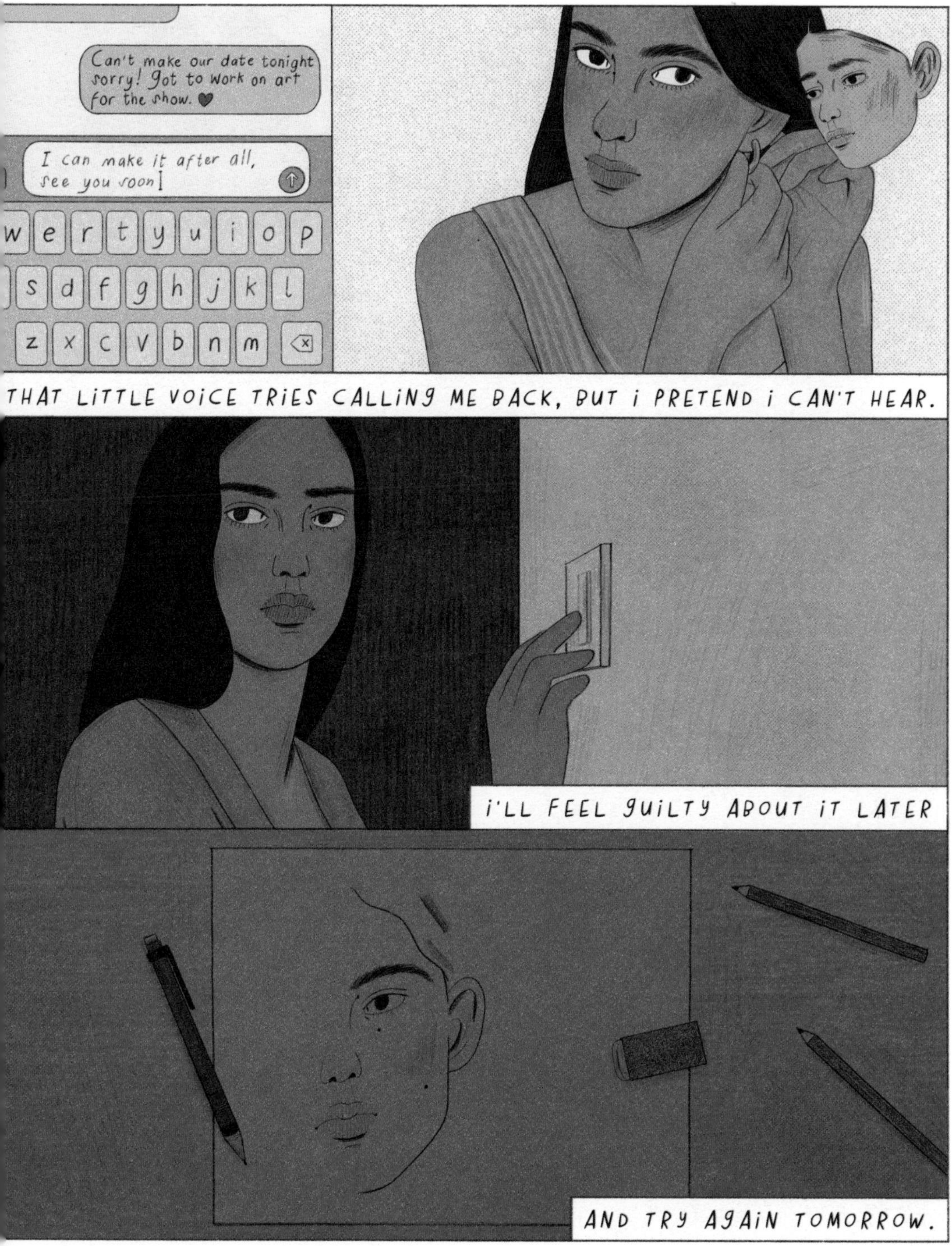
Can't make our date tonight sorry! Got to work on art for the show.
I can make it after all, see you soon
THAT LITTLE VOICE TRIES CALLING ME BACK, BUT I PRETEND I CAN'T HEAR.
I'LL FEEL GUILTY ABOUT IT LATER
AND TRY AGAIN TOMORROW.

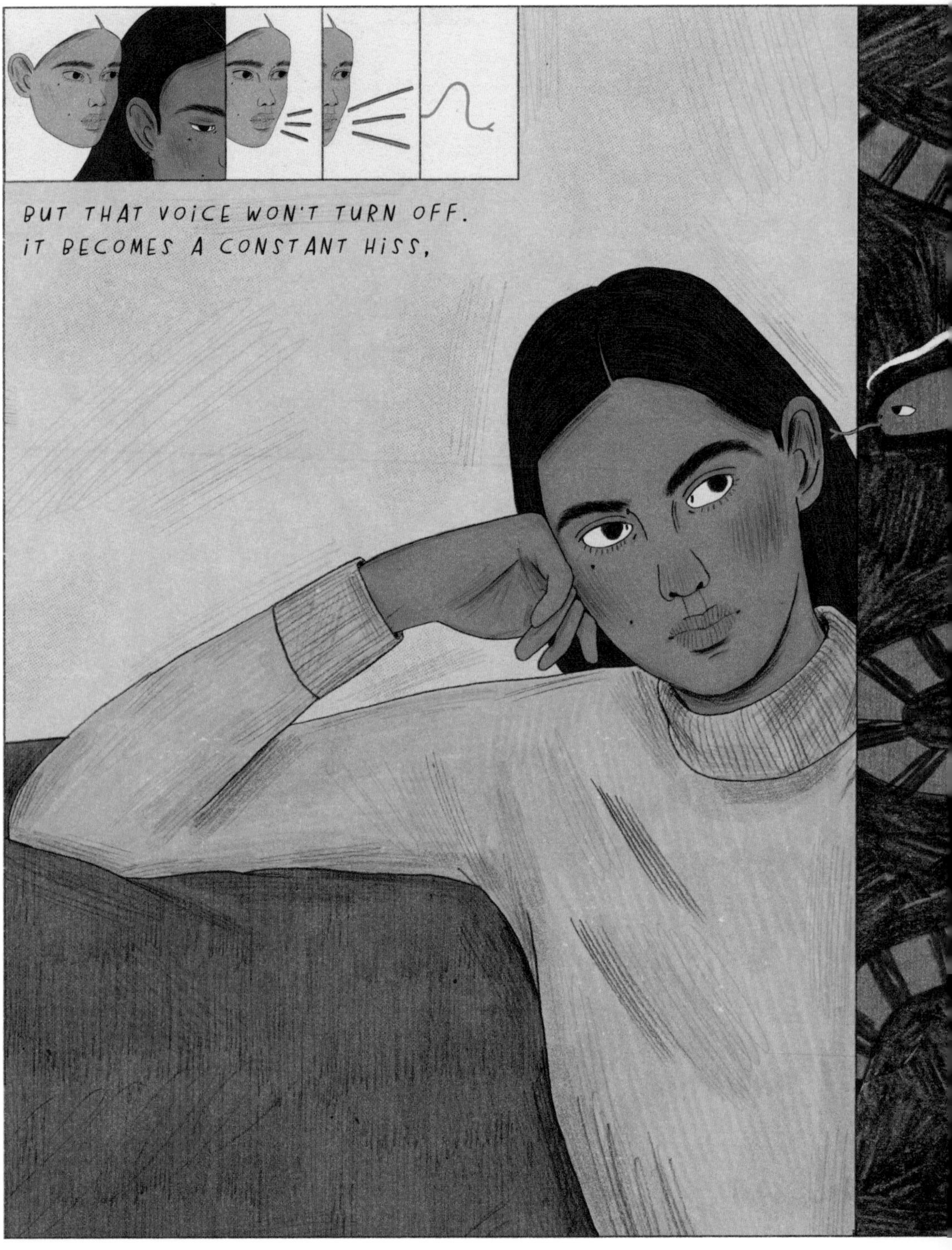
BUT THAT VOICE WON'T TURN OFF.
IT BECOMES A CONSTANT HISS,

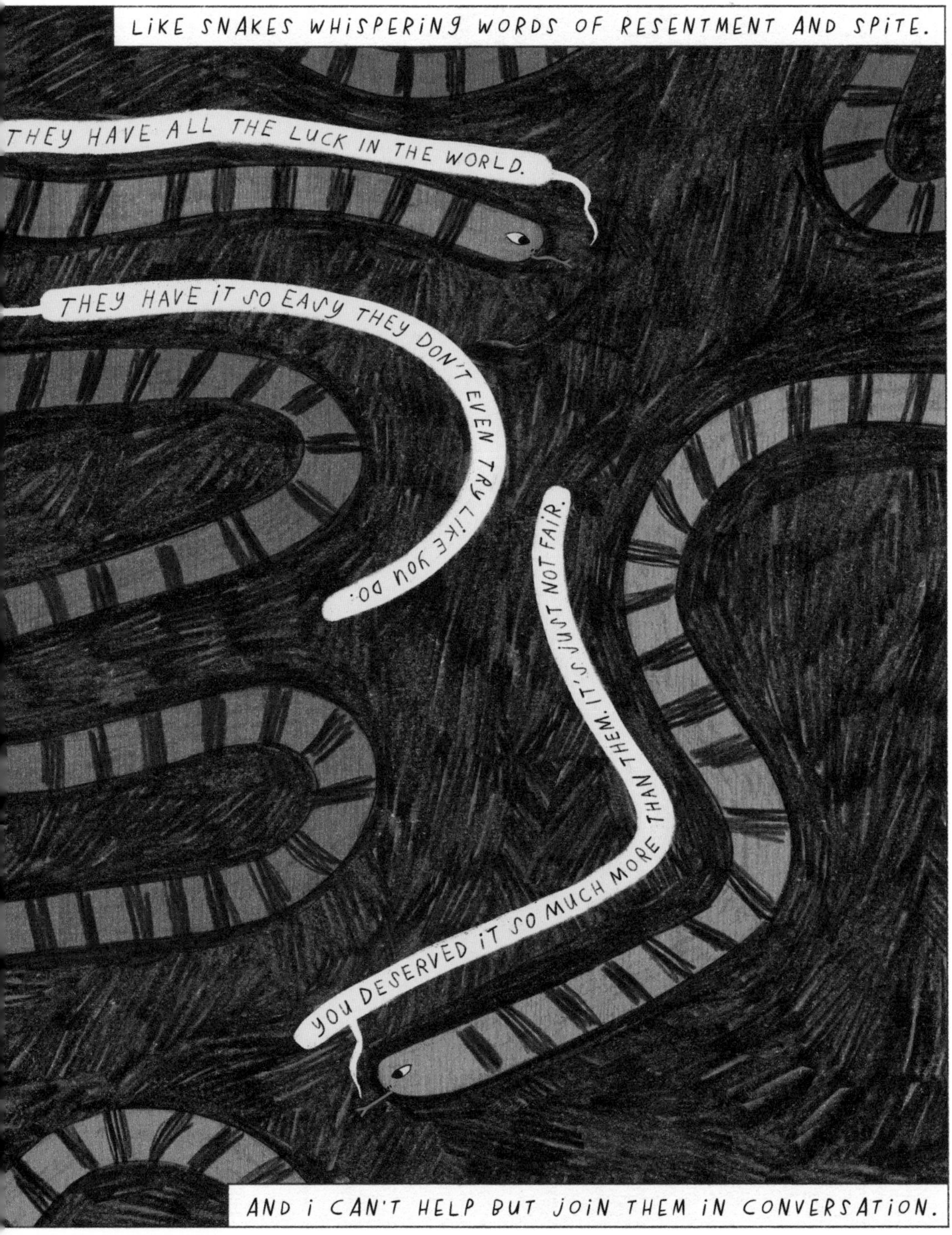
LIKE SNAKES WHISPERING WORDS OF RESENTMENT AND SPITE.
THEY HAVE ALL THE LUCK IN THE WORLD.
THEY HAVE IT SO EASY THEY DON'T EVEN TRY LIKE YOU DO.
YOU DESERVED IT SO MUCH MORE THAN THEM. IT'S JUST NOT FAIR.
AND I CAN'T HELP BUT JOIN THEM IN CONVERSATION.

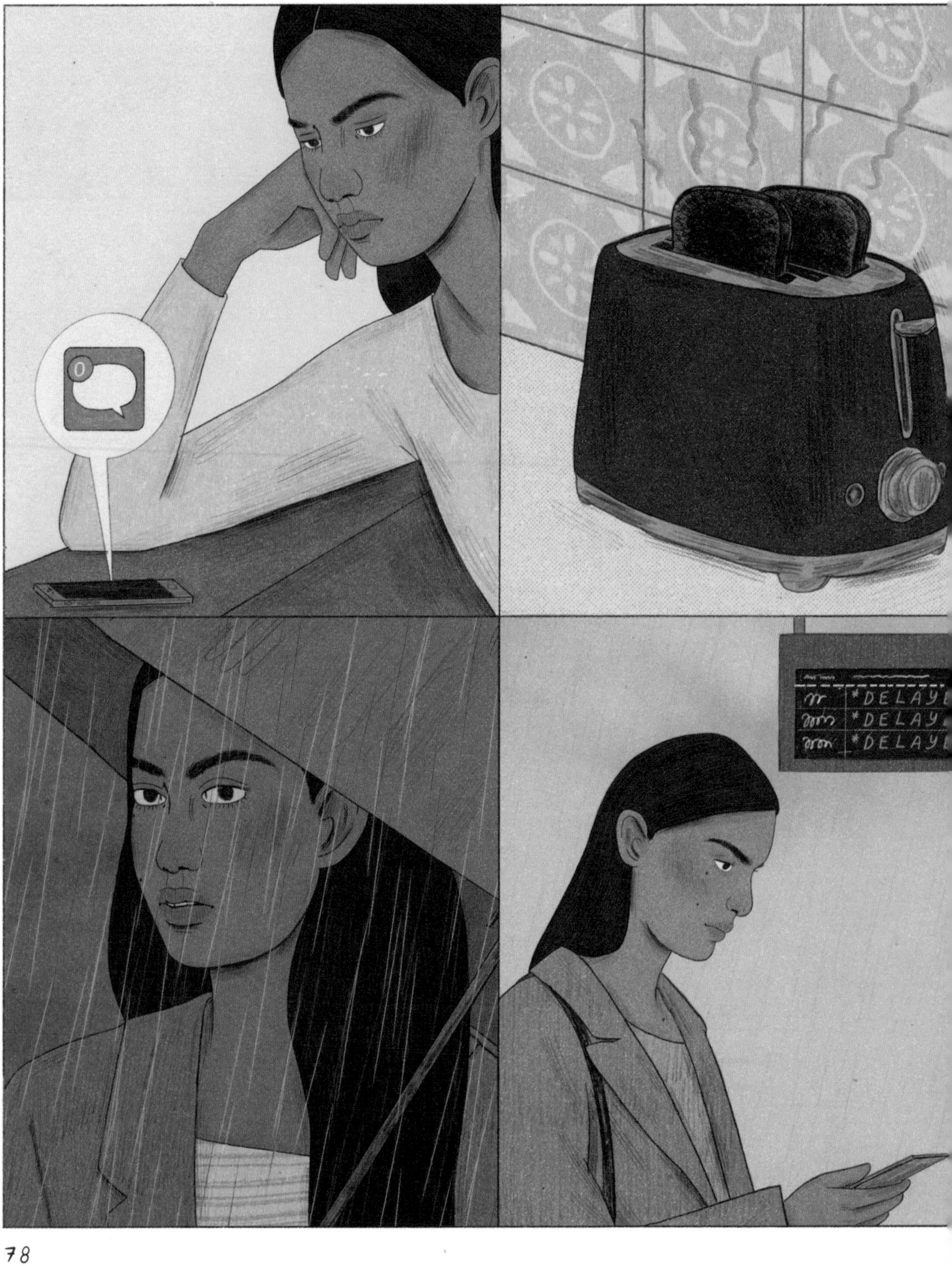
*DELAY
*DELAY
*DELAY

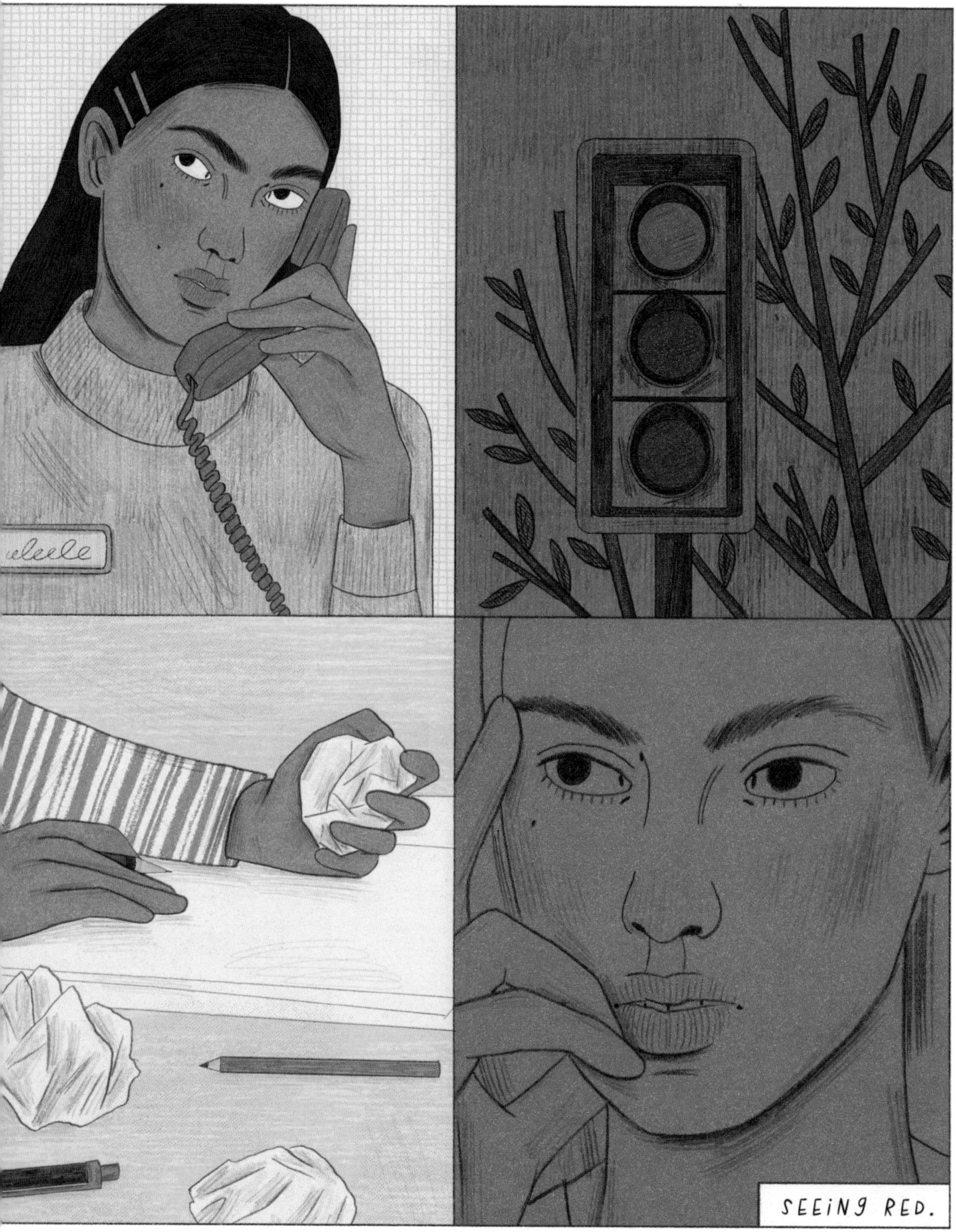
SEEING RED.

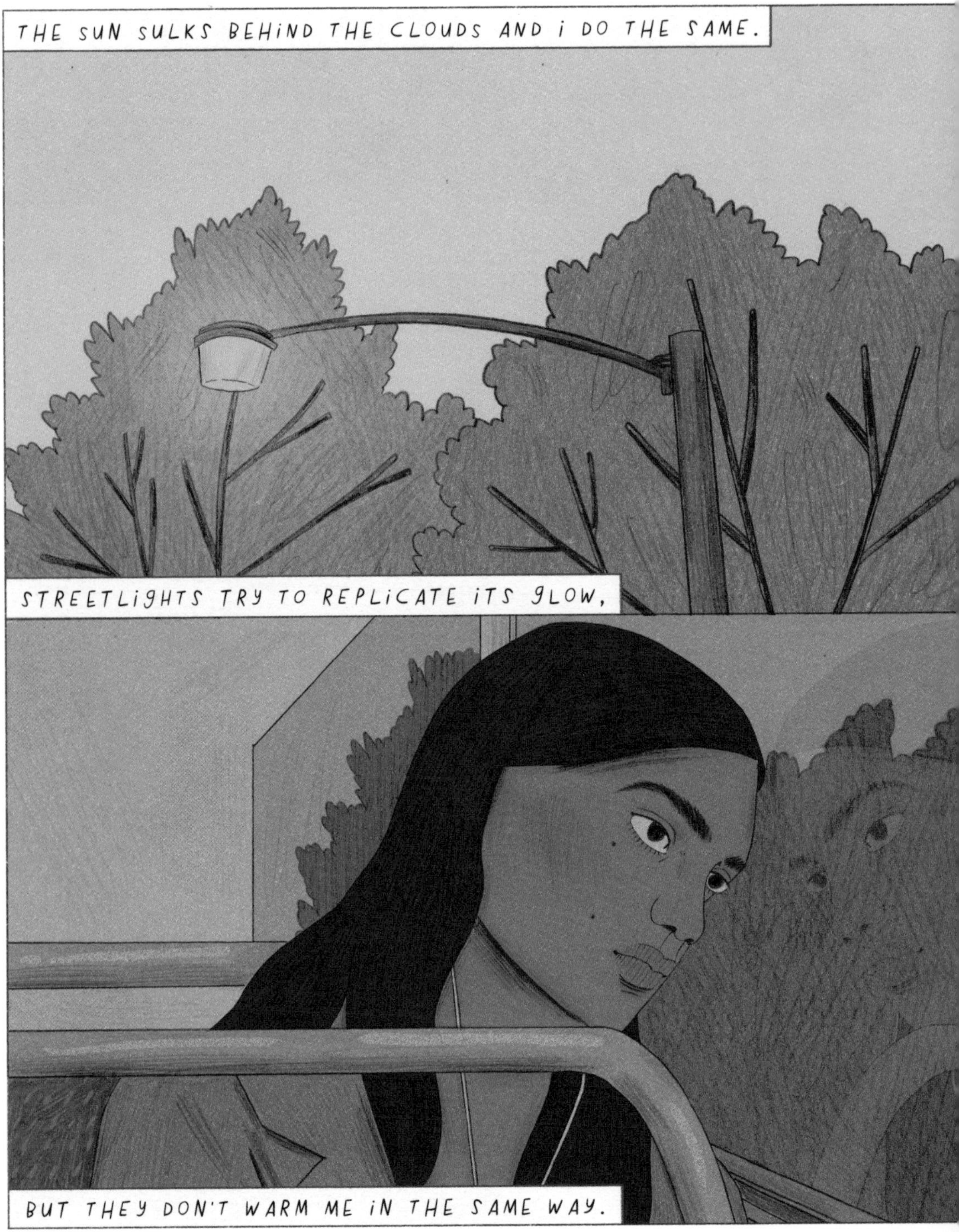
THE SUN SULKS BEHIND THE CLOUDS AND i DO THE SAME.
STREETLiGHTS TRY TO REPLiCATE iTS GLOW,
BUT THEY DON'T WARM ME iN THE SAME WAY.

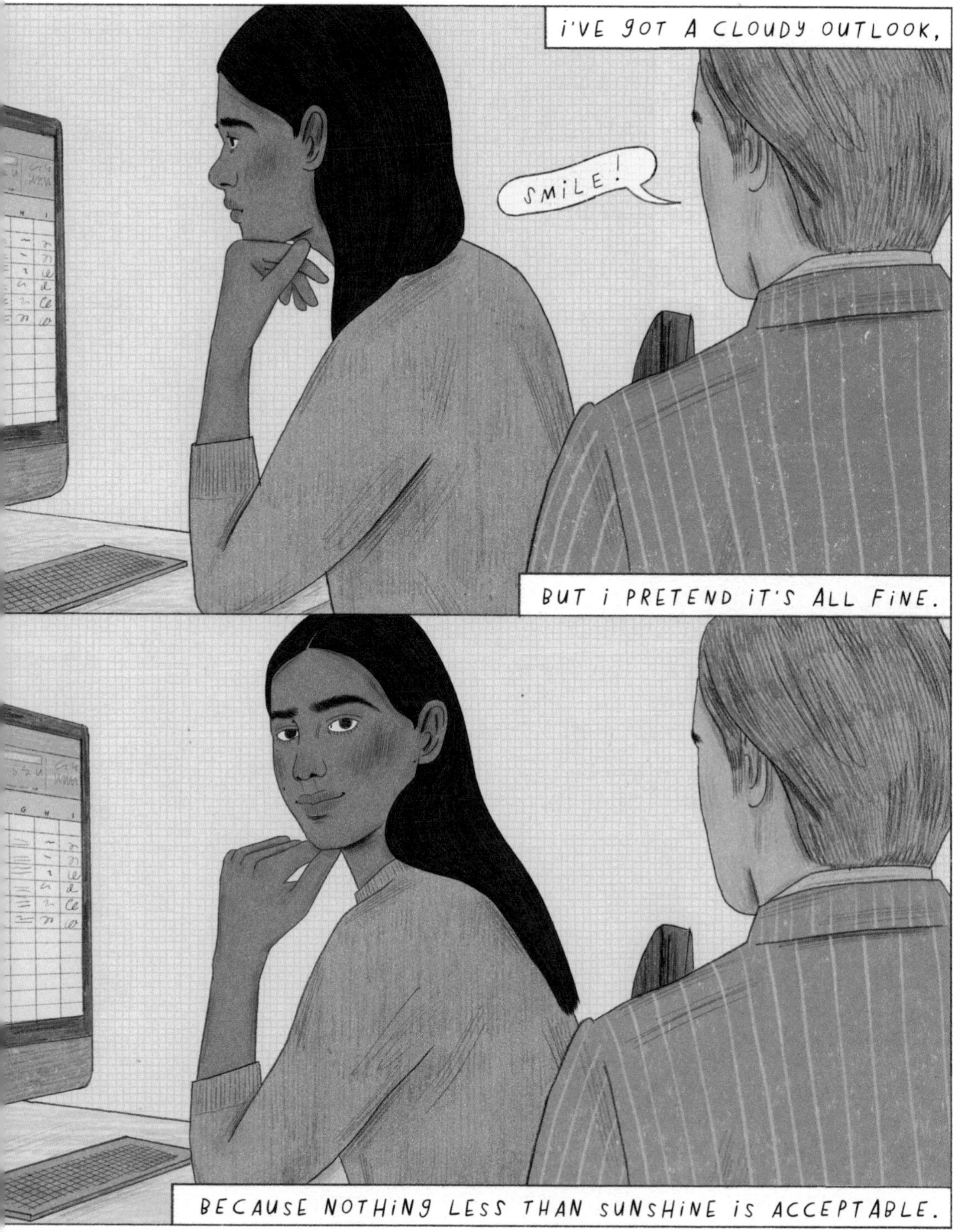
i'VE GOT A CLOUDY OUTLOOK,
SMiLE!
BUT i PRETEND iT'S ALL FiNE.
BECAUSE NOTHiNG LESS THAN SUNSHiNE iS ACCEPTABLE.

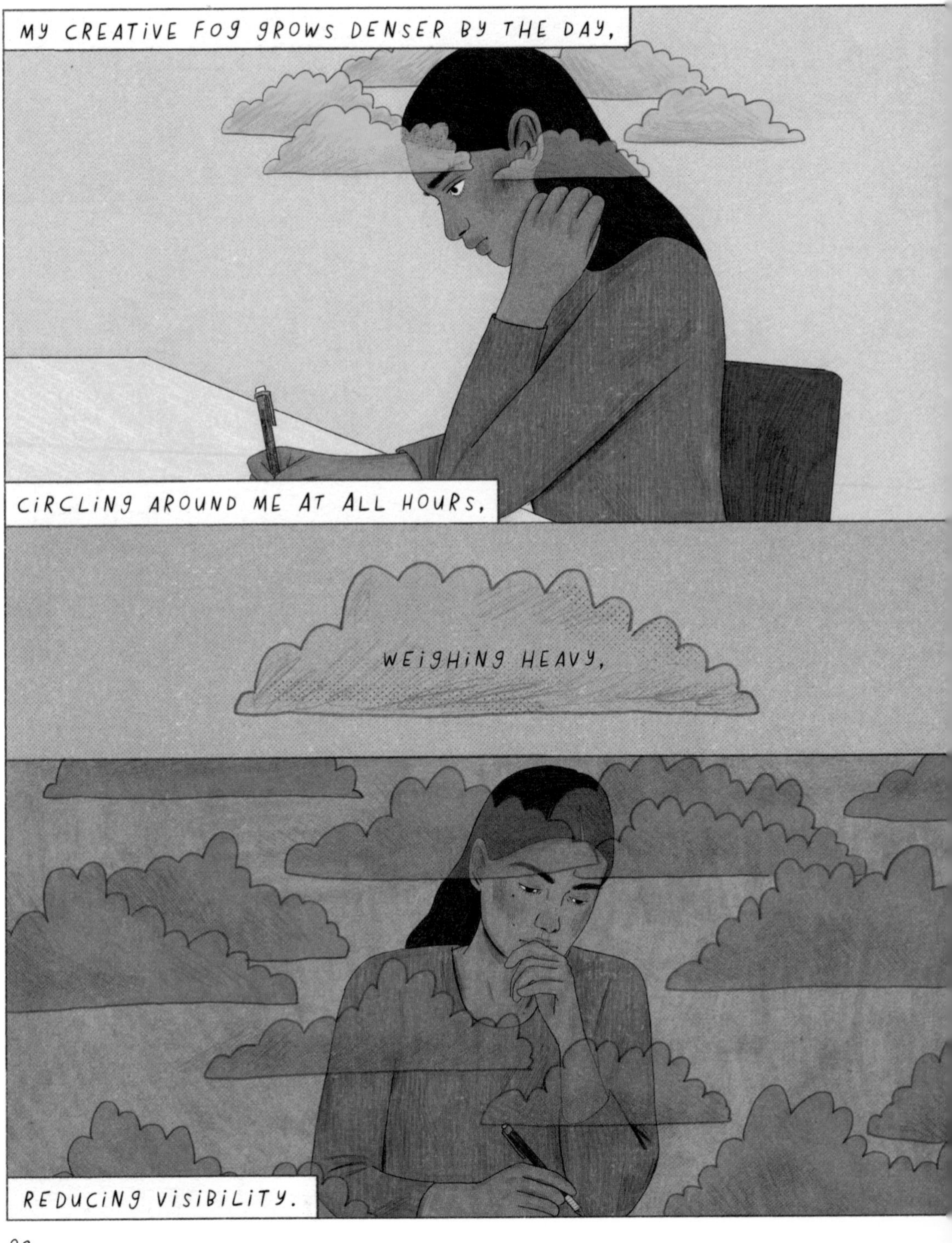
MY CREATIVE FOG GROWS DENSER BY THE DAY,
CIRCLING AROUND ME AT ALL HOURS,
WEIGHING HEAVY,
REDUCING VISIBILITY.

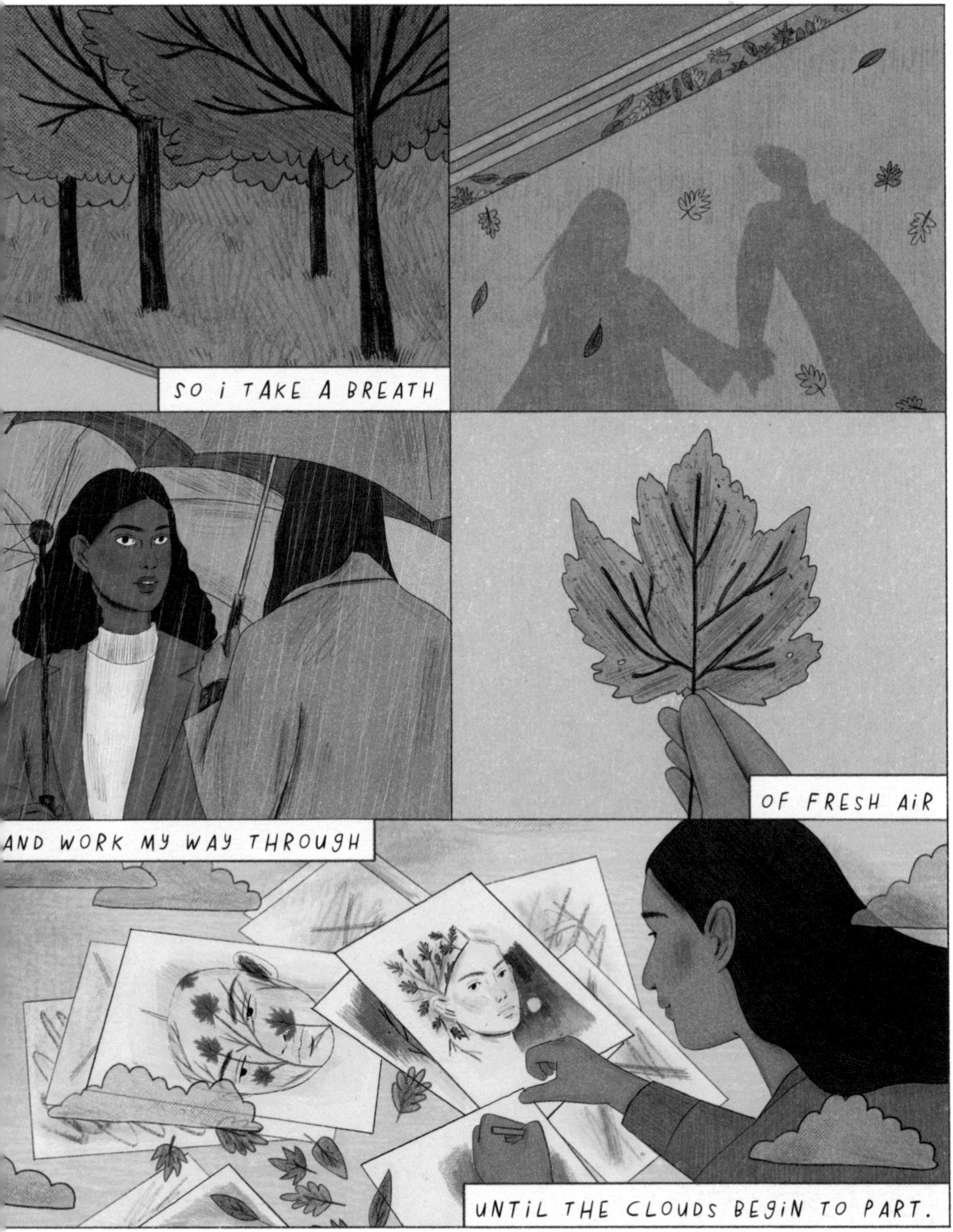
SO i TAKE A BREATH
OF FRESH AiR
AND WORK MY WAY THROUGH
UNTiL THE CLOUDS BEGIN TO PART.

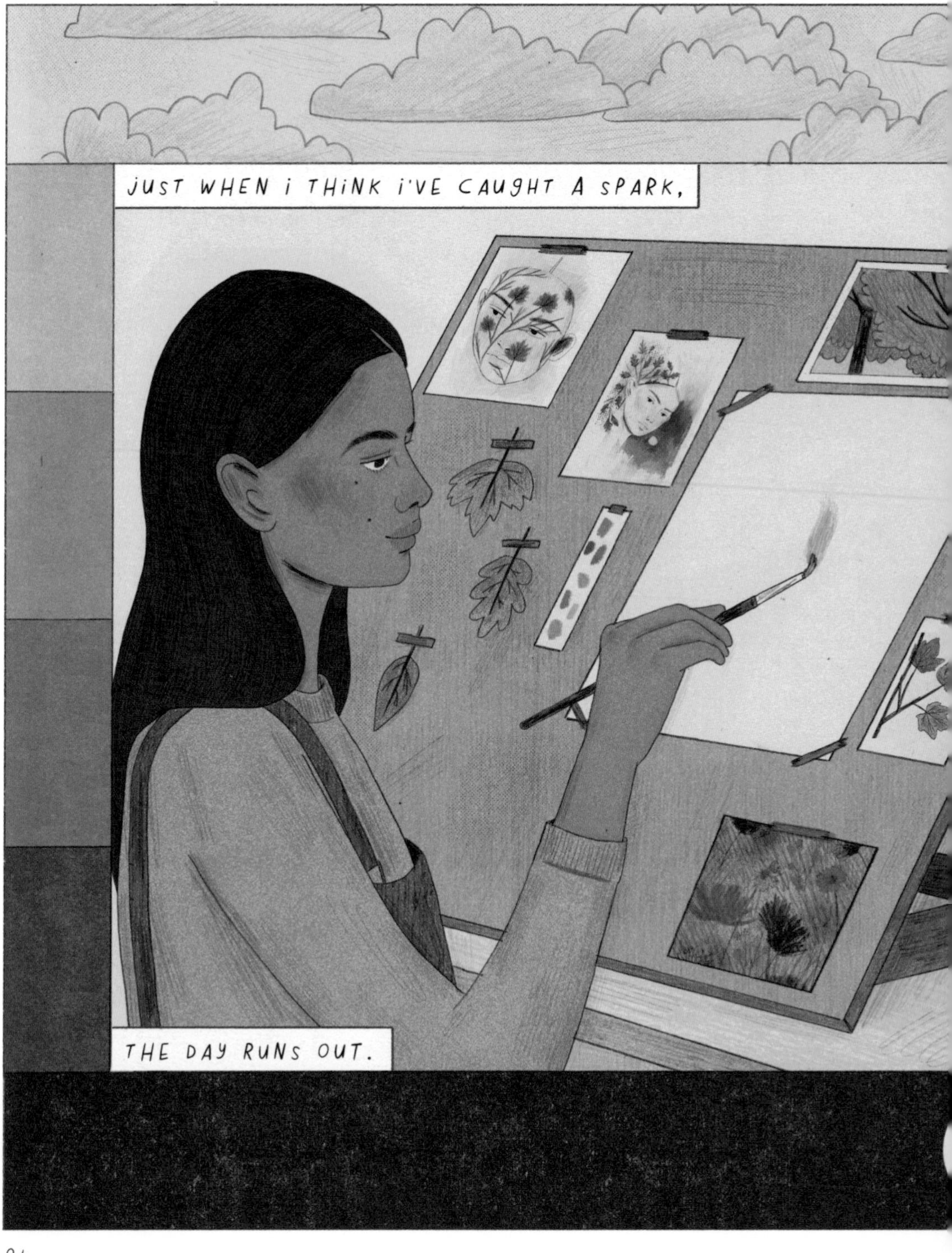
JUST WHEN I THINK I'VE CAUGHT A SPARK,
THE DAY RUNS OUT.

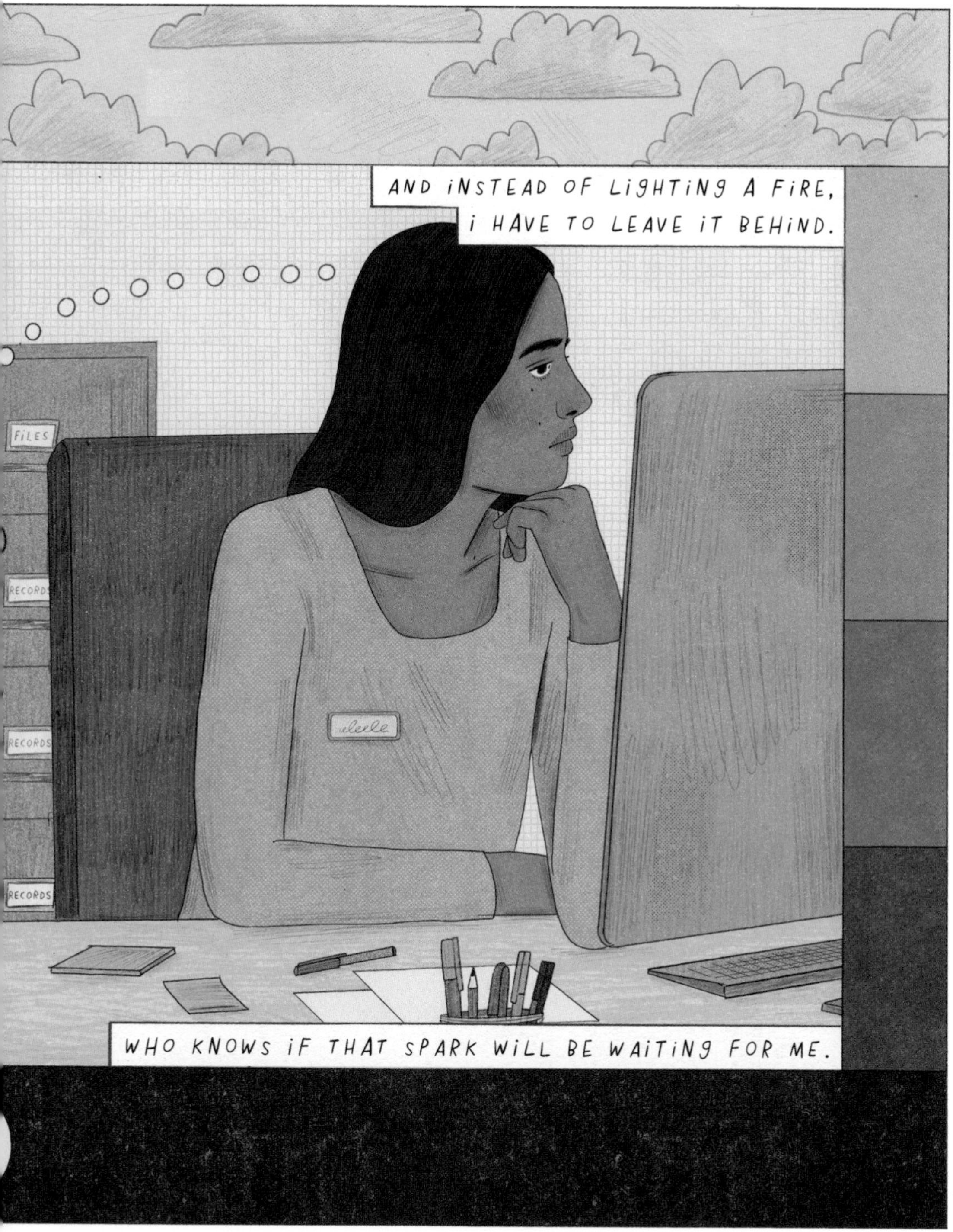
AND INSTEAD OF LIGHTING A FIRE,
I HAVE TO LEAVE IT BEHIND.
FILES
RECORDS
RECORDS
RECORDS
WHO KNOWS IF THAT SPARK WILL BE WAITING FOR ME.

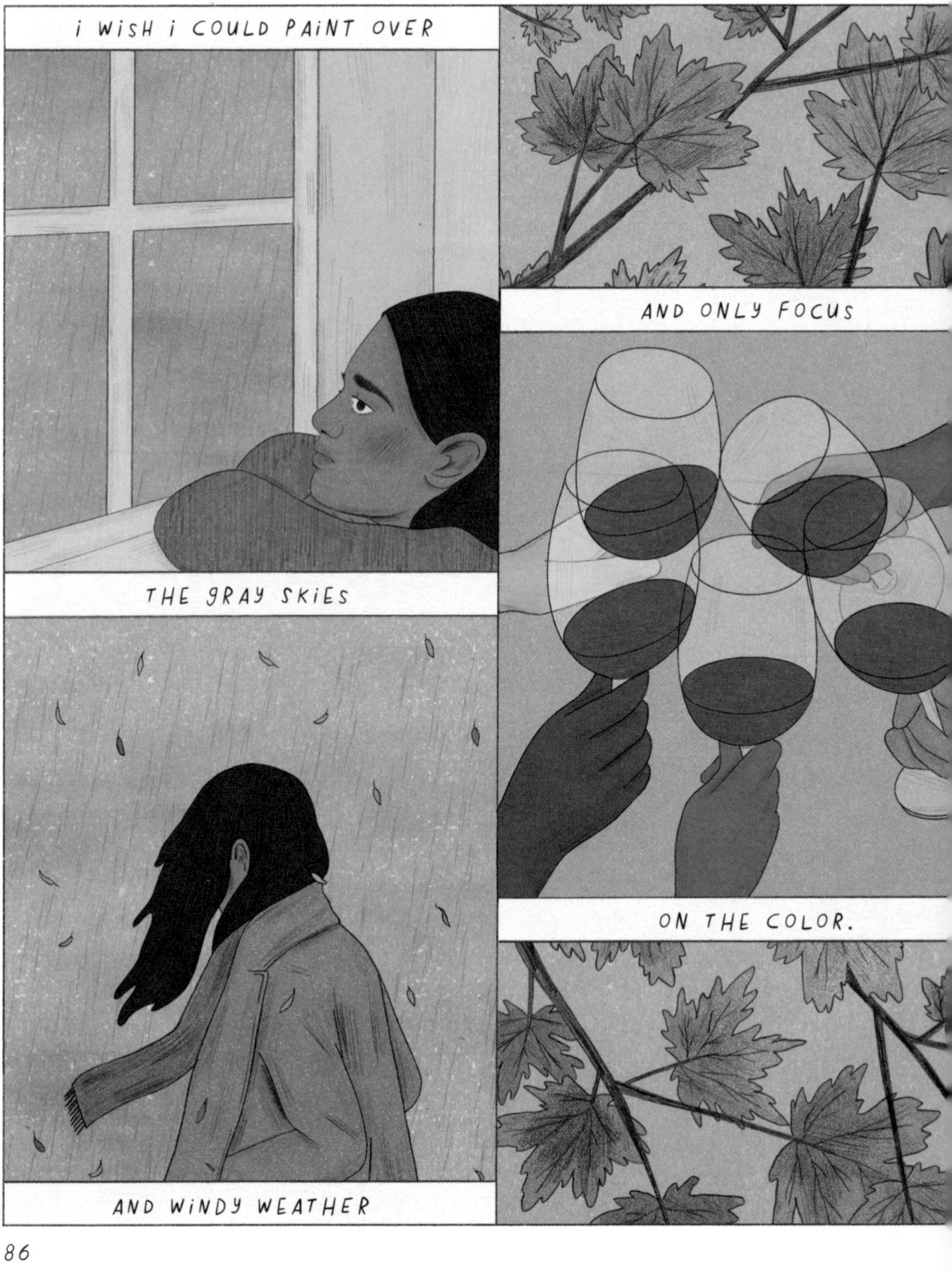

i WISH i COULD PAiNT OVER
THE gRAY SKiES
AND WiNDY WEATHER
AND ONLY FOCUS
ON THE COLOR.

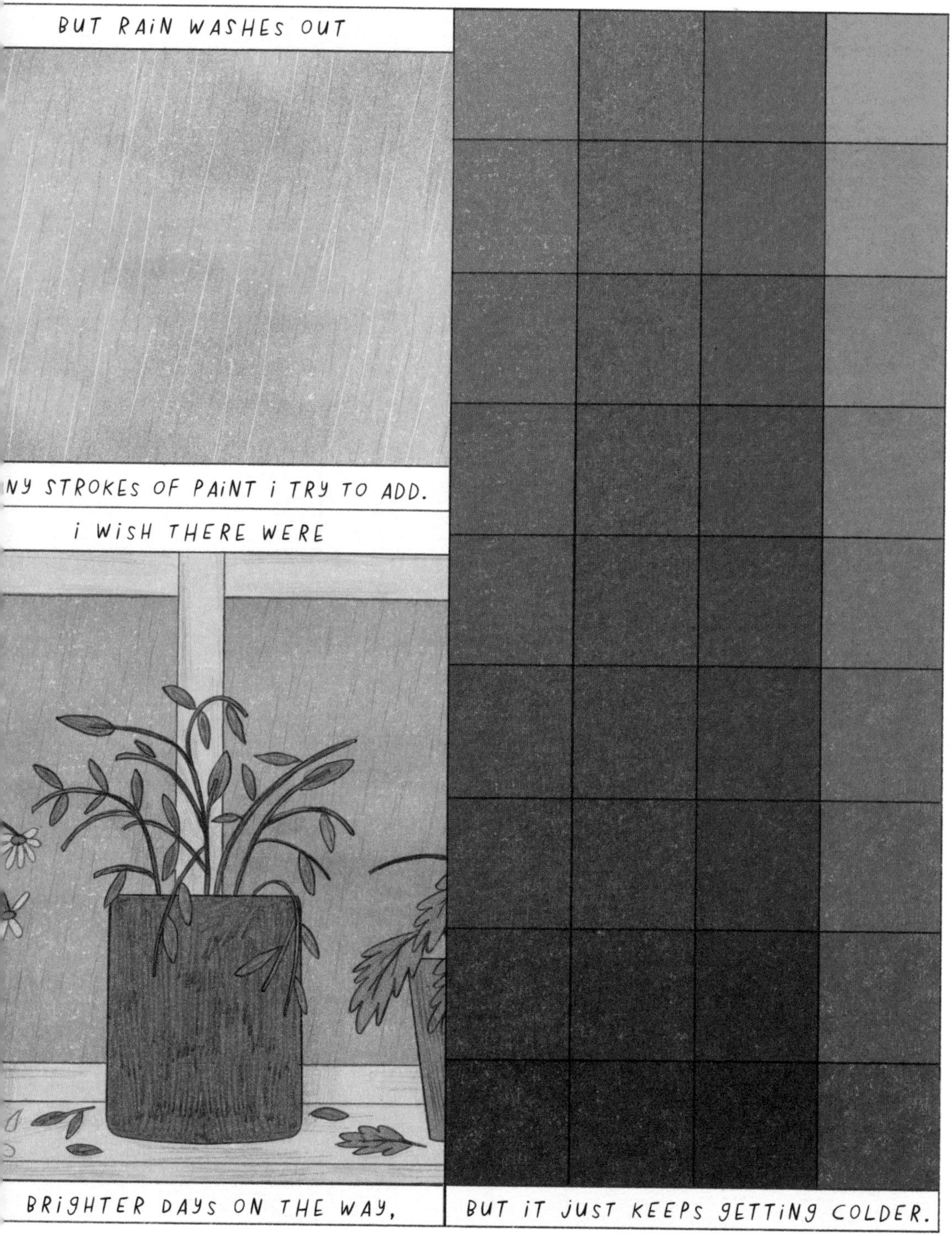
BUT RAIN WASHES OUT
NY STROKES OF PAINT I TRY TO ADD.
I WISH THERE WERE
BRIGHTER DAYS ON THE WAY,
BUT IT JUST KEEPS GETTING COLDER.

CHAPTER FIVE

WINTER

AS THE TEMPERATURE CONTINUES TO
DROP, IT'S A DIFFICULT SEASON FOR
GROWTH.

THE CLOUDY SKIES OF AUTUMN ARE
REPLACED BY WINTER'S FOG, OBSCURING
ANY REMAINING LIGHT AND FILLING
THE AIR WITH A BITTER CHILL.

THE SEASON DOESN'T OFFER MUCH;
DAYLIGHT QUICKLY GIVES WAY TO DARKER
HOURS. PLANTS BURROW INTO A WINTER
SLUMBER AS THEY WAIT FOR WARMER
DAYS TO REVIVE THEM.

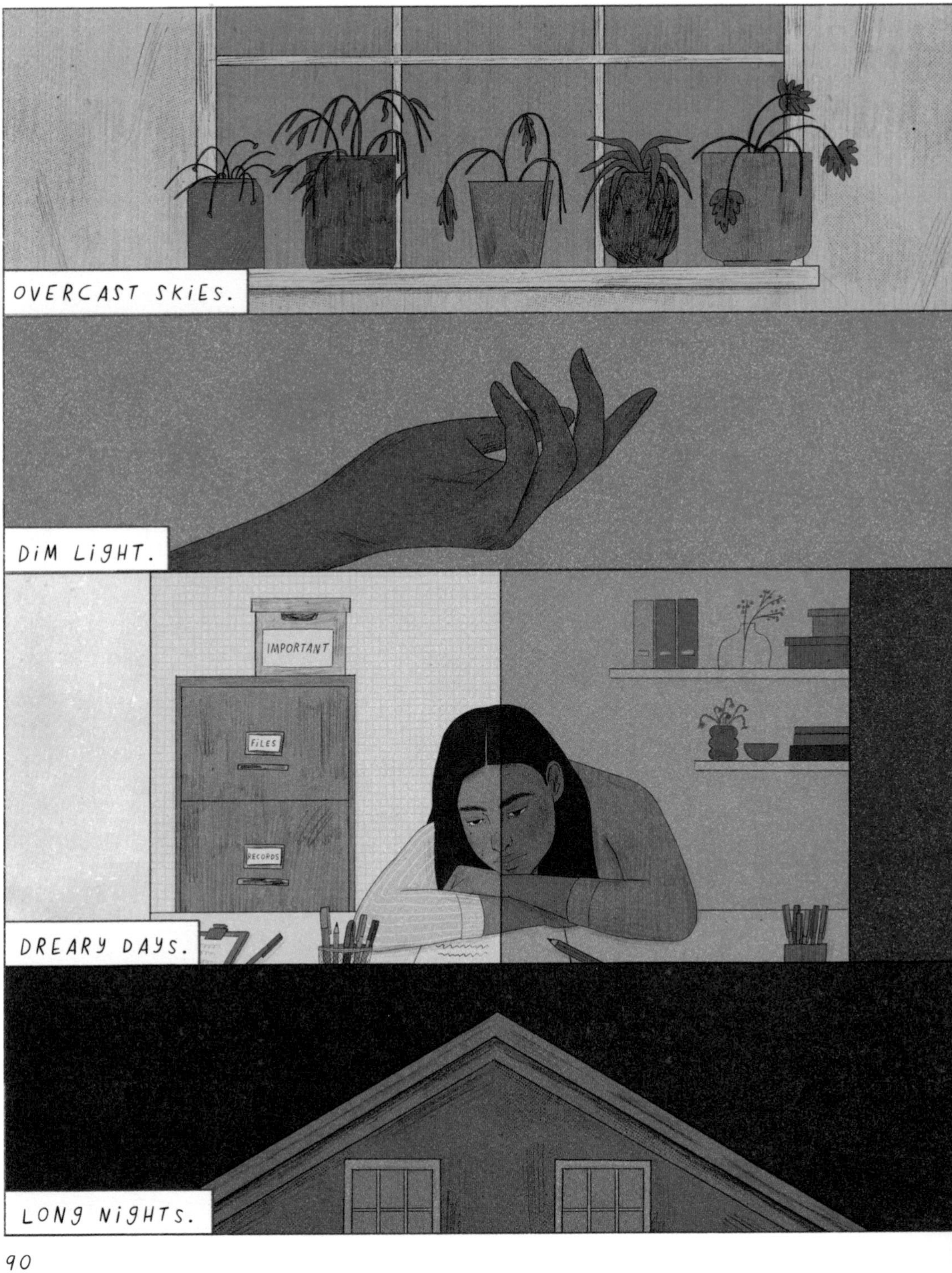
OVERCAST SKIES.
DIM LIGHT.
IMPORTANT
FILES
RECORDS
DREARY DAYS.
LONG NIGHTS.

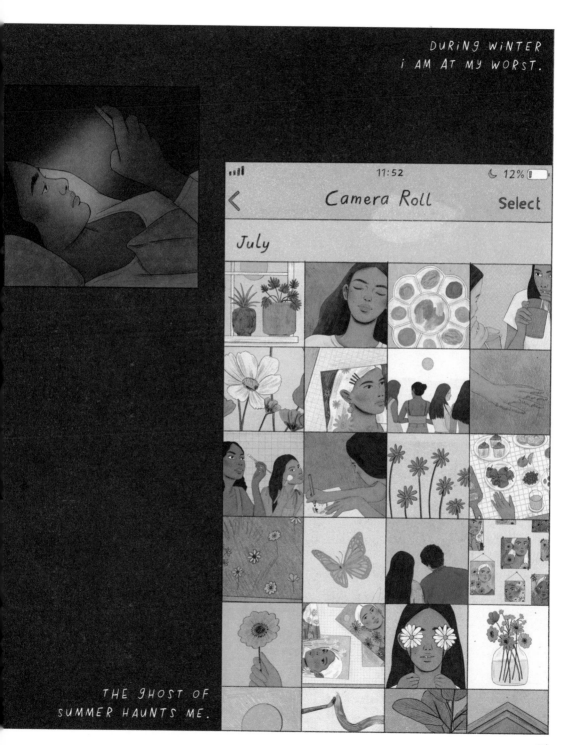

DURING WINTER
i AM AT MY WORST.

11:52   🌙 12% 🔋

< Camera Roll   Select

July

THE gHOST OF
SUMMER HAUNTS ME.

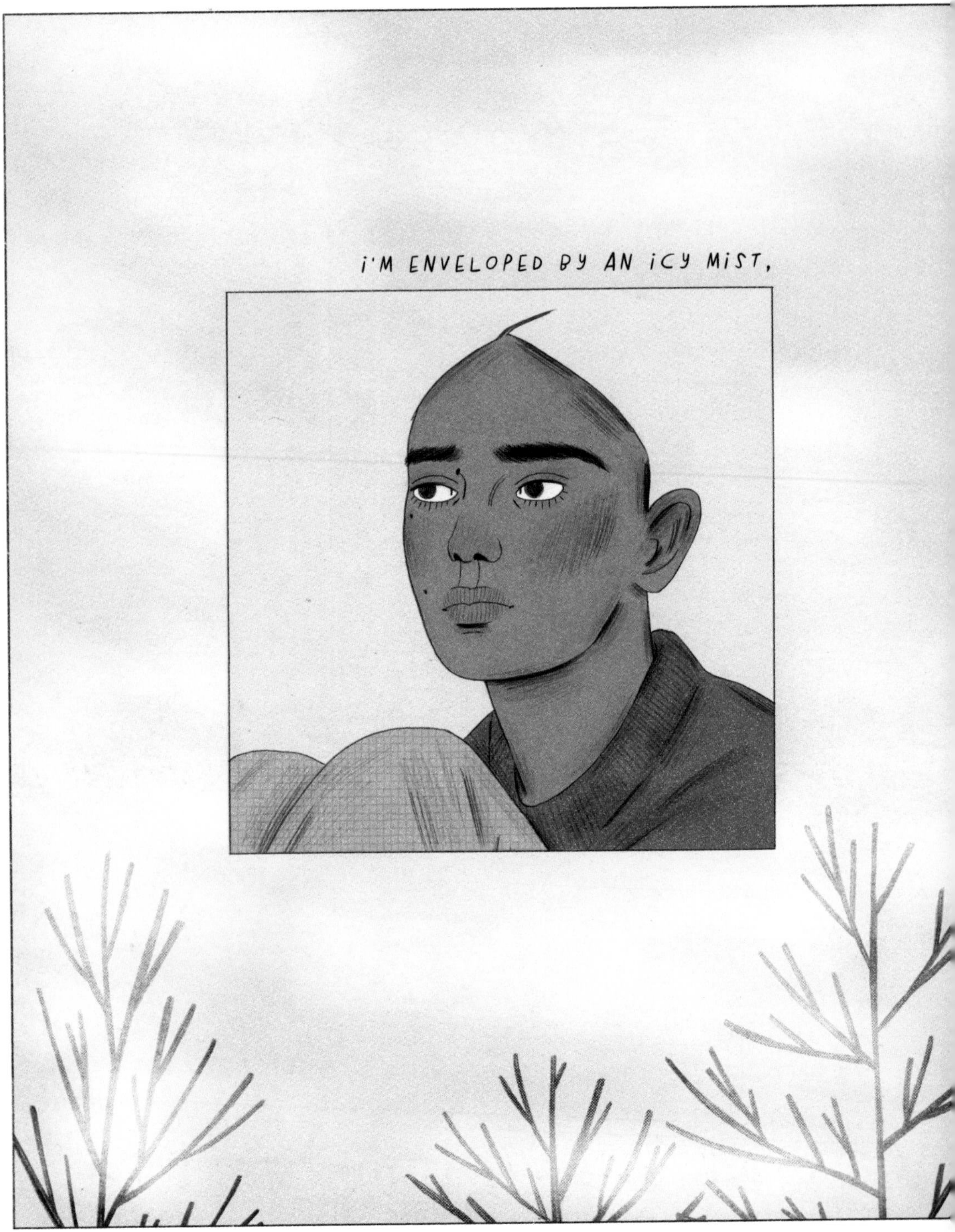
I'M ENVELOPED BY AN ICY MIST,

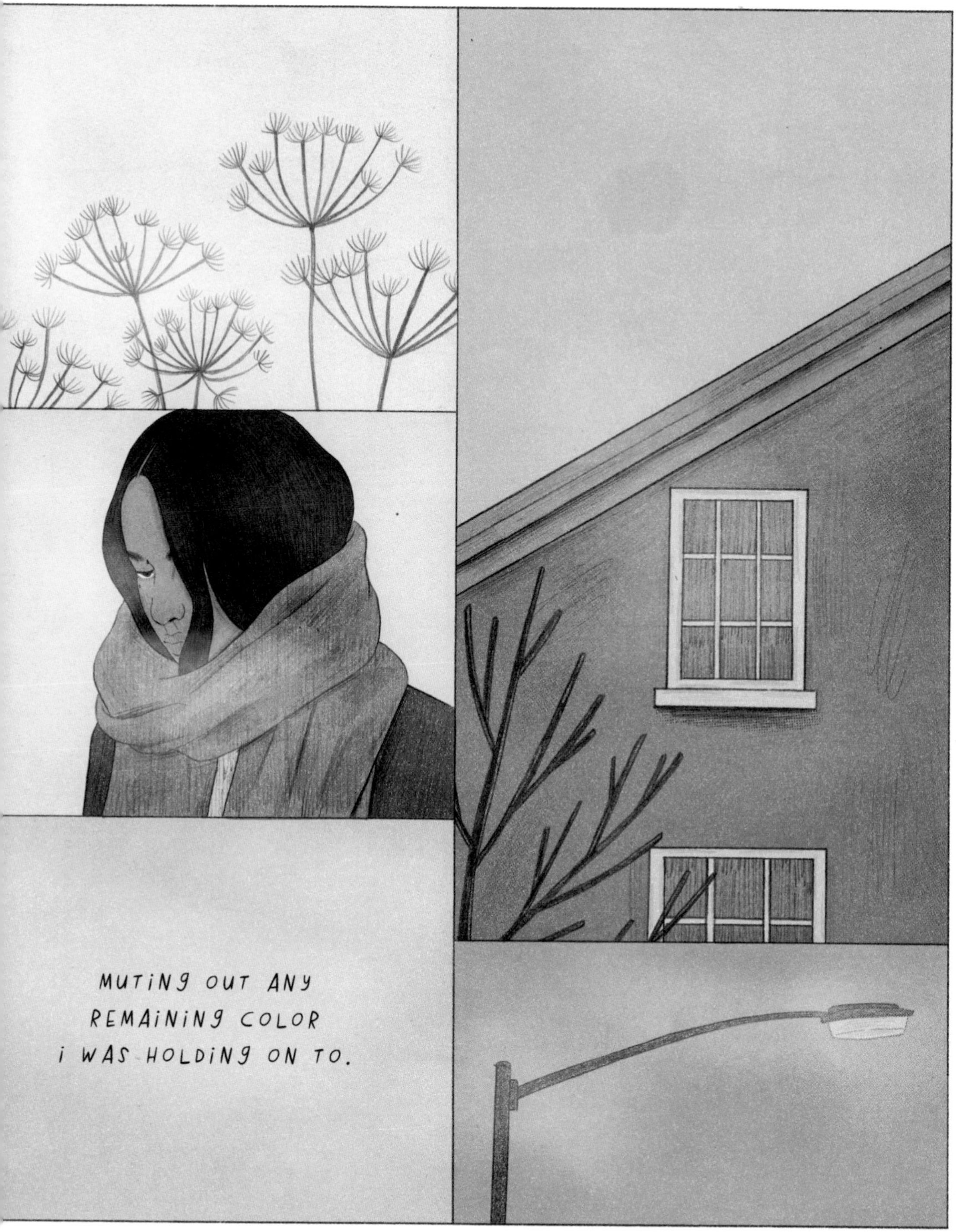
MUTING OUT ANY
REMAINING COLOR
I WAS HOLDING ON TO.

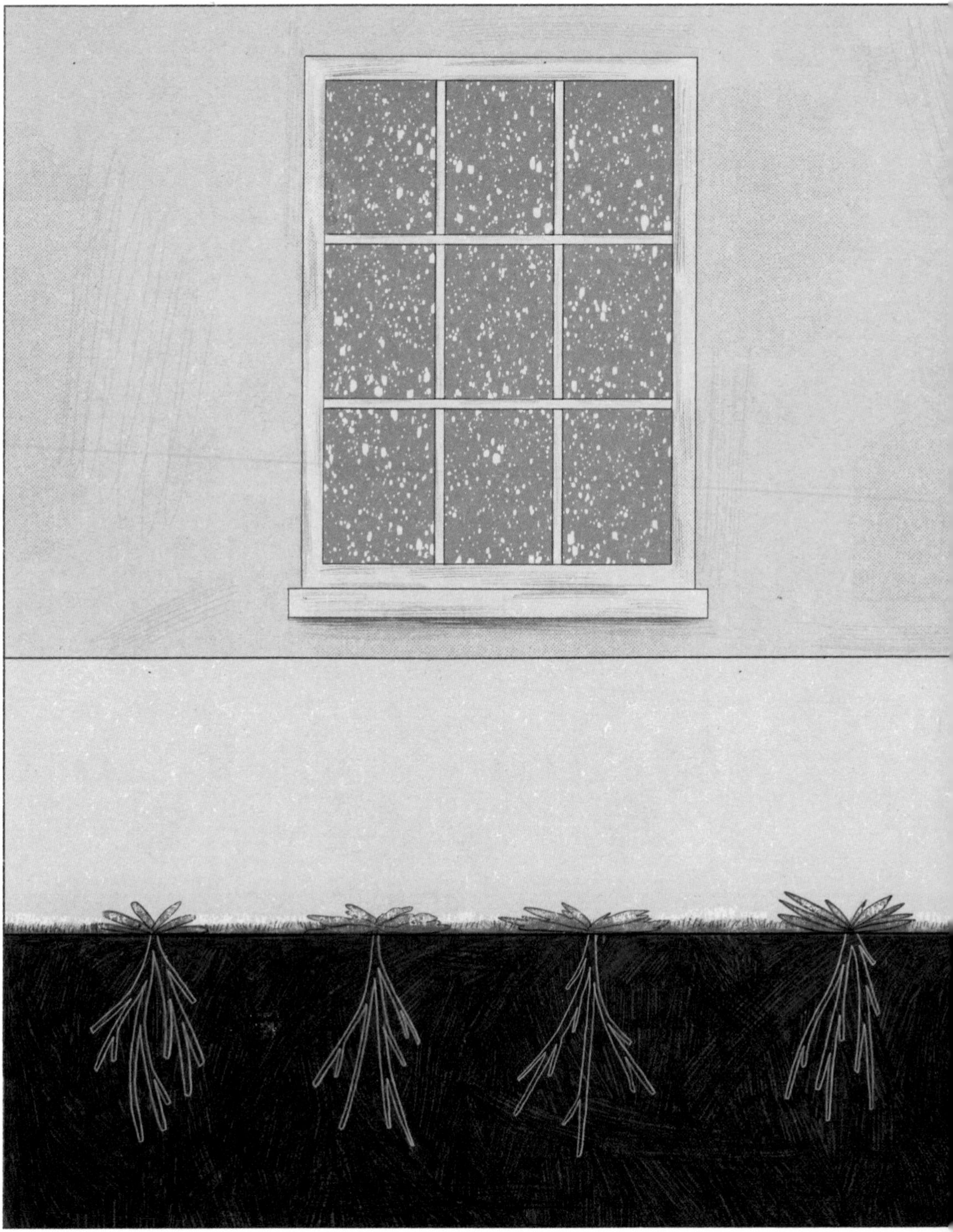

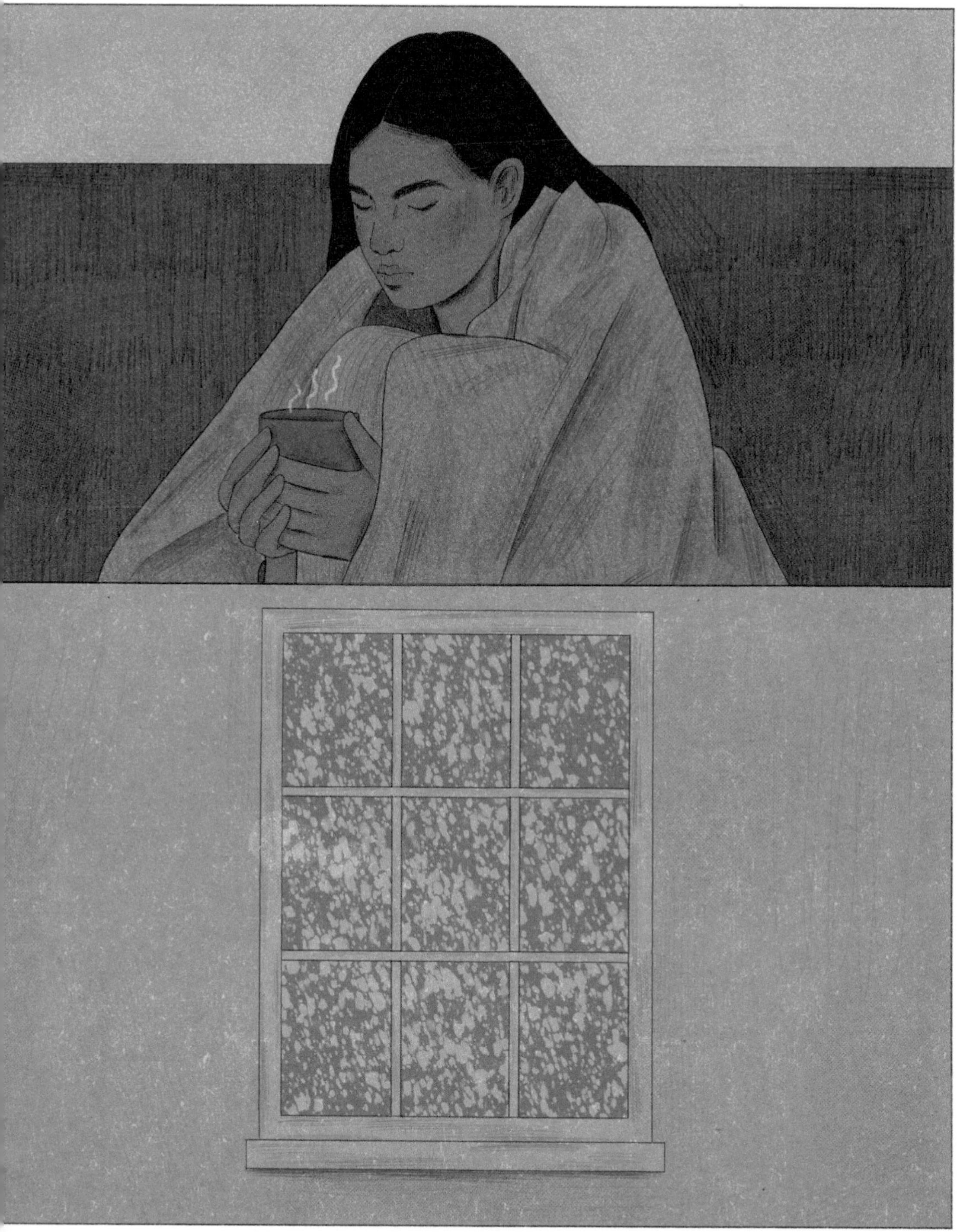

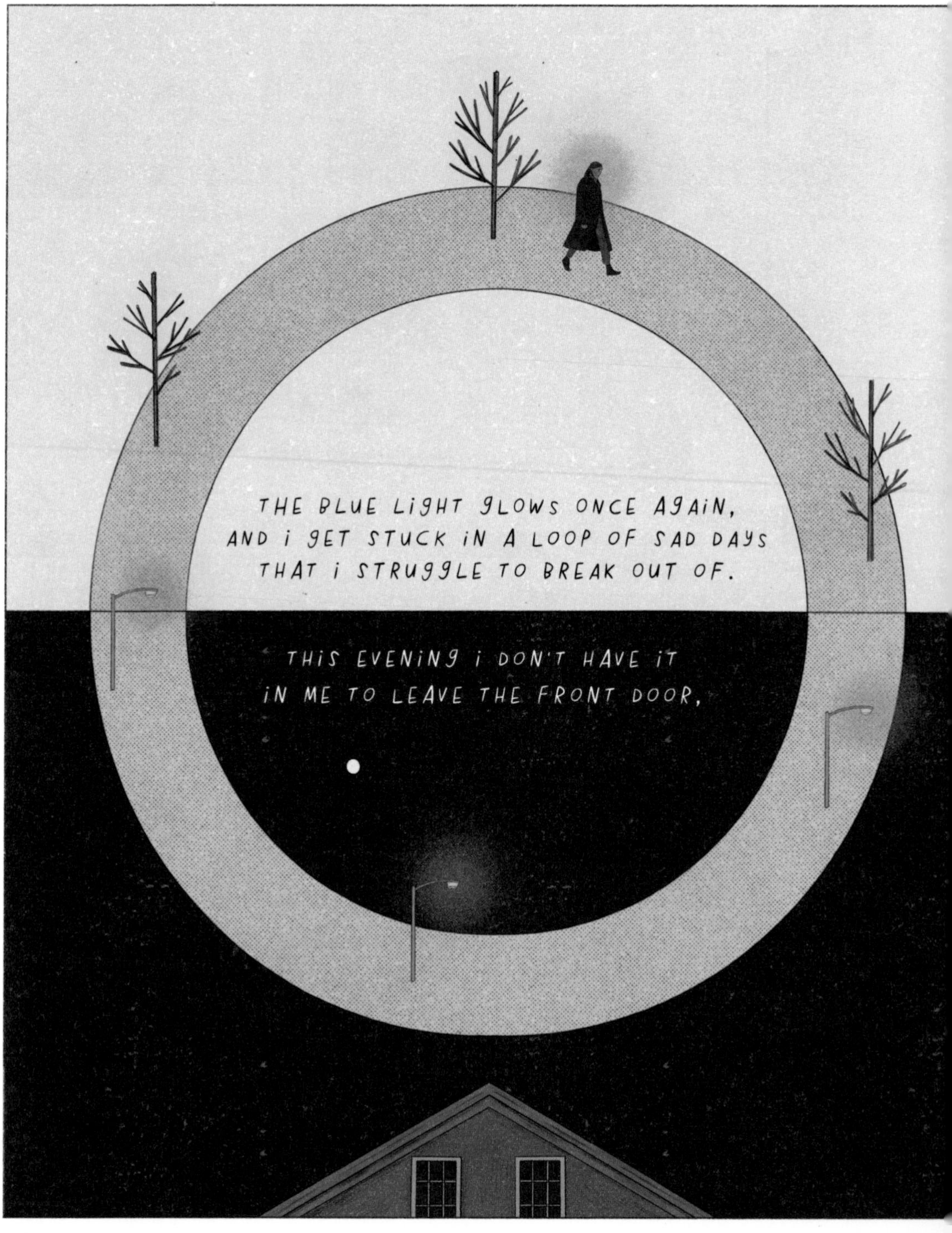
THE BLUE LIGHT GLOWS ONCE AGAIN, AND I GET STUCK IN A LOOP OF SAD DAYS THAT I STRUGGLE TO BREAK OUT OF.
THIS EVENING I DON'T HAVE IT IN ME TO LEAVE THE FRONT DOOR,

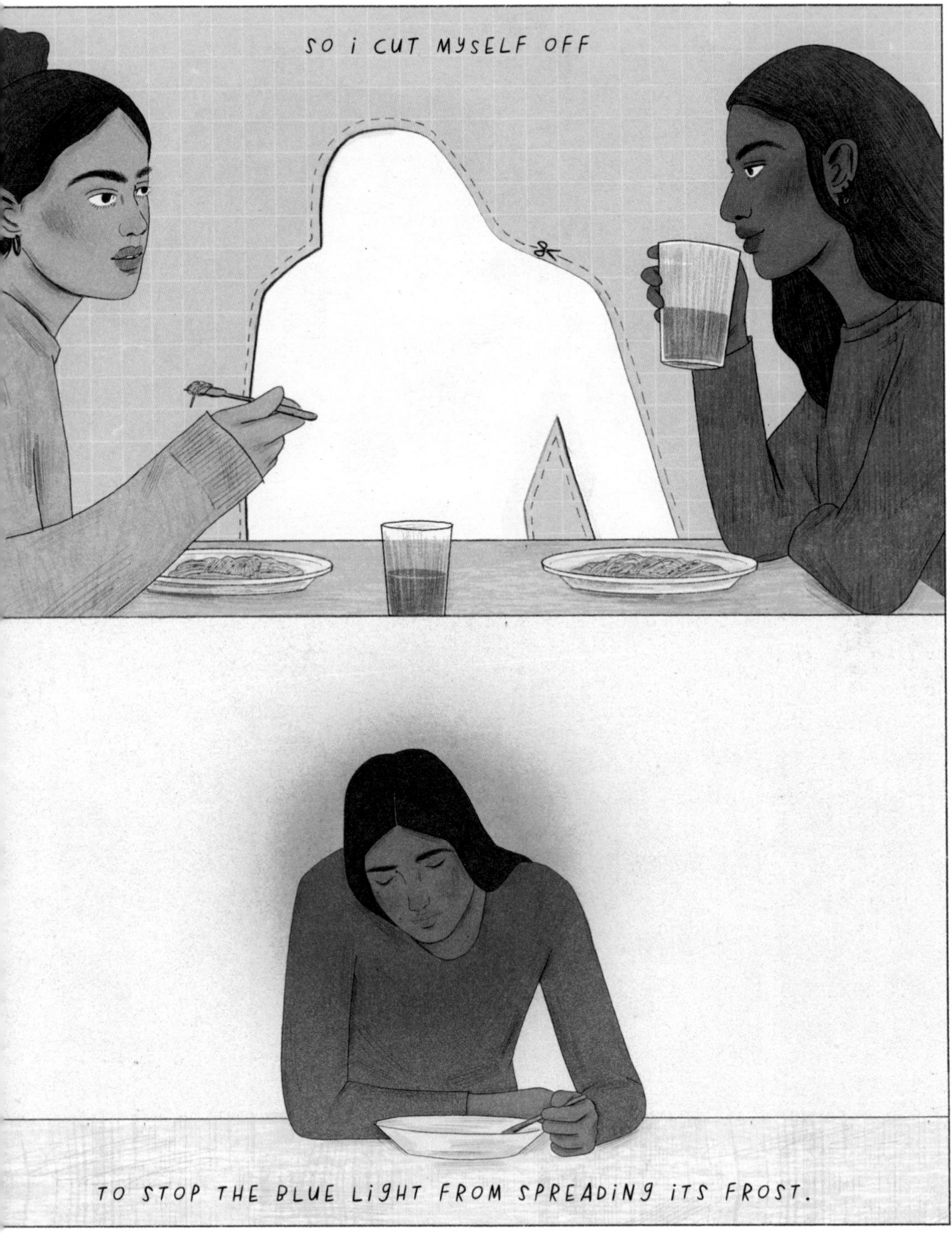
SO i CUT MYSELF OFF
TO STOP THE BLUE LiGHT FROM SPREADiNG iTS FROST.

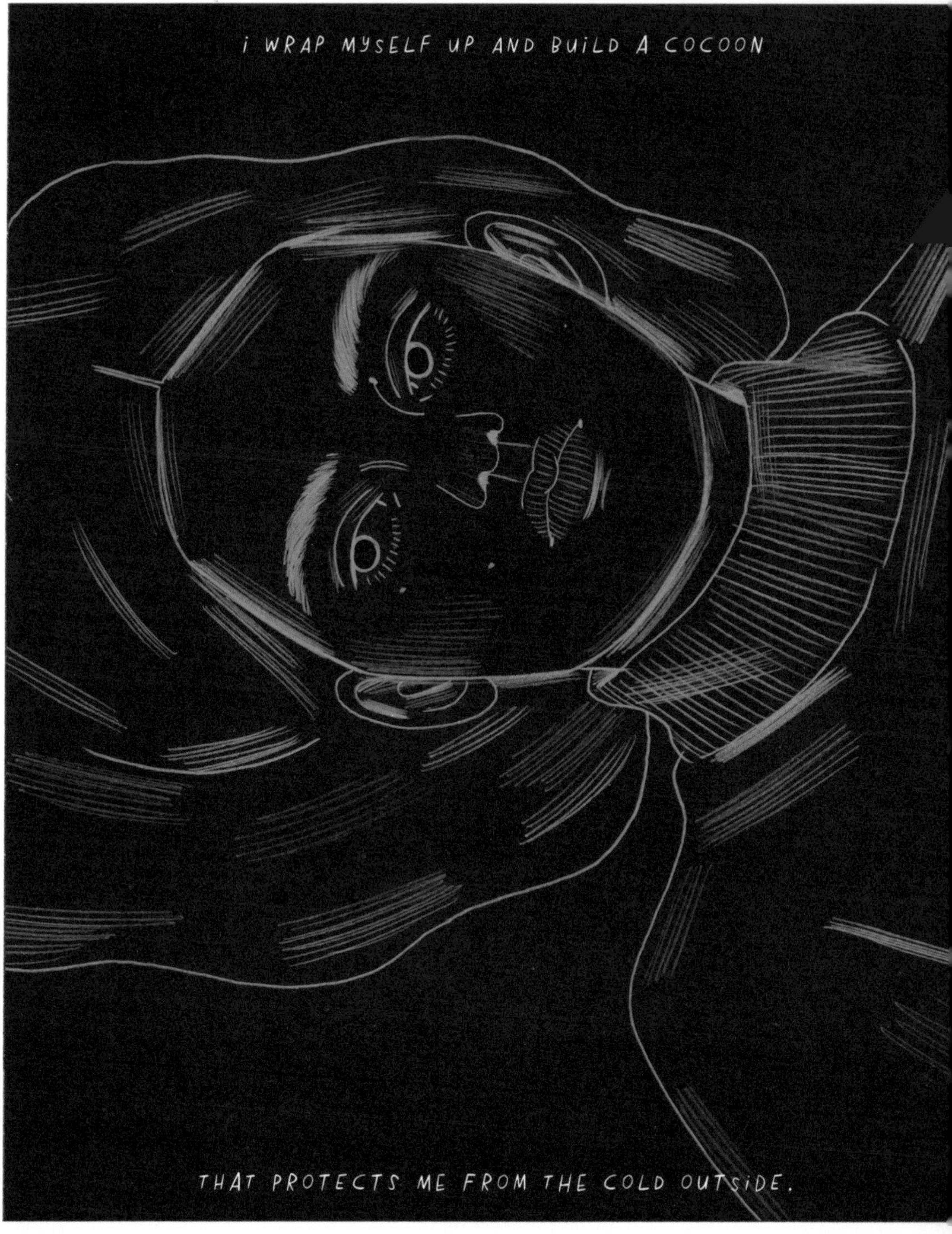
i WRAP MYSELF UP AND BUiLD A COCOON
THAT PROTECTS ME FROM THE COLD OUTSiDE.

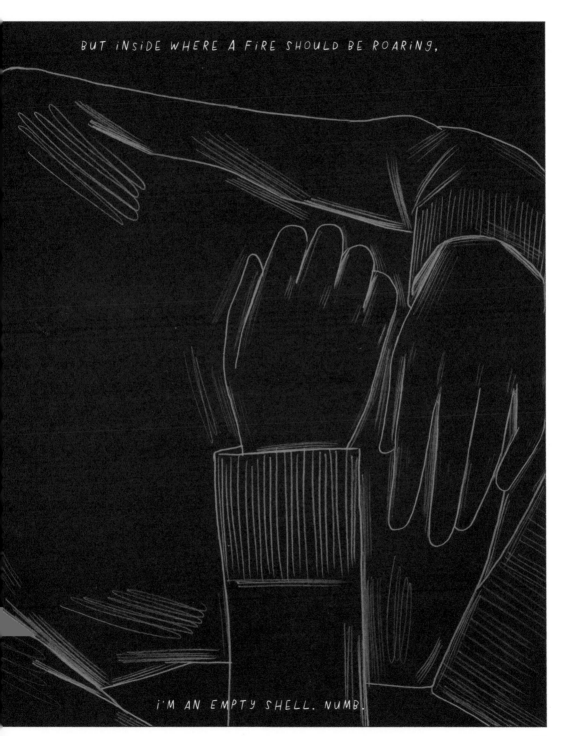

BUT INSIDE WHERE A FIRE SHOULD BE ROARING,

I'M AN EMPTY SHELL. NUMB.

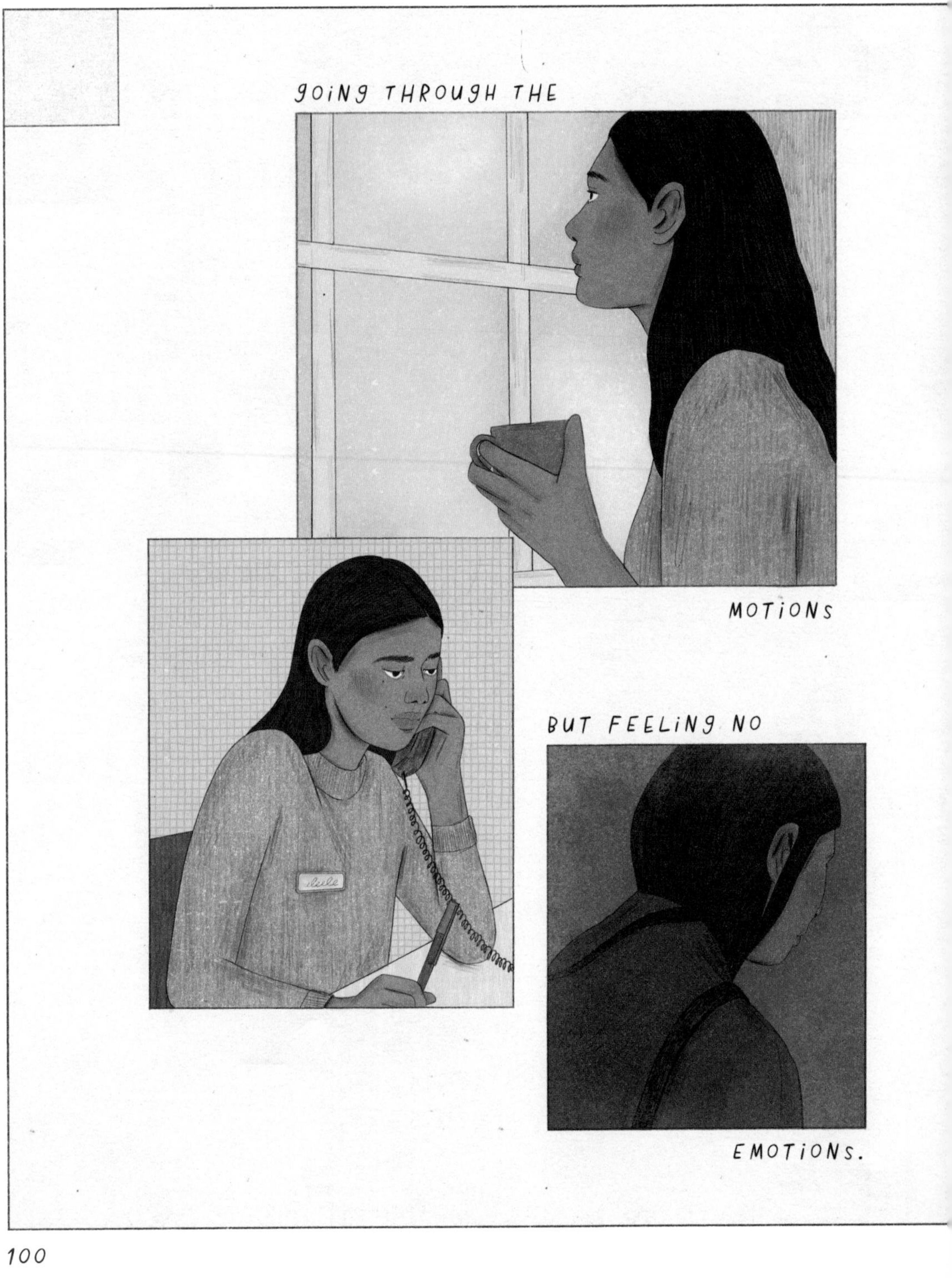
GOING THROUGH THE
MOTIONS
BUT FEELING NO
EMOTIONS.

A MONOTONOUS

ROUTiNE,

STUCK ON REPLAY.

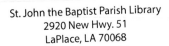

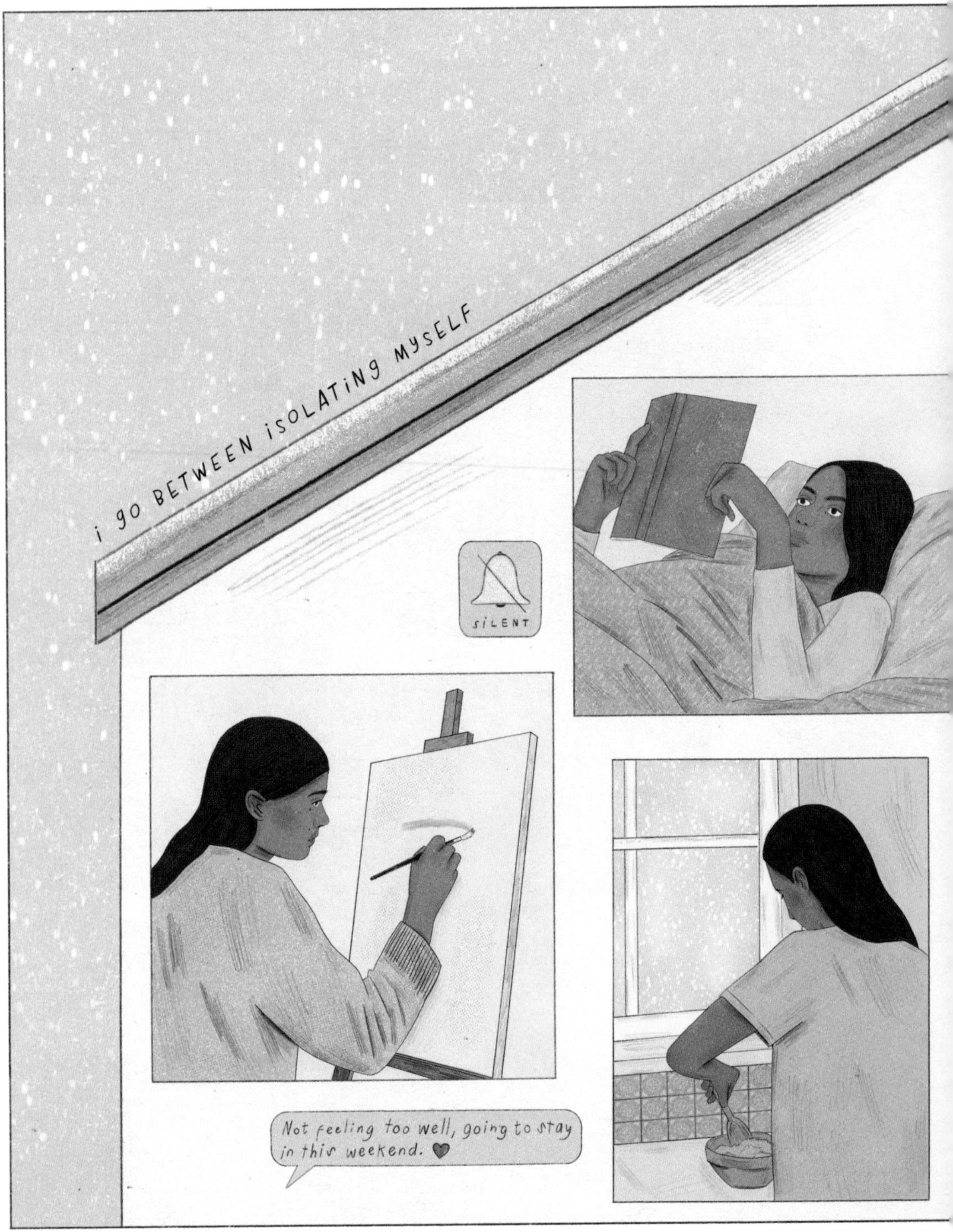
i go BETWEEN iSOLATiNg MYSELF
SiLENT
Not feeling too well, going to stay in this weekend.

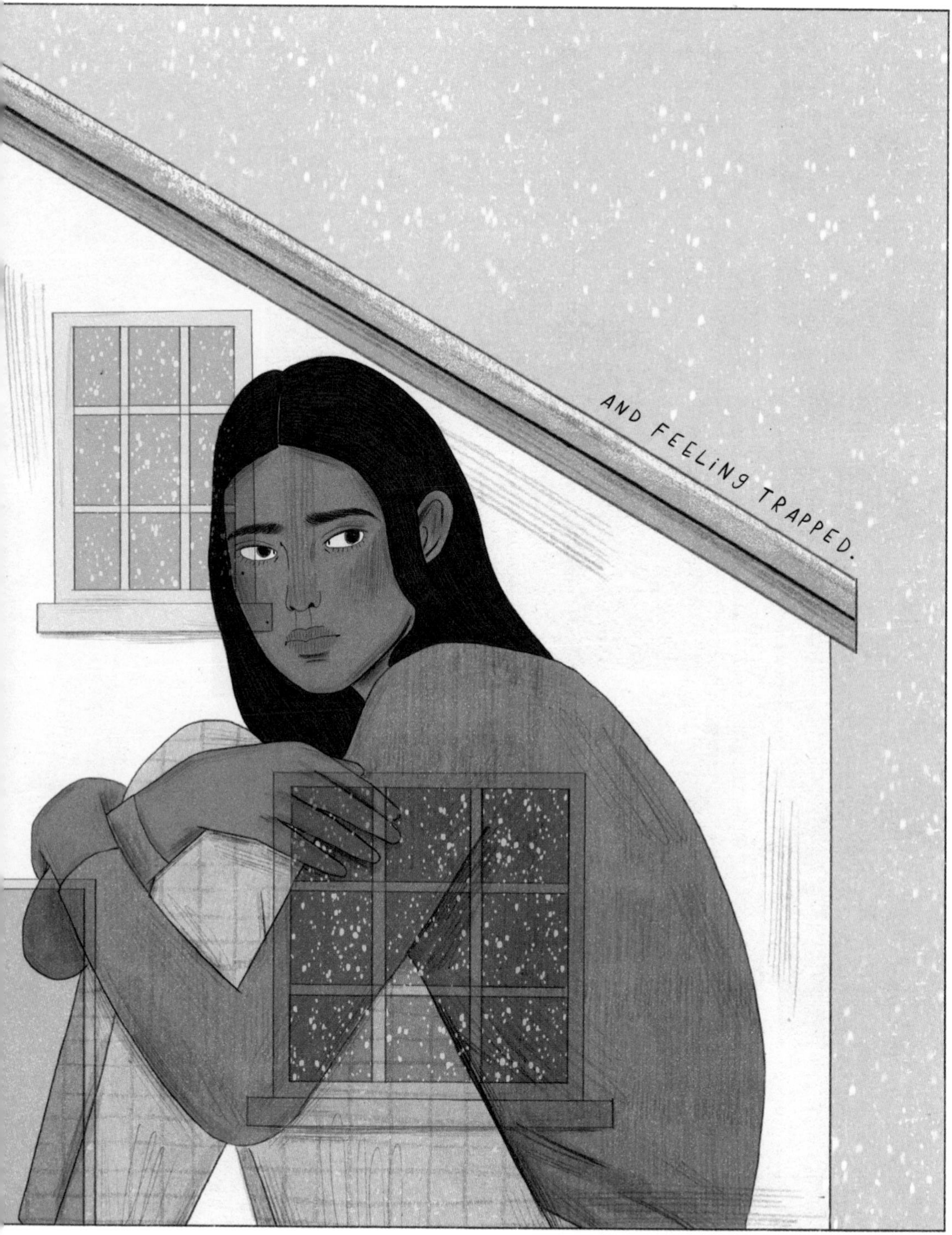
AND FEELING TRAPPED.

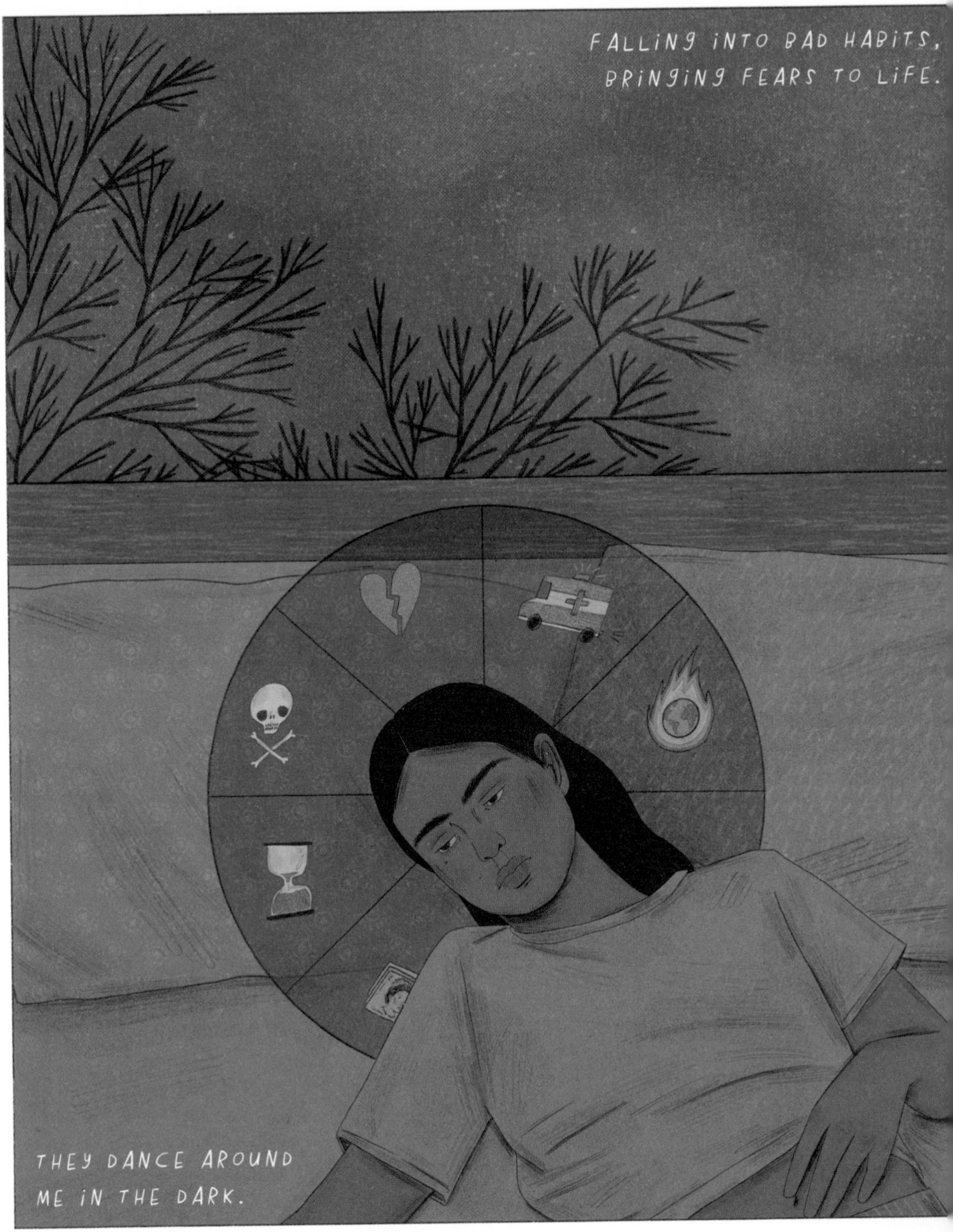
FALLING INTO BAD HABITS,
BRINGING FEARS TO LIFE.
THEY DANCE AROUND
ME IN THE DARK.

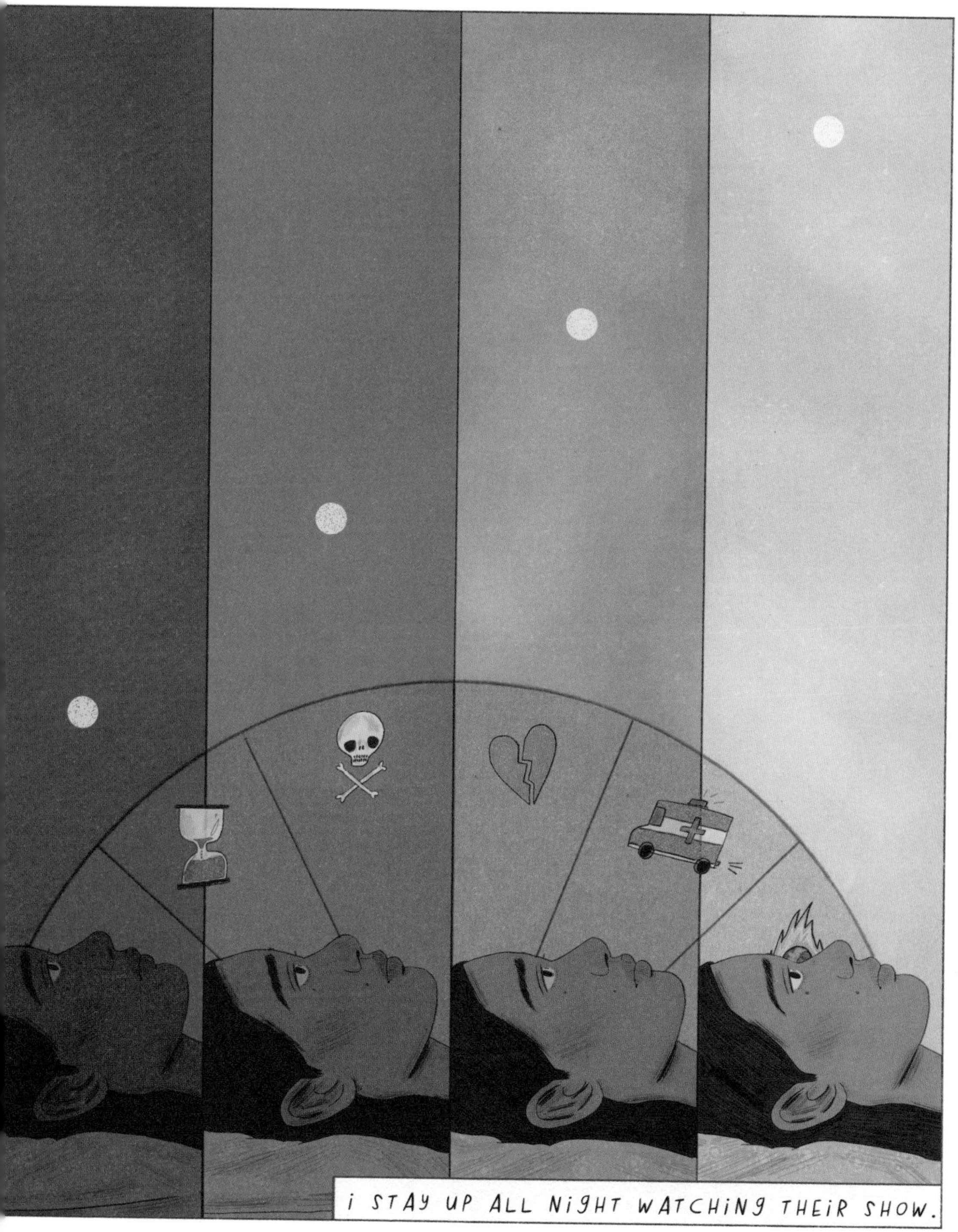
i STAY UP ALL NiGHT WATCHiNG THEiR SHOW.

I REALIZE
EVERYONE IS HUDDLED
IN THEIR OWN COCOON.

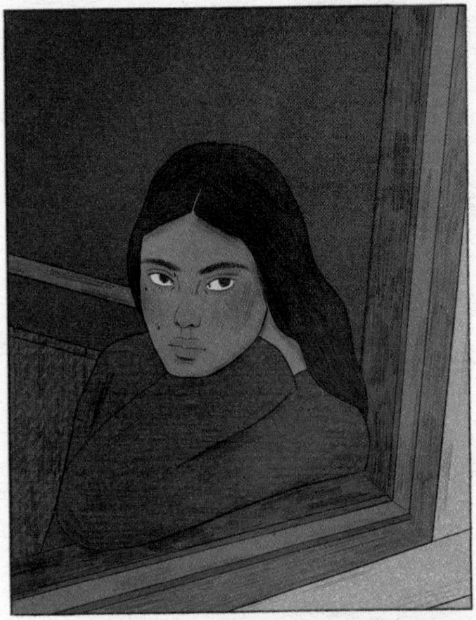

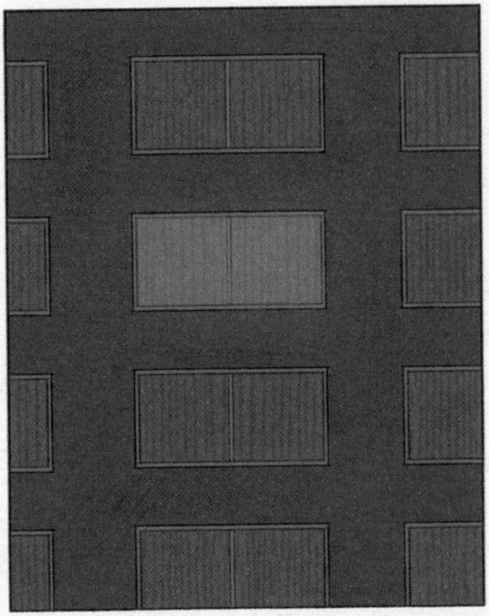

THEY'RE EITHER
HAPPY IN THE WARM

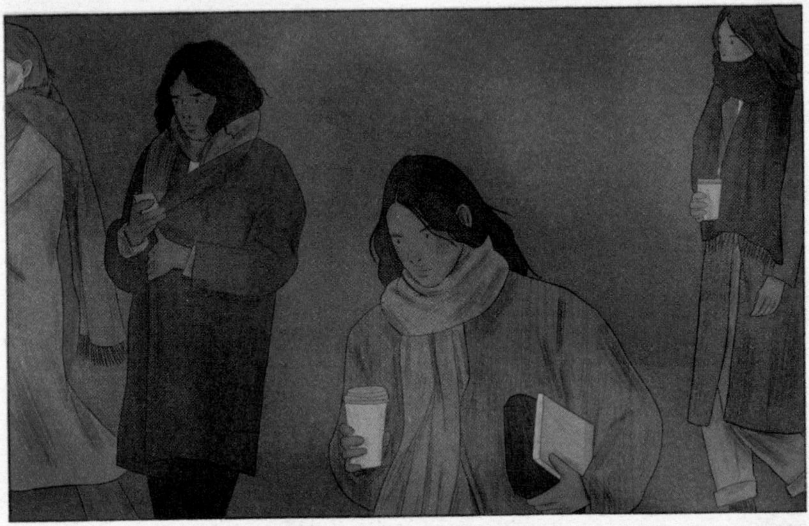

OR WAITING TO THAW IN BETTER DAYS.

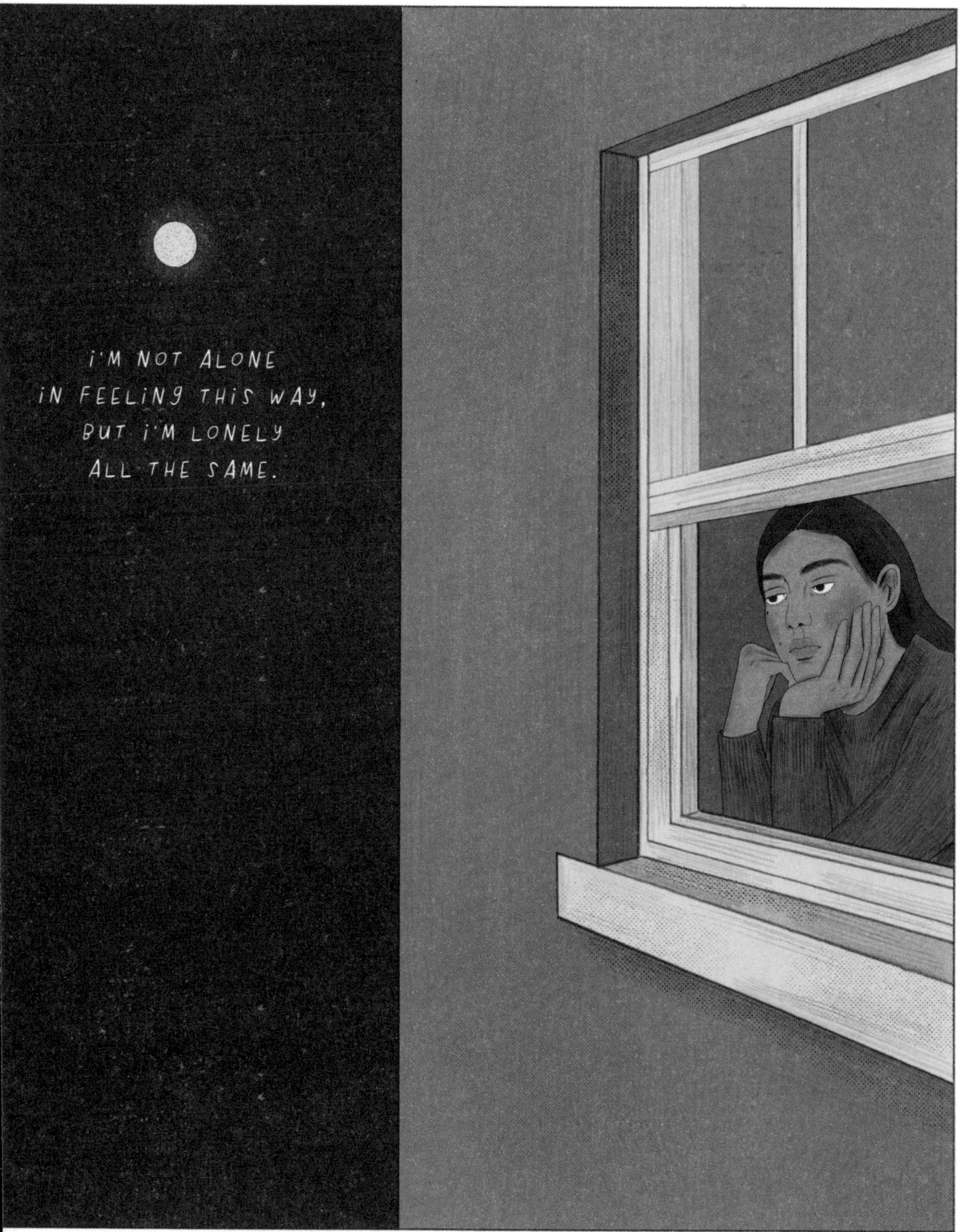
I'M NOT ALONE
IN FEELING THIS WAY,
BUT I'M LONELY
ALL THE SAME.

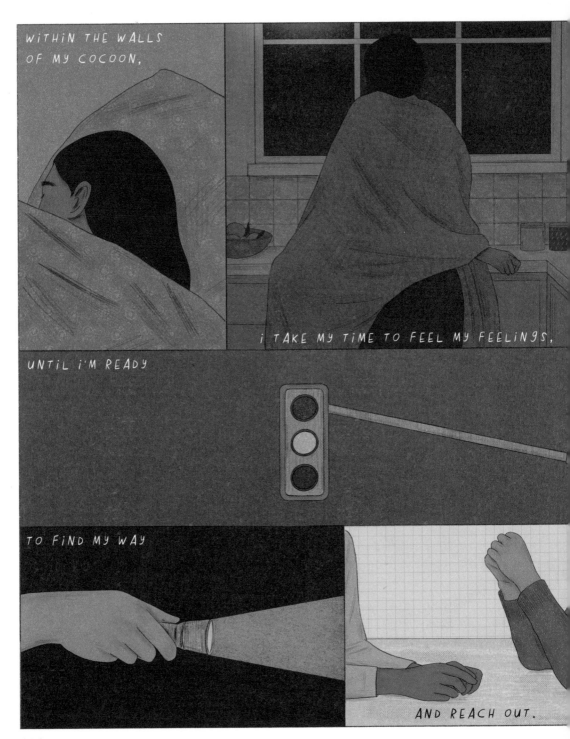

WITHIN THE WALLS
OF MY COCOON,

I TAKE MY TIME TO FEEL MY FEELINGS,

UNTIL I'M READY

TO FIND MY WAY

AND REACH OUT.

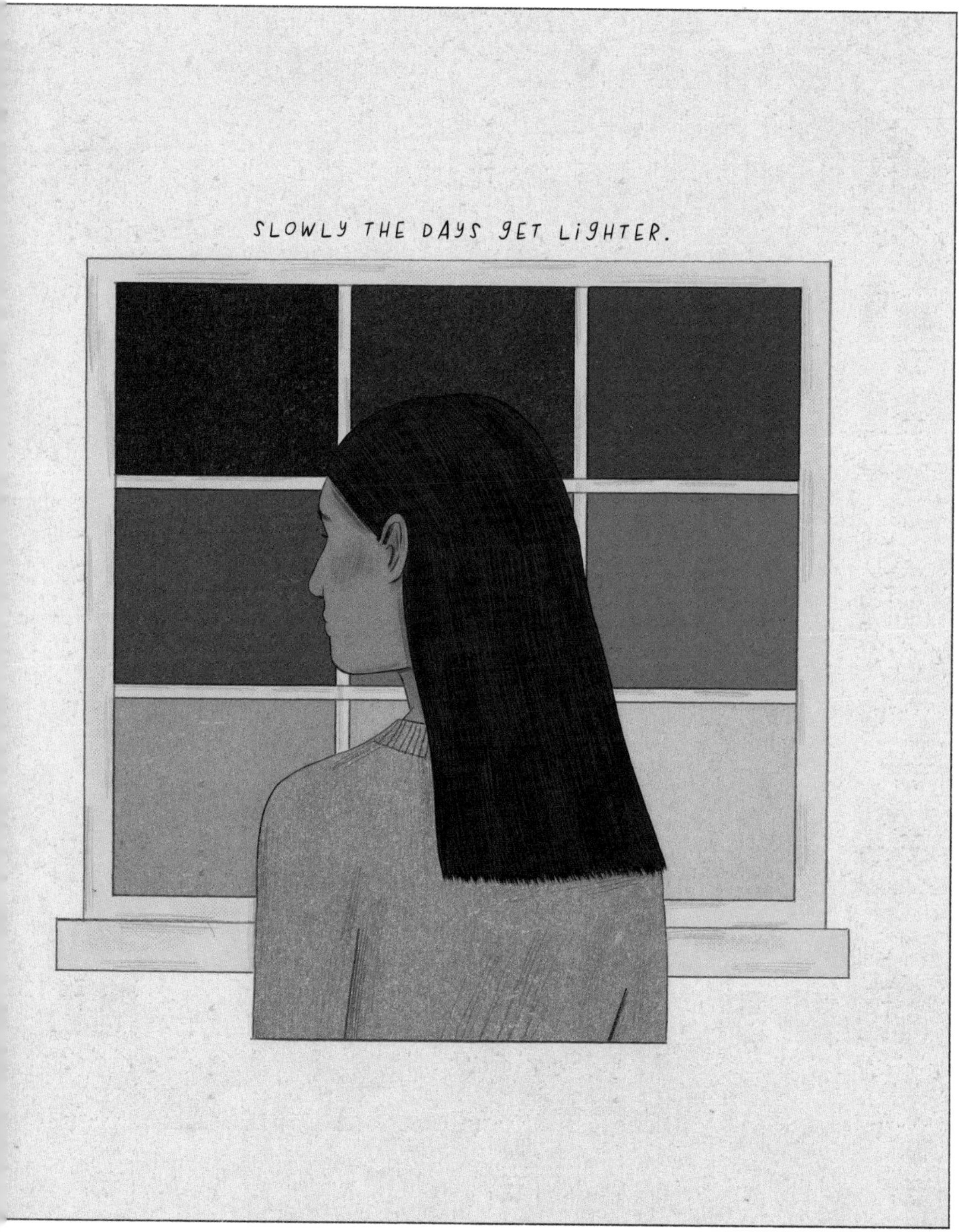
SLOWLY THE DAYS GET LIGHTER.

CHAPTER SIX

SPRING

THE RETURN OF LONGER DAYS AND
EXTRA HOURS OF SUNLIGHT TRIGGERS
RENEWAL. TREES BUD AND FLOWERS
PREPARE TO BLOOM.

ROOTS ARE REACQUAINTED WITH
WARMER SOIL AS THE DREARY WINTER
IS DISMISSED AND BRIGHTER DAYS ARE
WELCOMED IN.

THERE IS A SENSE OF AWAKENING AS A
SLOW CAUTIOUS RETURN TO ROUTINE
COMMENCES WITH THE ASSURANCE OF
WARMER WEATHER ON THE WAY.

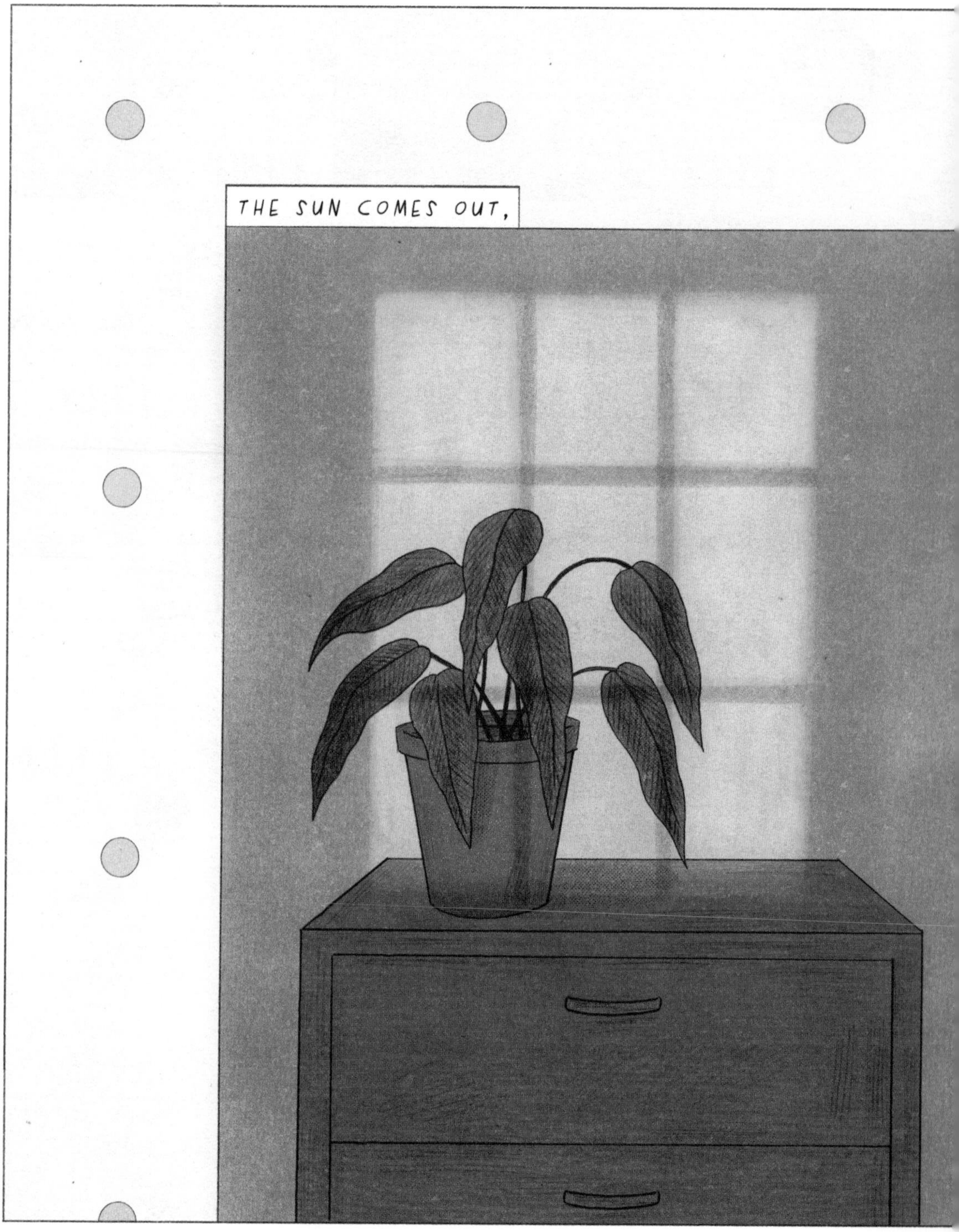
THE SUN COMES OUT,

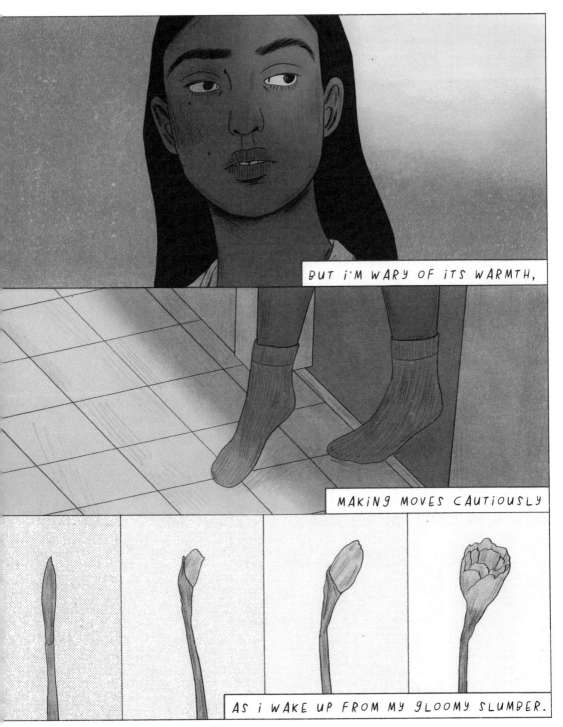

BUT i'M WARY OF iTS WARMTH,

MAKING MOVES CAUTIOUSLY

AS i WAKE UP FROM MY gLOOMY SLUMBER.

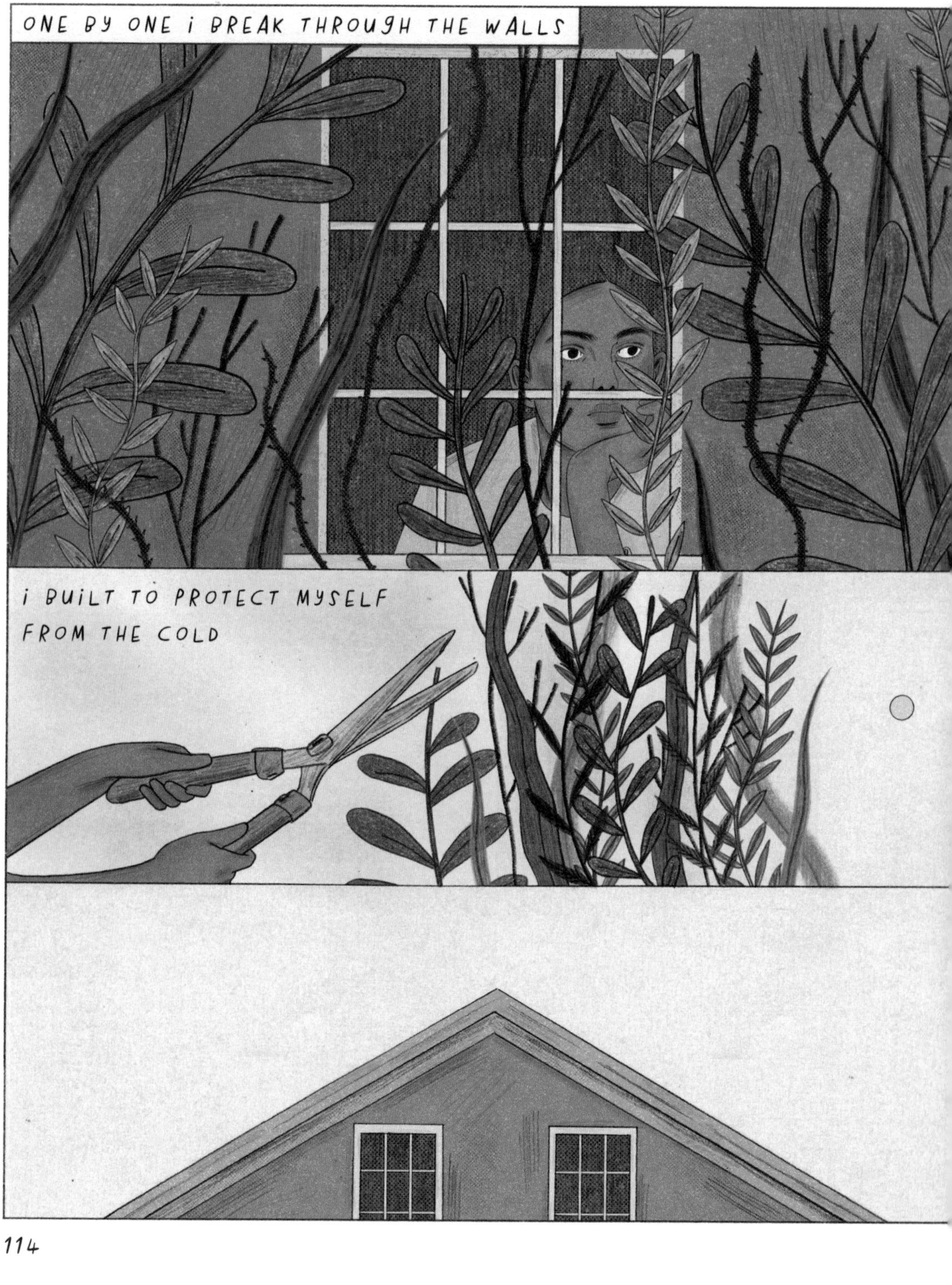
ONE BY ONE i BREAK THROUGH THE WALLS
i BUILT TO PROTECT MYSELF
FROM THE COLD

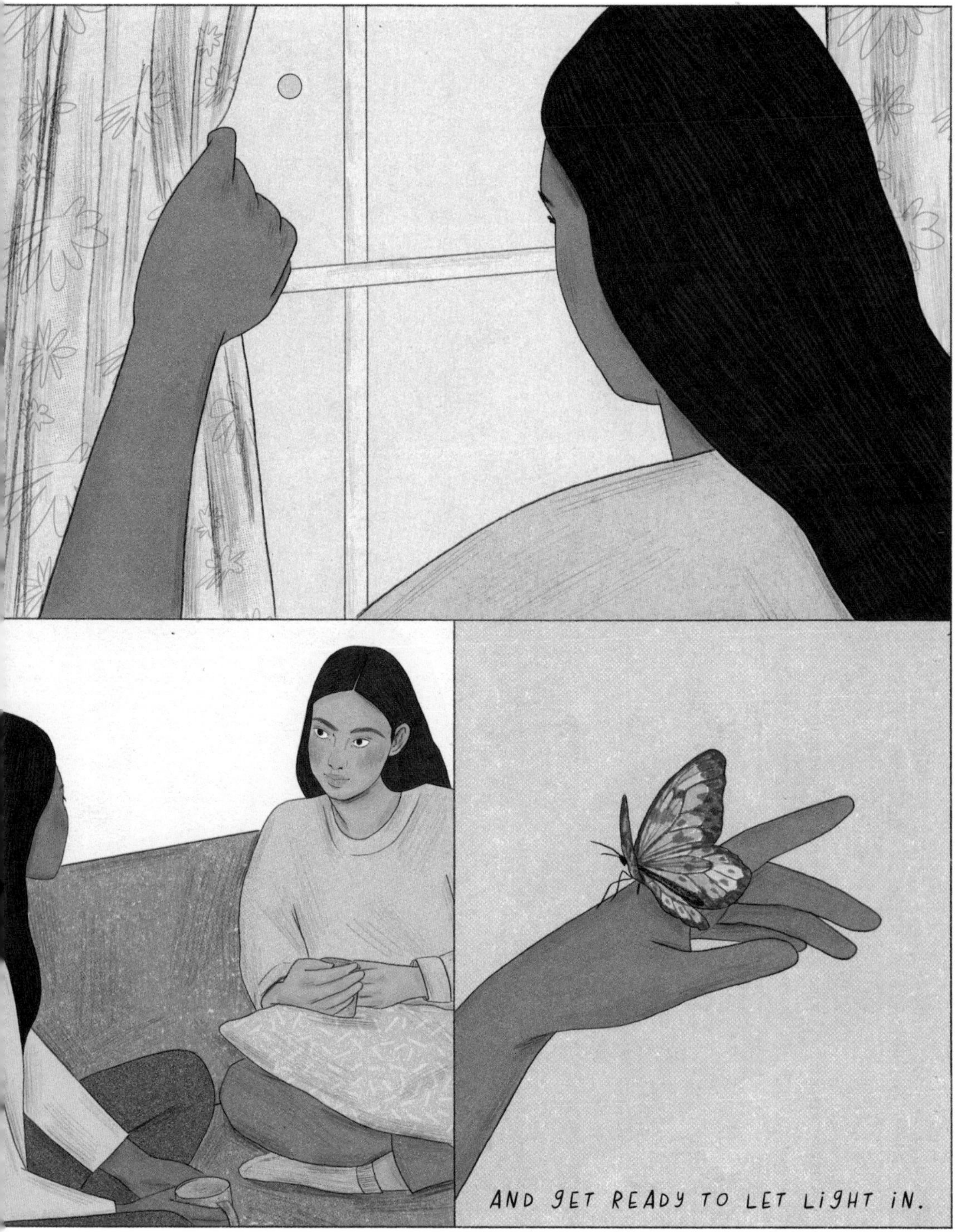
AND GET READY TO LET LIGHT IN.

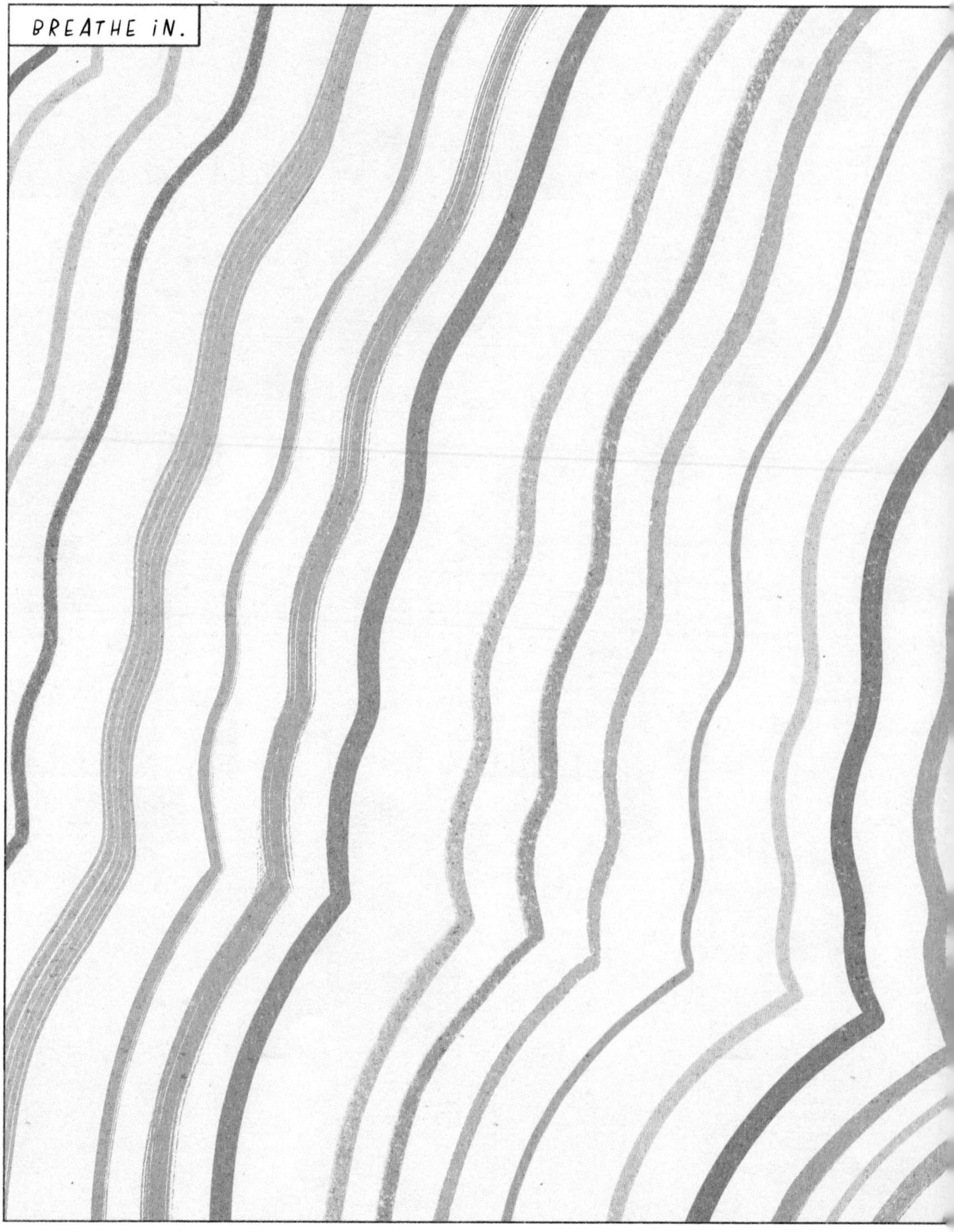
BREATHE IN.

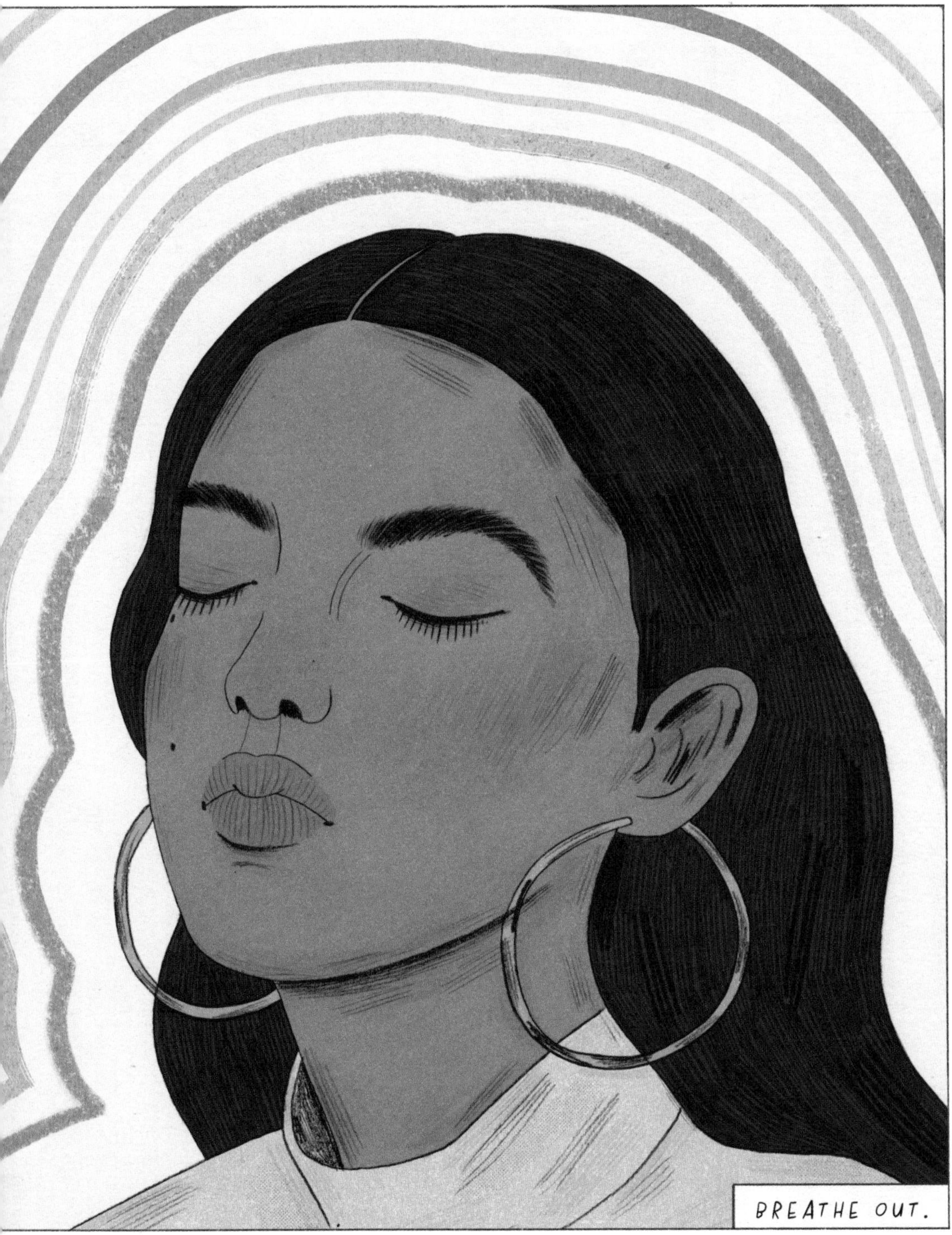
BREATHE OUT.

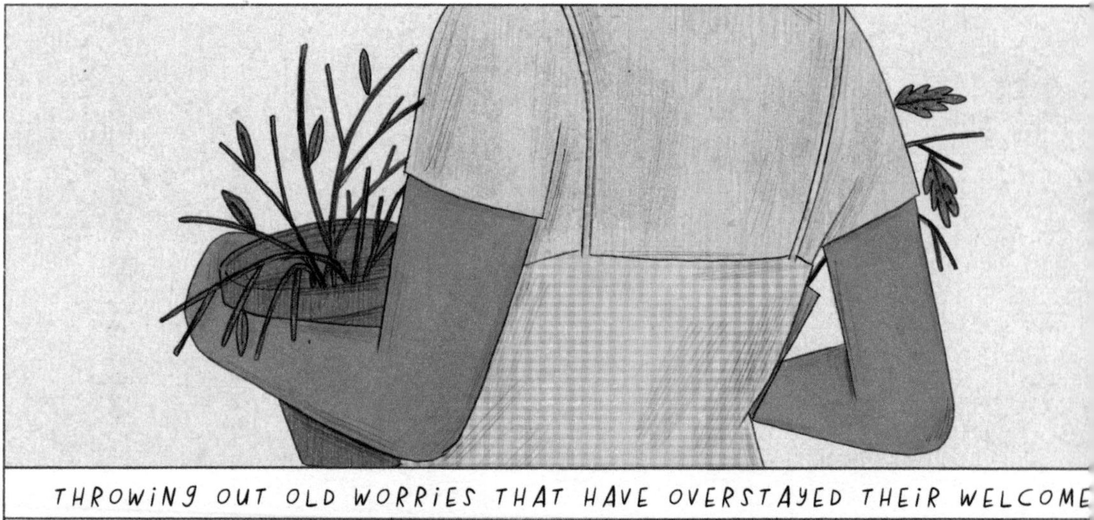
THROWING OUT OLD WORRIES THAT HAVE OVERSTAYED THEIR WELCOME

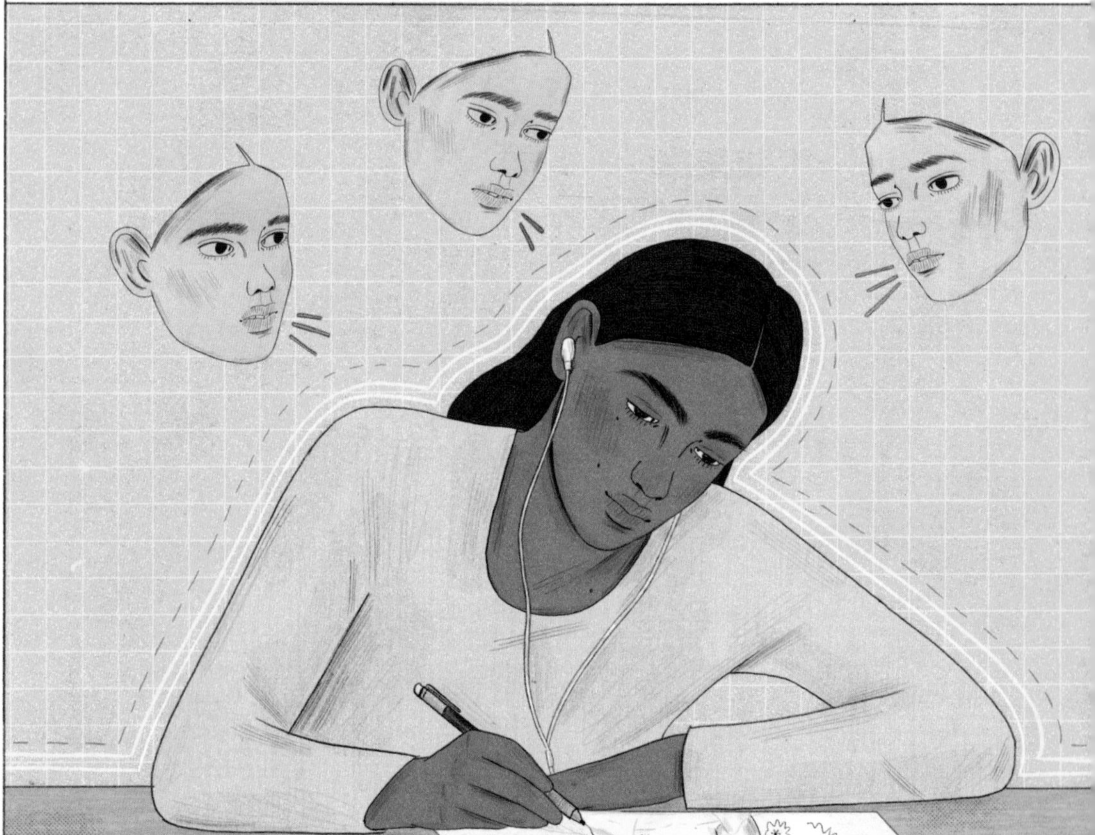
SOME AREN'T SO EASY TO LET GO OF, BUT I GIVE THEM LESS OF MY TIME

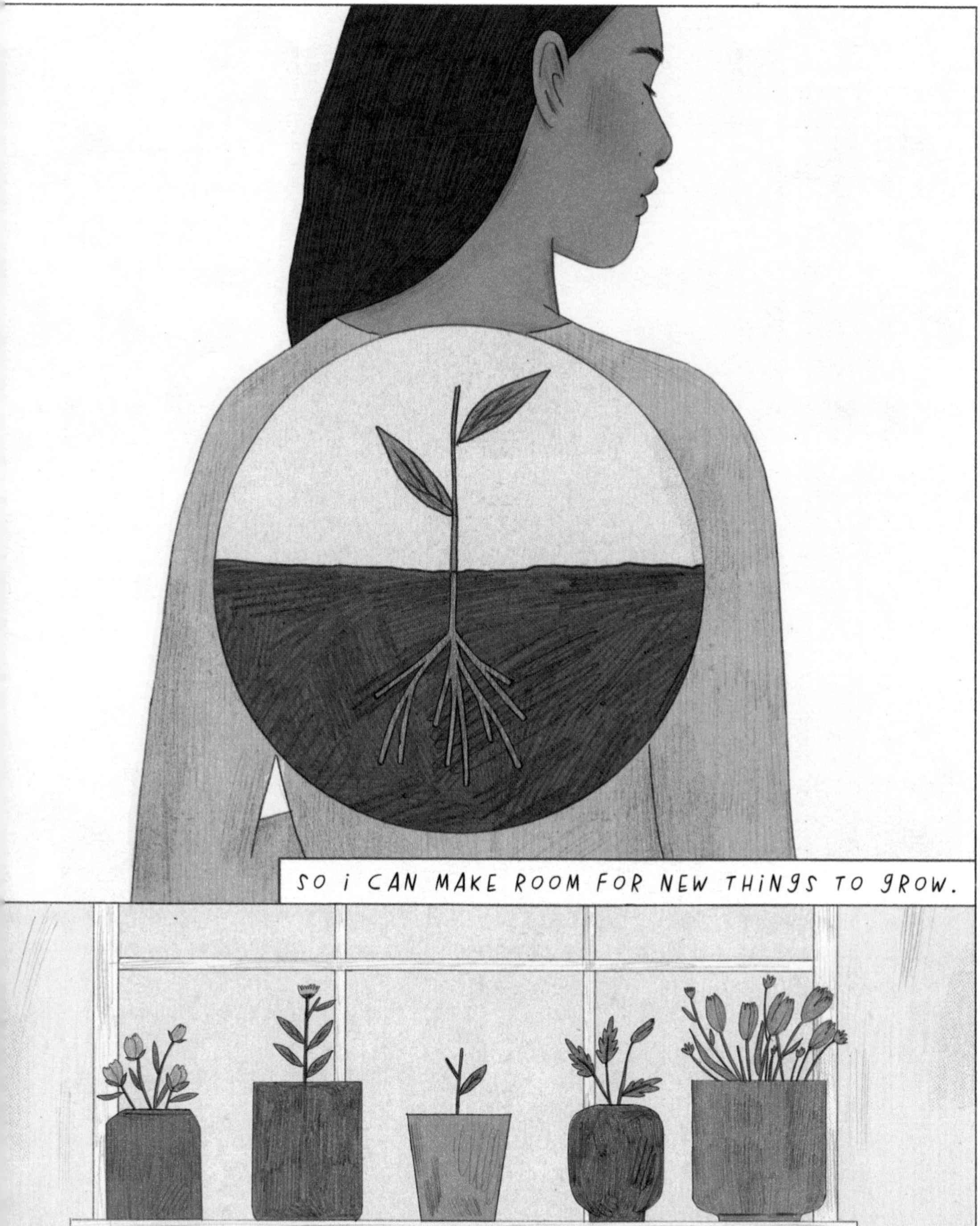
SO i CAN MAKE ROOM FOR NEW THiNGS TO gROW.

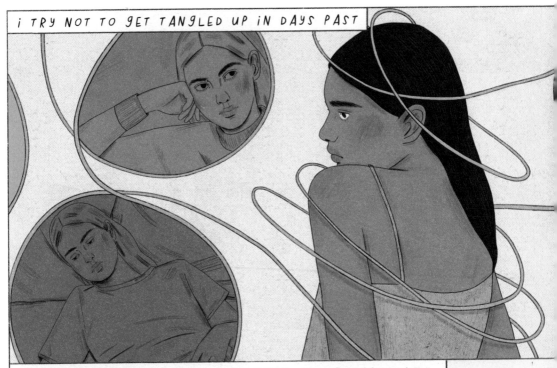

I TRY NOT TO GET TANGLED UP IN DAYS PAST

OR SPEND TOO MUCH TIME FIGURING OUT FUTURE ONES.

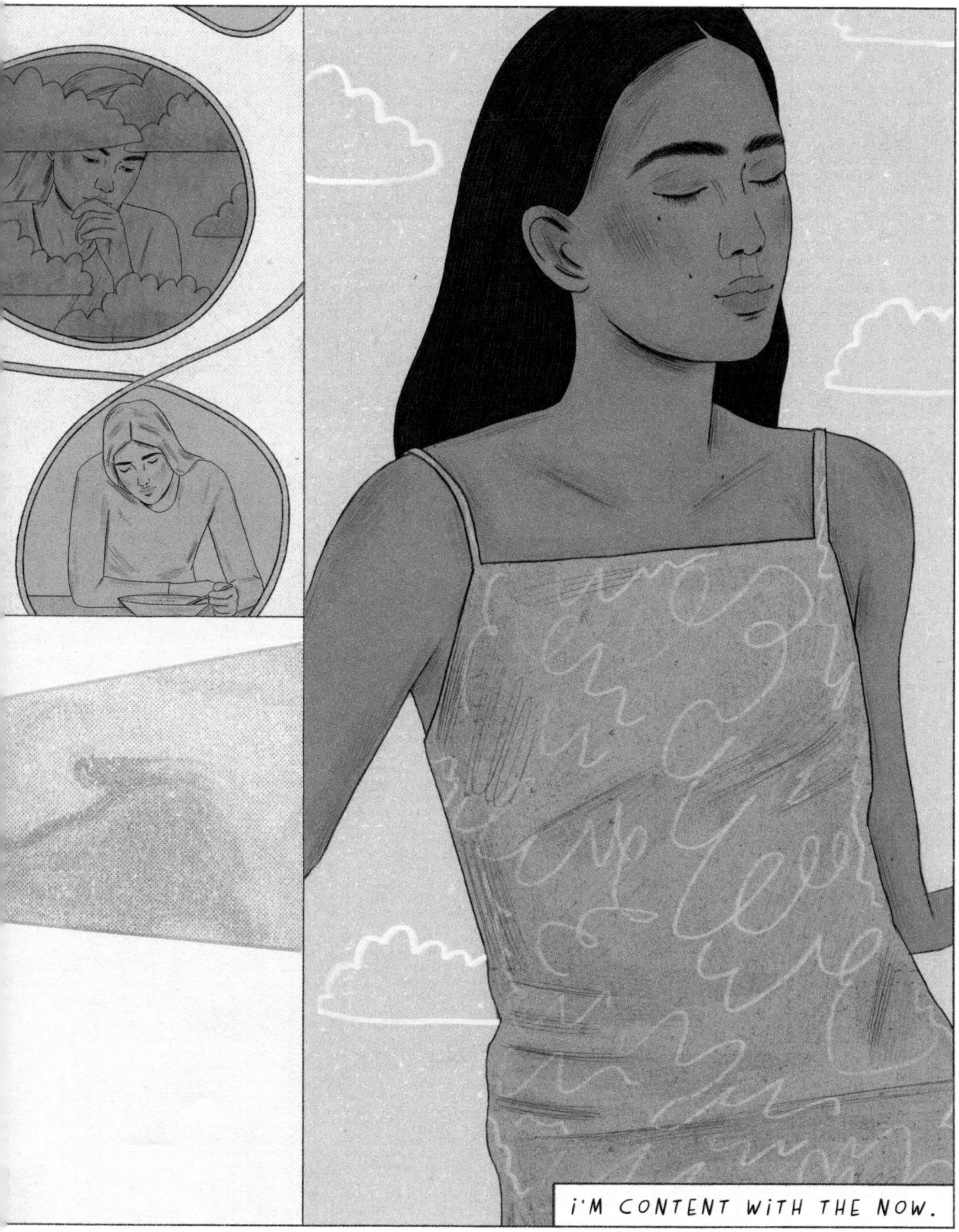
i'M CONTENT WiTH THE NOW.

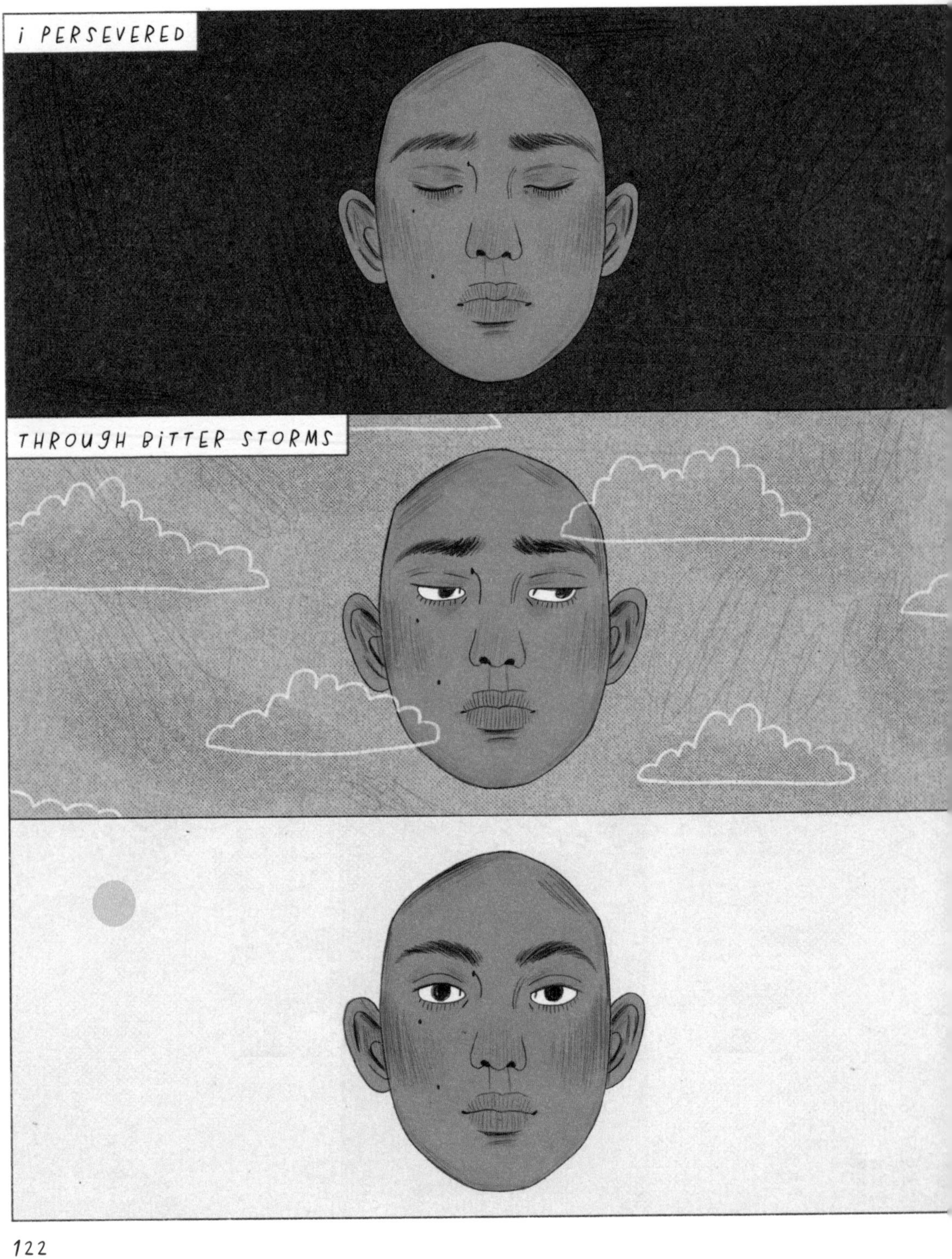
i PERSEVERED
THROUGH BITTER STORMS

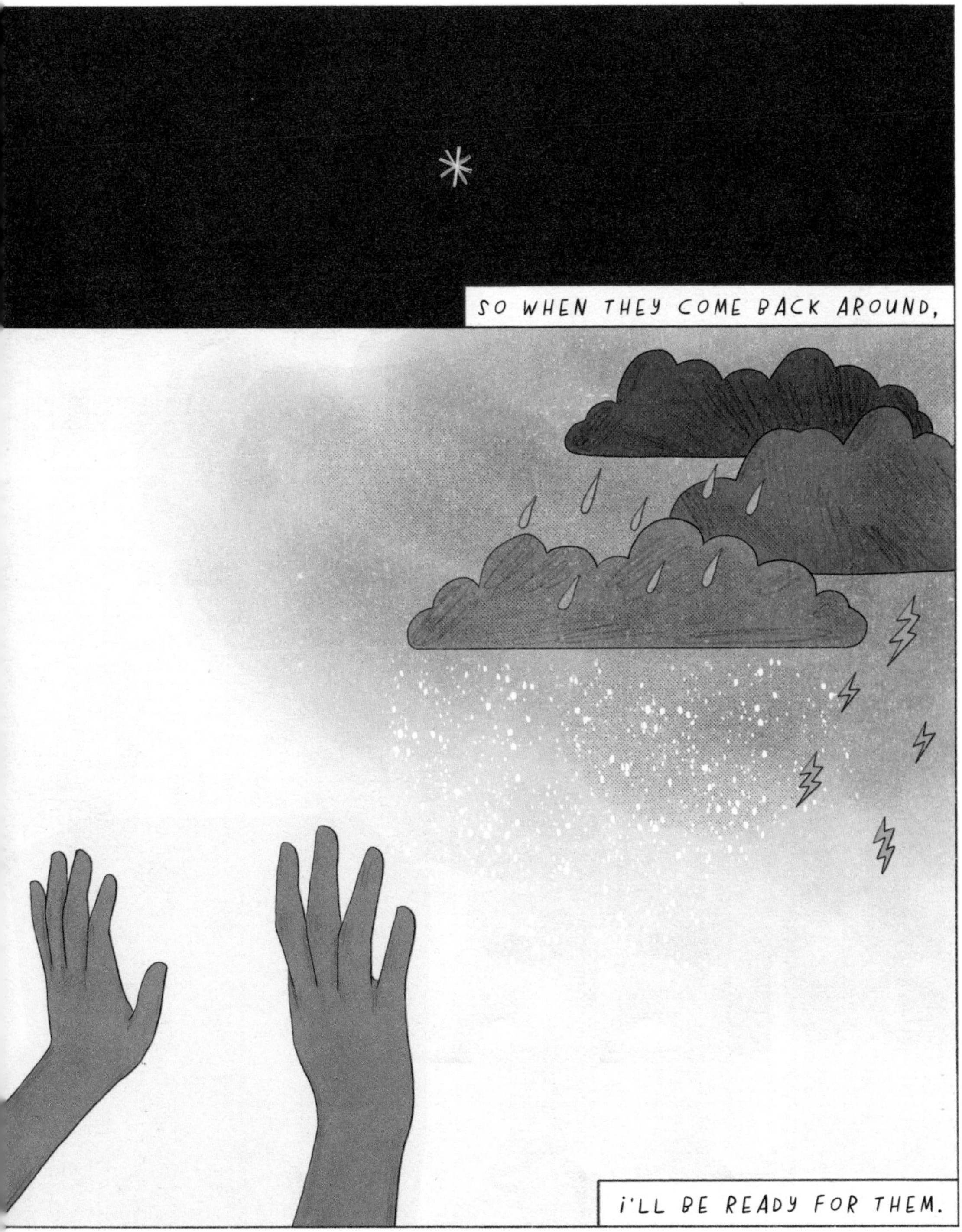

SO WHEN THEY COME BACK AROUND,
I'LL BE READY FOR THEM.

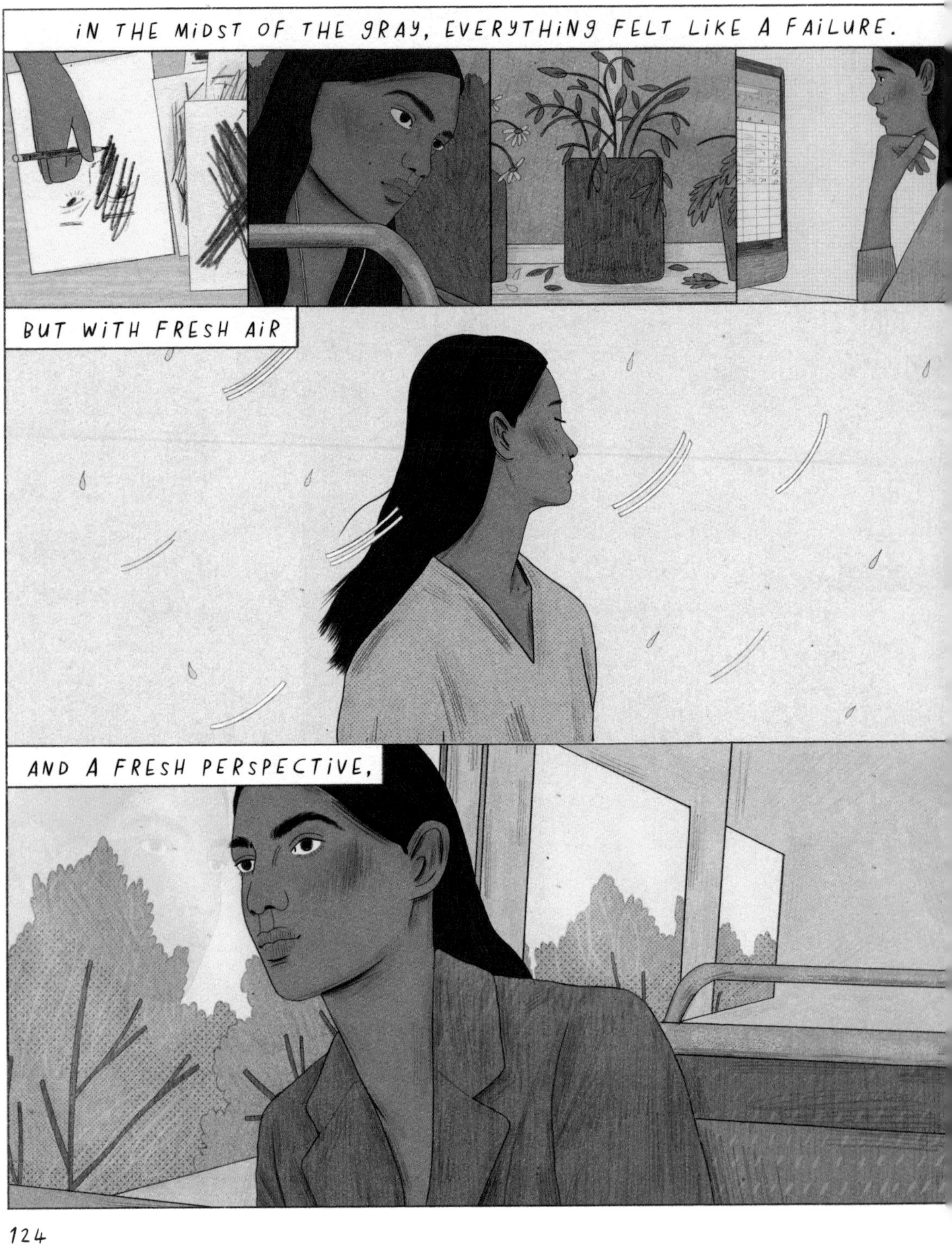
IN THE MIDST OF THE GRAY, EVERYTHING FELT LIKE A FAILURE.
BUT WITH FRESH AIR
AND A FRESH PERSPECTIVE,

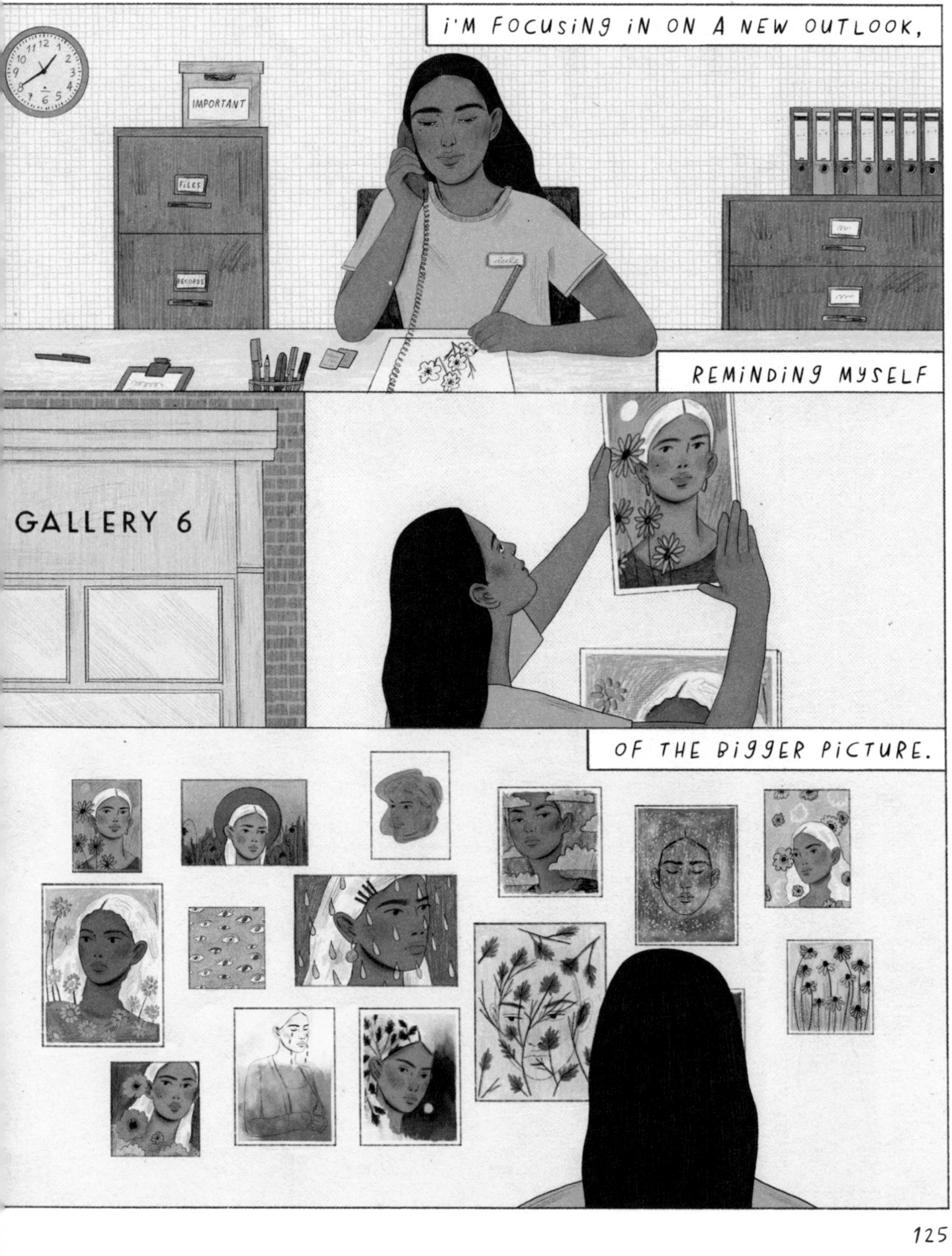
I'M FOCUSING IN ON A NEW OUTLOOK,
IMPORTANT
FILES
RECORDS
REMINDING MYSELF
GALLERY 6
OF THE BIGGER PICTURE.

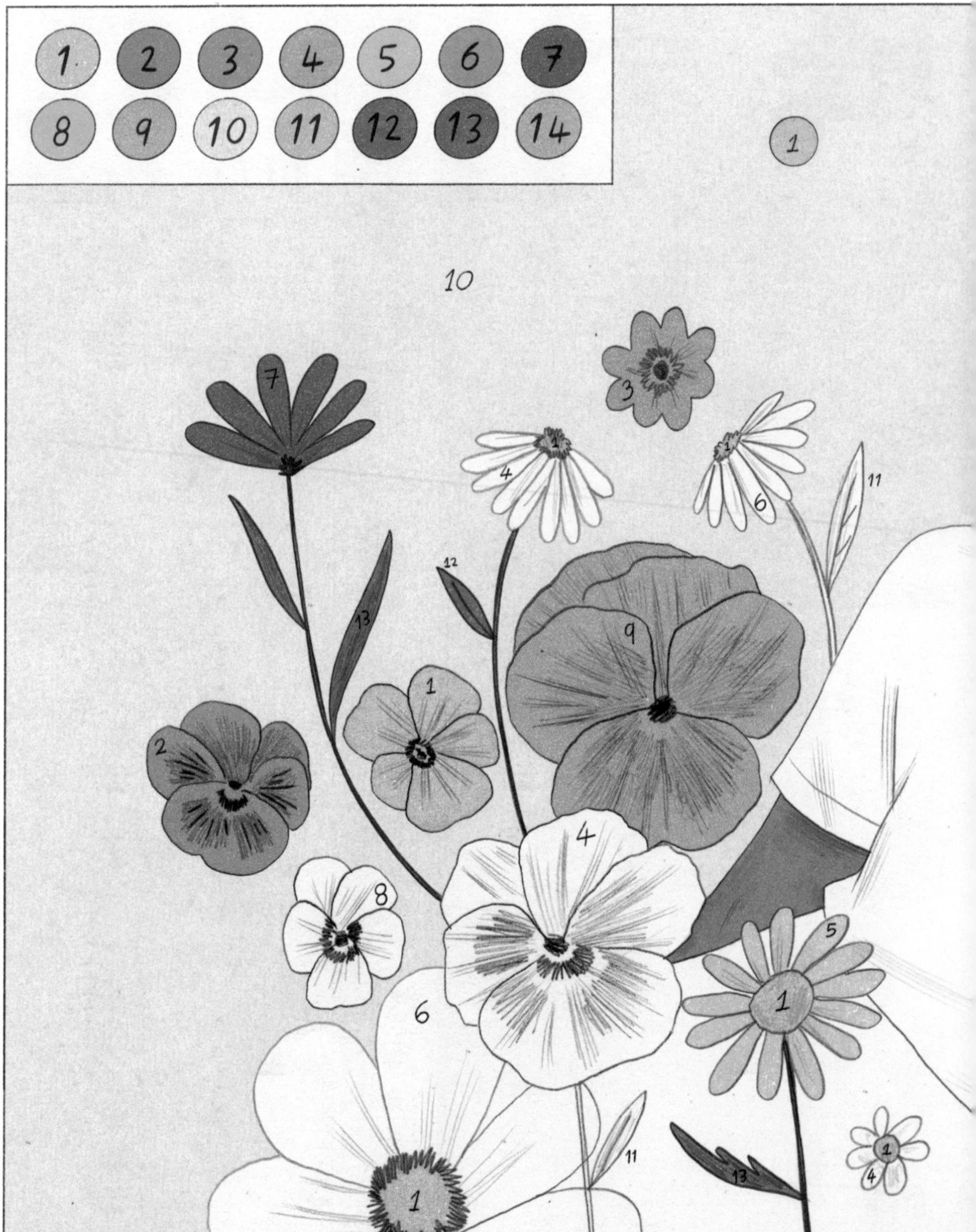
1
2
3
4
5
6
7
8
9
10
11
12
13
14
1
10
7
3
1
4
1
6
11
12
13
9
1
2
4
8
5
1
6
1
11
13
1
4

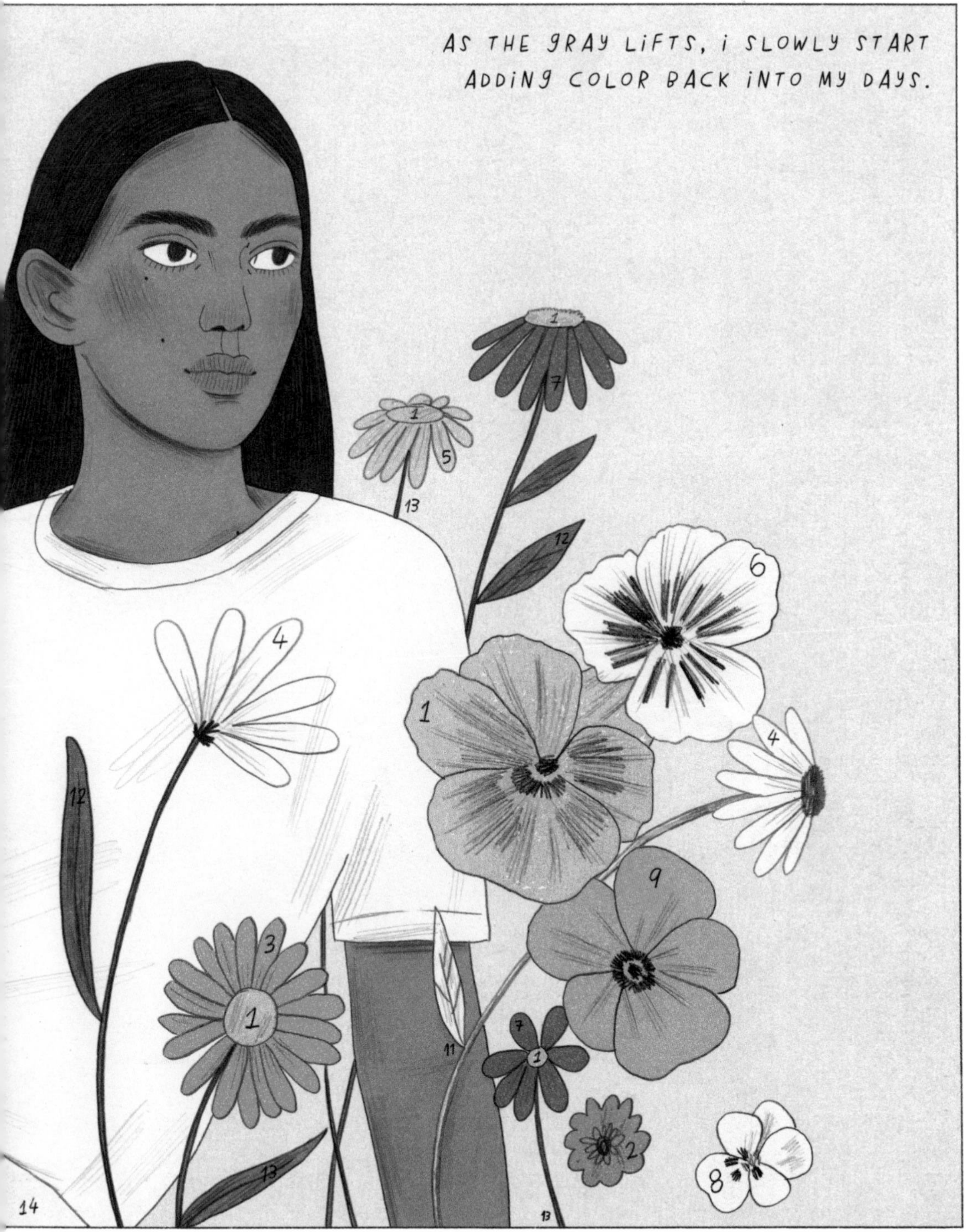
AS THE GRAY LIFTS, I SLOWLY START ADDING COLOR BACK INTO MY DAYS.

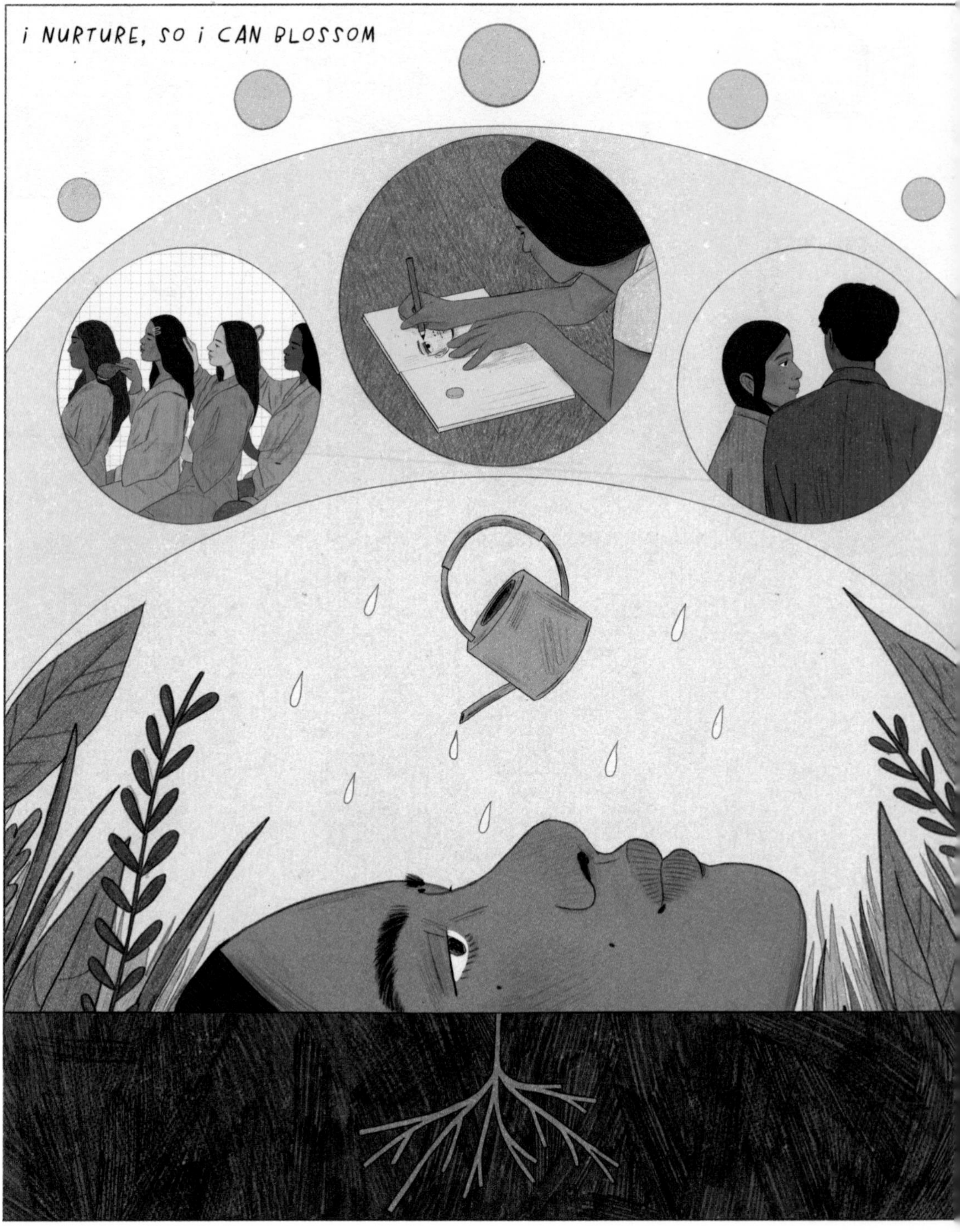
i NURTURE, SO i CAN BLOSSOM

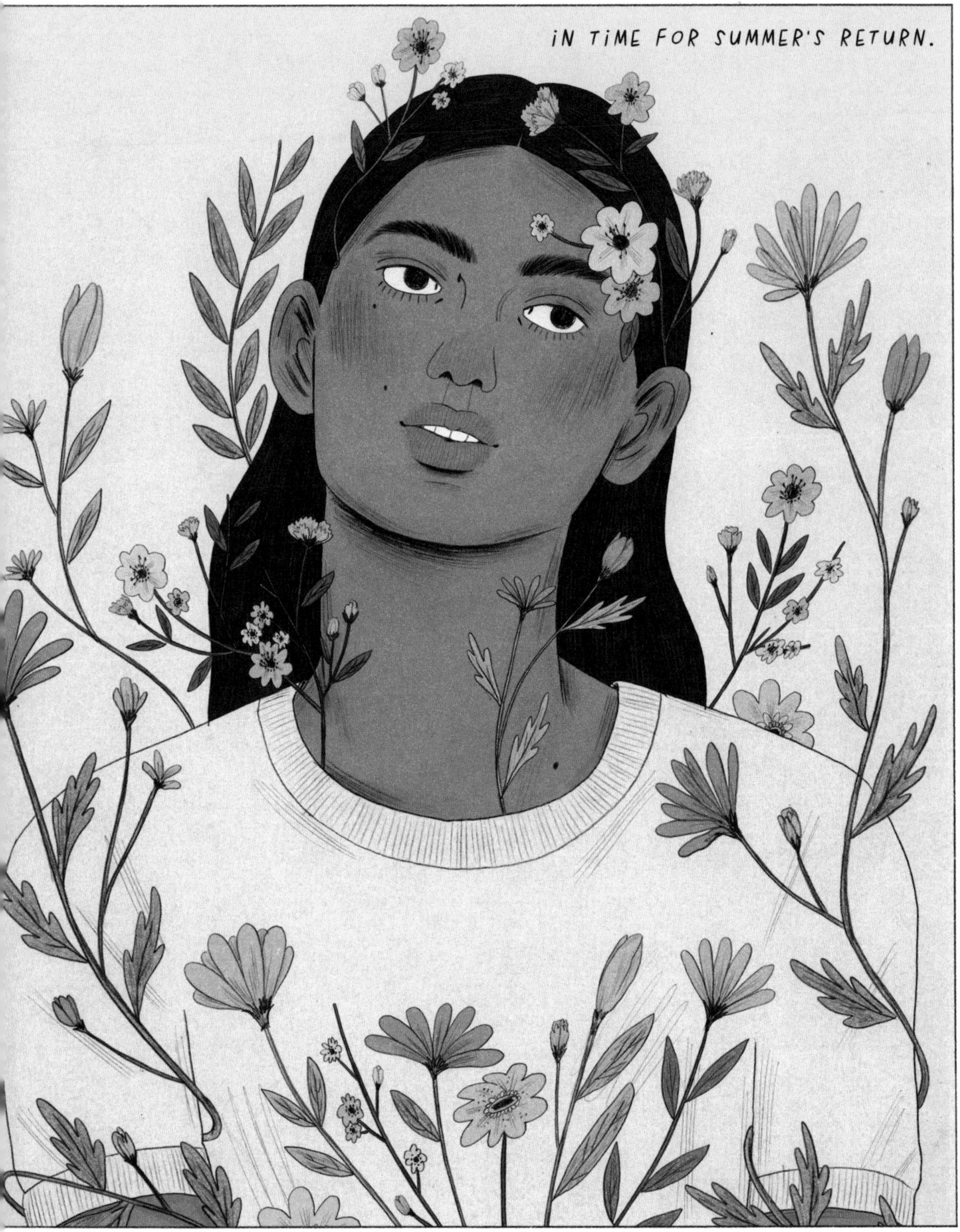
IN TIME FOR SUMMER'S RETURN.

ACKNOWLEDGMENTS

I WOULD LIKE TO THANK THE FOLLOWING:

MUM, FOR FILLING MY CHILDHOOD WITH PICTURE BOOKS AND ART SUPPLIES. THANK YOU FOR NURTURING MY CREATIVITY.

LAURA, THANK YOU FOR ALWAYS BEING THE BEST SOUNDING BOARD.

CAITLIN MCKENNA AND EMMA CARUSO, MY INCREDIBLE EDITORS. THANK YOU FOR YOUR INSIGHTFUL FEEDBACK AND SUPPORT THROUGHOUT. I HAVE LOVED WORKING WITH YOU BOTH SO MUCH.

MONICA ODOM, MY WONDERFUL LITERARY AGENT! THANK YOU FOR HELPING ME SHAPE _FEELINGS_ IN ITS EARLY STAGES.

TO EVERYONE WHO HAS FOLLOWED MY WORK ALONG THE WAY, I AM SO THANKFUL FOR YOUR SUPPORT!

ABOUT THE AUTHOR

MANJIT THAPP IS AN ILLUSTRATOR FROM THE
UNITED KINGDOM. SHE GRADUATED WITH A BA IN
ILLUSTRATION FROM CAMBERWELL COLLEGE OF
ARTS. HER ILLUSTRATIONS COMBINE TRADITIONAL
AND DIGITAL MEDIA, AND HER WORK HAS BEEN
FEATURED BY INSTAGRAM, DAZED, VOGUE INDIA,
AND WONDERLAND. SHE ILLUSTRATED THE LITTLE
BOOK OF FEMINIST SAINTS.